CHRISTIAN FREEDOM

Essays in Honor of Vernon C. Grounds

Edited by
Kenneth W.M. Wozniak
Stanley J. Grenz

UNIVERSITY PRESS OF AMERICA
LANHAM • NEW YORK • LONDON

University Press of America,® Inc.

4720 Boston Way
Lanham, MD 20706

3 Henrietta Street
London WC2E 8LU England

Printed in the United States of America

Library of Congress Cataloging in Publication Data

Christian freedom.

Bibliography: p.
1. Freedom (Theology) 2. Mission of the church.
3. Church and the poor. 4. Grounds, Vernon C.
I. Wozniak, Kenneth W. M., 1952- . II. Grenz,
Stanley, 1950- . III. Grounds, Vernon C.
BT810.2.C48 1986 233'.7 86-24584
ISBN 0-8191-5696-5 (alk. paper)
ISBN 0-8191-5697-3 (pbk. : alk. paper)

All University Press of America books are produced on acid-free paper which exceeds the minimum standards set by the National Historical Publications and Records Commission.

Acknowledgments

Acknowledgment is made to the following for permission to reprint copyrighted material:

To the *Journal of Psychology and Theology* for permission to reprint "Towards a Biblical Model of Counseling," from the *Journal of Psychology and Theology*, Spring, 1980, 8(1), 45-52, copyright 1980 by the *Journal of Psychology and Theology*.

To Christianity Today, Inc. for permission to reprint "When It's Time to Confront" from *Well-Intentioned Dragons*, copyright 1985 by Christianity Today, Inc. Published by Word, Inc.

To Jim Conway for permission to publish "Ministering to Women in Mid-Life Transition: A Challenge to Evangelicals," copyright 1986 by Jim Conway.

Contents

Vernon C. Grounds

Foreword

Senator Mark O. Hatfield

When I learned that a *Festschrift* was being developed in honor of the contributions Dr. Vernon Grounds has made to the lives of so many, my thoughts turned immediately to the third chapter of I John where the apostle writes:

> This is how we know what love is: Jesus Christ laid down his life for us. And we ought to lay down our lives for our brothers. If anyone has material possessions and sees his brother in need but has no pity on him, how can the love of God be in him? Dear children, let us not love with words or tongue but with actions and in truth. (I John 3:16-18)

In this passage the apostle identifies a problem among some early church members. He exhorts his "brothers" not to be guilty of what James calls "faith without deeds," for although their words may have accurately expressed God's loving gospel, they were empty words because they were not accompanied by authenticating deeds. The apostle states that they hardened their hearts against responding with deeds of love to the needy.

Regrettably, the problem identified in this passage is one with which the church continues to struggle. For many people in the church simply speak the gospel of Christ's love rather than practice it. Evidence suggests that John's indictment against his early church readers is still applicable.

Although the United States is one of the most affluent nations in the world with polls showing that more than 50 million Americans identify themselves as being "born again," problems of poverty, hunger, discrimination and loneliness still plague our society.

In America today one out of every four children lives in poverty. Last year in New York City 17,000 children sought emergency shelter and estimates indicate that over thirteen million children go to bed in slum houses each night. A recent study showed that over 13 million poor living in our rural areas had inadequate diets, abnormally small babies and a high infant mortality rate. Currently the median income for black families is about $8,000 less than that for white families. The suicide rate in America has risen dramatically. Suicide among teenagers has risen over 140% in the last two decades and over 300% the last 30 years. These statistics, as troubling as they appear, still do not fully portray the largely hidden agony of millions of Americans.

The church's struggle to bring the gospel of Christ to bear in both word and deed is evidence of the spiritual battle being waged in our world. The enemy seeks to dilute the transforming power of redemption in Christ by divorcing an individual's spiritual needs from one's physical needs. Such a bifurcation of the gospel has led church leaders and members to see no relationship between a person's need for Christ and one's need for food, clothing, shelter, companionship and health care.

Thankfully, God has not left his church alone in this struggle. He has given the church the Scriptures for direction and the Holy Spirit for strength, and has raised up ministers of the gospel to challenge us. One such minister is Dr. Vernon Grounds. He has been a contemporary prophet within the evangelical community in calling the church back to a Biblical faith that brings the loving gospel of Christ to bear on the contemporary issues and concerns of our society.

In the spirit of the apostle's exhortation, Dr. Vernon Grounds has been a faithful and loving minister of the gospel. As a seminary president, a professor, a pastor, an author and a leader in the Conservative Baptist Association, he has challenged countless individuals with the message and mission of the church of Christ. His gift for verbalizing Christ's gospel of redemption, for expositing the totality of Biblical faith and revelation, and for applying those truths to contemporary life has motivated many to respond to the needs of the poor, the oppressed and the lonely in the name of Christ.

It is certainly fitting for a collection of articles examining the Christian's freedom to be compiled in honor of Dr. Grounds, for it is through the liberating love of Christ that we have been freed to love others in both "deed and truth." Dr. Grounds has been a living testimony of this reality to the church of Christ and to the world.

Preface

During the last three years the idea for this *Festschrift* has germinated, grown and matured. Throughout the development process one thought has remained constant among a host of variables: the desire to honor Vernon C. Grounds.

Thirty-five years ago Dr. Grounds began his tenure as dean, president and finally president emeritus at the Conservative Baptist Theological Seminary in Denver, Colorado. In those years the lives of many hundreds of students have been touched by this man. He challenged his students to struggle with the truth as well as the demands of the Christian faith, while always seeking to love others as Jesus had done. His challenge goes beyond the student's seminary years, and extends throughout life in all aspects of human experience and interaction.

A small number of Vernon Grounds' former students have joined efforts to express in this volume some of what they have learned through that struggle. To varying degrees the articles included all center on the theme of Christian freedom. It is appropriate that this theme was selected, for it captures much of what the life and ministry of Vernon Grounds are about. A nebulous concept, to be sure, Christian freedom defies precise definition, yet holds out to each of its pursuers the promise of all that the faith offers, tailored to the uniqueness of the individual. Such is the dream Dr. Grounds holds for each one who crosses his path.

The authors represent each of the decades Vernon Grounds has spent in Denver. Contributors were members of classes from the 1950s, '60s, '70s and '80s. In addition, the biography was written by one of Dr. Grounds' students prior to the years in Denver: Gordon R. Lewis. Dr. Lewis has remained a close friend and colleague of Dr. Grounds for many years while at Denver Seminary. The article of tribute is the work of Gordon MacDonald, President of

Inter-Varsity Christian Fellowship and a member of the 1966 graduating class.

Two sections comprise the main body of the book: theory and practice. These sections reflect the broad nature of Vernon Grounds' appeal, and by design express a range of perspectives on the overall theme. Some deal specifically with the theme of freedom. Others treat it only tangentially. The first section focuses to varying degrees on academic subjects; the second section presents more practical reflections. Both sections include contributions from the disciplines of theology, ethics and psychology, fields in which Dr. Grounds is accomplished. Our appeal is thus to a wide audience, including ministers, academics and lay people interested in any of the three disciplines.

We are privileged to include a foreword by the Honorable Mark O. Hatfield, United States Senator from Oregon, Vernon Grounds' personal friend. Our special thanks to Senator Hatfield for joining us in honoring Dr. Grounds in this way.

None of the contributors wishes Dr. Grounds' views or abilities to be judged by the content of this book. Students rarely exceed the abilities of their mentors, and to the degree that we fall short of the level of intellectual acumen and personal caring of our teacher this book is deficient. Yet we offer it to him with humble gratitude, cherishing the honor of having been touched by his life.

Many are worthy of our thanks for their help throughout this project. A few, however, deserve special mention. We wish to thank Dr. Haddon Robinson, President of Denver Conservative Baptist Seminay, as well as the entire seminary family, for a level of support without which this *Festschrift* would not have been completed. Additionally we wish to thank Donna Fodness, Mark Mulholland and Donald Blomberg for their sacrificial efforts in helping to prepare the manuscript.

Kenneth W. M. Wozniak
Stanley J. Grenz
August 1986

Contributors

Gerry Breshears, Ph.D., Assistant Professor of Systematic Theology, Western Conservative Baptist Seminary

John D. Carter, Ph.D., Professor of Psychology, Rosemead Graduate School of Professional Psychology

Richard Cizik, M.Div., Director of Legislative Research, National Association of Evangelicals' Office of Public Affairs

Jim Conway, Ph.D., President, Mid-Life Dimensions/Christian Living Resources

Jeannette E. France, M.R.E., Assistant Librarian, Denver Conservative Baptist Seminary

Stanley J. Grenz, Ph.D., Associate Professor of Systematic Theology and Christian Ethics, North American Baptist Seminary

Mark O. Hatfield, United States Senator from Oregon

Roger E. Hedlund, D.Miss., International Coordinator, Church Growth Research Centre

William W. Klein, Ph.D., Associate Professor of New Testament, Denver Conservative Baptist Seminary

Gordon R. Lewis, Ph.D., Professor of Systematic Theology, Denver Conservative Baptist Seminary

Gordon MacDonald, D.D., President, Inter-Varsity Christian Fellowship

David Murchie, Ph.D., Professional Violinist

A. W. Parmenter II, Th.M., Pastor, Flagstaff Christian Fellowship

Fran Sciacca, M.A., Educator, Colorado Springs Christian School

Marshall Shelley, M.Div., Associate Editor, *Leadership* journal

Kenneth W. M. Wozniak, Ph.D., Vice President and Telecommunications Planning Manager, City National Bank

Tribute

Vernon Grounds: The Greatest Kind of Preacher

Gordon MacDonald

It seems as if the name Vernon Grounds has always been a significant part of my vocabulary. When I was a child the name was a household word. I often heard it mentioned in conversations my father and mother had with associates in the world of ministry. What impressed me even as a youngster was that the references to the man were always cast in a positive perspective; he was trusted, admired and loved, then, as he is now.

But the Grounds name became much more real to me at the time of my first personal encounter with him. A preacher's kid, I was somewhere in the age range of nine or ten years when he came to our church to give a series of Bible studies to the congregation. I vividly recall where I was sitting (front row left), what he talked about (1 Corinthians 3, "All things are yours"), and how he spoke (a clear, deliberate, often humorous delivery). I remember these details because, strange as this might seem, it was the first time I understood a sermon from beginning to end. Think of it: a child actually liking the preacher and his sermon.

Even now I can visualize myself sitting in that sanctuary with a copy of the Bible open on my lap, quietly muttering "so this is what a sermon is supposed to be." It was a marvelous moment. I was discovering that a Biblical exposition could be interesting, that it could make sense to a pre-teen mind and heart!

That night, almost forty years ago, the preacher, Vernon Grounds, won me for a friend. From that moment I was a part of an informal network of enthusiastic admirers -- people sincerely grateful for the chance to know him, to listen to his spoken and fleshed out sermons.

His frequent visits to our home were enthusiastically anticipated, because the busy educator took an interest in me. Unlike many other highly active men, he had time to ask questions, to respond to matters of youthful significance, and to make sure that I felt myself to be an important person in his world of relationships.

My curiosity and fascination for him grew in my adolescent days, as the two families (the MacDonalds and the Grounds') moved to the same city. He was to assume responsibilities as dean at Denver Seminary, and my father was to take up pastoral responsibilities at a Denver church. Those years brought frequent social gatherings which included the MacDonalds and the Grounds, and I was able to sit on the edge of adult conversation. Rarely was I disappointed as I watched the gentle and mentally sharp Vernon engage in a plethora of subjects. He was usually the one who managed to make the final observation that put all the pieces of a topic into proper order.

Spiritually and intellectually the superior in any group, Vernon was (and still is) usually ahead of others in his study, thinking and analysis. And it frequently caused him trouble with critics whose attacks were biting, but rarely a match for the Grounds mind. Because they did not understand the issues which were important to him (or did not trouble themselves to understand), there were those who relied on a variety of substandard adversarial techniques: name calling, threats and political posturings. I found it all quite unattractive, and, along with others, often hurt for my friend.

But what deeply marked me as I watched and listened close up to the responses of Vernon Grounds to his critics was his refusal -- his absolute refusal -- to fight back. Answer their questions? Elaborate when asked on more technical points? Explain the meaning and purpose of difficult concepts and terms? Yes; always yes. But respond in kind when attacked personally? Never!

Years later I would read the words of A. W. Tozer -- "The man of God never fights back at his enemies..." -- and immediately match the observation with Grounds' performance, when criticism of his thinking and view of the gospel was at an all time point of stridency.

The strongest retort I ever heard from my friend, Vernon, came one Sunday evening when he sat among friends. Someone had quoted to him the most recent comments of his harshest adversary, a pastor in the city who seemed to gain his own following by lacing his sermons together with accusations and judgments toward others. When Vernon had pondered the pastor's remarks he said, "Perhaps we should honor the brother with a ticket to the Holy Land. And perhaps it would be best if the ticket were one-way."

Like others I have known criticism, both deserved and undeserved, during my adult years. When tempted to fight back, the Vernon Grounds' performance has always been my ultimate model. How often I have said to myself, "Vernon didn't respond in moments like these; I won't either."

I passed through a personal crises at the age of eighteen, a cross-roads experience which could have caused my life to move in a totally different direction than it has ventured in the past thirty years. My faith was in jeopardy; my ability to trust people was seriously wounded; my sense of how to react to circumstances about me was clouded. I have often wondered where that crises would have taken me, if Vernon Grounds had not called me on the phone one day and suggested a breakfast together.

As I can accurately recall the front row seat and text of a Vernon Grounds sermon when I was nine years old, I can also recount the restaurant, the position of the table and the subject matter of that morning's conversation. It was a forty-five minute encounter that re-ordered my world. Looking back I now realize this was the morning when the man, having now moved from a seminary deanship to the seminary presidency, became my mentor. I say that gingerly, because there are hundreds of other men and women who might jealously read my possessive sounding words and cry out, "He's MY mentor too!"

That breakfast was full of questions (a Grounds trademark). "Do you feel that...?" Or, "How have you handled...?" Or, "Don't you suppose that he/she is also...?" It was a style of conversation which later I came to realize was vintage Vernon: his slouched posture, head often supported by one hand, elbow on the table--the epitome of casualness, of unhurried concentration--a personna that suggested that nothing in the schedule of the day was more important than this immediate exchange of thought.

Any quest at a Vernon Grounds breakfast, then or now, finds the moments intense and invigorating. You have to be there to appreciate the process. The breakfast-invitee is soon spilling out the contents of one's soul with the sense that the breakfast-invitor has absolutely nothing else to do for the rest of the day, but to listen to the trivia and travail of a hurting person. There is no manipulation here, no crass dependence upon therapeutical technique, but simply a matter of honest caring.

And that's what happened to me the first time I was the invitee. The bottom line of that particular breakfast meeting in Lakewood, Colorado, was memorable. I concluded that I had a friend who believed in me and who said it was OK to feel as I felt, to question as I was questioning, and to make decisions as I came to the point of deciding. There was the confidence-building reminder that the God of Jesus Christ was in charge of my personal history, that he knew my address, that nothing happening to me would ever be a waste. I would be able to drain from my personal crises, he said, elements of wisdom and experience that would make me a better man some day. He was right. It was the first of many breakfasts and of many such conversations.

Incidentally, the man always picked up the check on occasions such as these. His favorite excuse for check-grabbing was simple: "the seminary over-pays me," he would appear to confide, "and some day you'll probably be overpaid too; THEN you can pay." At the time I actually believed him!

In a world seemingly marked with undependability, Vernon always followed through on his promises and commitments. "I'll call you next week," meant that he called next week. "I'll send you a copy of a book that will..." meant that a book would be in the mail within a day. "You should think about doing..." meant that he would ask on the next occasion of meeting whether or not I had done the doing.

The man always centered the attention on his guest, and I quickly began to realize that every meeting between the two of us made me and my world the agenda. Soon I created a game which Vernon Grounds knew nothing about. I tried to see how long I could sustain a conversation with questions that caused him to talk about himself, rather than me talk about myself. I rarely got beyond eight or ten minutes. Sooner or later, with an adroit movement, skillfully executed something like an agile basketball player moving around the guard, he would turn the talk in my direction. Was the game of question-asking mine, or was it his? I never was quite sure.

Like many other students I entered Denver seminary because of Vernon Grounds. Somewhere along the line I had made an important decision: I would unashamedly model my life and pastoral style after his. His way of speaking, of caring, of expressing faith appealed to realities deep within my private world, and I heard myself saying, "I would like to be like him when I grow up." And like others I became a "watcher," a listener, a learner.

I listened, for example, when he sat in his book-lined study with my then-fiancee, Gail, and me, talked of our pending marriage and offered insights into the nature of our future relationship. "Gail," he said as he affectionately hugged both of us in something akin to a wrestler's headlock, "if this riff-raff of a man ever mistreats you, call me; I'll beat him into submission for you." What made all of us respond so deeply to moments like that?

I watched Vernon convene a seminary chapel the day after President Kennedy died and speak on the subject, "In the day that King Uzziah died, I saw the Lord..." It was clear that he understood how young men and women needed to be stabilized, to see a present event in the light of eternity, how our concept of heroes and events had to be scaled into true size.

I was mesmerized in my learning experiences with Grounds, when he would walk into the classroom with ten to fifteen books in his arms (book marks--actually torn pieces of paper--in every book) a sheaf of (what seemed to be) disorganized legal-sized pages, handwritten (usually double-spaced), probably scrawled during a plane flight from the east coast the night before. Sitting down and assuming a somewhat weary stance he would peer out at the class and begin a loosely organized conversation which might or might not fit what the syllabus indicated was the point of the day.

His courses had actual titles and outlines, but they never seemed to interfere with what Vernon thought might add to our education. I once suggested to him that his courses would have been better titled, "Things about the current state of affairs in the world that interest me." Whatever he talked about we loved, and we learned. We discovered in that classroom that the preacher, the spiritual director of people, the leader of an organization has to have a grasp of the real world, as it is marked with the agony of suffering, the possibilities of new discoveries, the places where the love of Christ can make a difference.

As he read to us from his endless lists of books and papers covered with scrawl, we the students sensed we were watching a man think out loud, wrestling with the many imponderables of our time. We too began to learn how to think in moments like that.

A visit to the president's office was an awesome experience to a new student (and still is to a middle-aged man like me). One wandered into the area of the books -- always the books. Rows and rows of them! They appeared at first to be carelessly shelved, but the suspicion was instantly dispelled when one discovered that Dr. Grounds seemed to know exactly where to put his finger on any one of them. Did you have a question for him? "I have a book you should read," he'd say. And soon the two of you would be pulling a volume or two off the shelf which he would shove into your hand.

In a day when seminary students were mainly male, more than one young, newly-married wife learned to quake in terror when she heard that her husband had been to the president's office. She could safely (or unsafely) assume that he would return resolving to have a library like Vernon's. "Buy books, buy books, buy books," I once heard him tell an entering class of students whose wives were present. "Even if you have to mortgage your marriage bed to get the money, keep buying books." It was hyperbole to him in order to make a point. Not a few students took him literally. In any event, he taught each of us to love books and to love the Book of Books.

When other professors sternly warned me to stay away from a student pastorate during my graduate days, Vernon cried "go for it; you can do it." And Gail and I did. When others believed strongly in the professionalization of relationships, Grounds crossed all barriers, touching, kidding, mocking the stodginess of the academic system, questioning, sharing weaknesses and doubts. We soon learned that he savored every moment and wanted us to join him.

When certain others in the conservative world of theology were unwilling to venture into challenging areas of experimental thought which were sometimes promoted by people not of our faith, Vernon wondered what there was to be afraid of. He would remind us of the belief of the church fathers: that all truth was God's truth and was not to be feared. A person walking intimately with the Savior in one's personal disciplines could hardly fear wandering when it came to honest exploration in the world of thought and discovery.

Now of course that view of learning and personal growth sometimes terrified those in the Seminary administration who had to worry more than Vernon Grounds did about the reactions of generous donors. They were aware (and perhaps Grounds was too) of those who sometimes inadvertently use their dollars to stifle creative exploration into efforts to integrate faith and real-world living. More than one always-play-it-safe benefactor probably gave money to other institutions rather than to Vernon's school, because its president would not play by certain rules. I admired him for not caving in to such pressure.

It is not that Grounds, as a seminary president, was a reckless or irresponsible man when it came to potential controversy. He was not an intellectual rabble-rouser, and he did not delight in upsetting the applecart of conviction or belief for the sheer pleasure of it. We've seen enough of that from some professors and philosophers.

But Grounds did and does understand something that some Christian educators and would-be shapers of young people have often been unwilling to face: that there are indeed times to take stands and risks when it comes to uncovering new insights into God's ways; that fresh minds and inquisitive spirits are more important than budgets and buildings; that sometimes you have to protect another as that one searches for the truth. Vernon obviously believed in doing this.

Perhaps there is no area where Vernon Grounds has preached sermons more vigorously than in the subjects of forgiveness, reconciliation and restoration. Across this country today are numbers of Christian men and women who at one time or another knew the blessing of success and effectiveness in their activities. But there came a point of failure, of defeat and of public humiliation. In most cases "friends" and co-workers turned against them. Theirs was often the experience of ostracism, loneliness, despair.

I have personally witnessed on more than one occasion the efforts of Vernon to reach out and touch such people. His was the gesture of gentleness and sensitivity. He was often the ONLY one who sought ways to help a fallen brother or sister get up again and put life back together. When others warned Vernon that he might soil his own reputation through such associations, he was adamant in walking with once-compromised people, so that they might have the experience of being trusted again. He has never been the judge; but he has always pursued the healer's arts.

Faults? Of course: He was a marginal administrator, I suppose, because people came before plans, structures and professional rules in his perspective. He was probably not a great fund-raiser, because he simply couldn't bring himself to engage in activities or conversations which had money as the whole objective. Maybe he was a bit less than totally candid, when he knew how deeply hurt some people could become, if the full truth were told and they were fired from administrative jobs or dismissed from the student body. And he was unable to say "no" to "friends" who asked him to travel long distances and expend enormous amounts of energy to speak at this conference and at that service, to counsel with this person and to consult with that group. Perhaps we "friends" did more to drain him of needed energy, than did any of his critics or the demands of his massive job, when we asked our favors and pled for his attention.

I once walked a New Hampshire trail with him as we talked of the future and his options when his seminary presidency would end. Naming one by one various people in his world, he told me of what they wanted him to do, what the school wanted from him, what the Conservative Baptist leaders suggested. I said, "Vernon, everyone has a great plan for your life. When do you take some time and ask what you and God want to do with the rest of your life?" He stopped walking and looked at me intently, as if the question had never crossed his mind before. "I guess I hadn't thought about that yet," he said.

At the time of my seminary graduation the president came to our small home for dinner. A sizable church in the midwest had asked if I would become a candidate for its pulpit. Even my greatest fan, my wife, had misgivings as to whether or not I had any business accepting responsibility of that magnitude, since I was only twenty-seven. He listened to our thoughts and threw his arms into the air saying, "Gail, your husband can do it, if you'll help him." His endorsement carried us; we went to that congregation and enjoyed six of our happiest years.

It was Vernon Grounds who shoved me on to New England to serve the Grace Chapel family in Lexington, Massachusetts, for twelve years. It was Vernon Grounds who took me aside at a convention at which we were both speaking and confided that he thought Inter-Varsity might be a good place for me to invest a bit of leadership energy.

Is there anyone who has known Vernon Grounds who has not been amazed as well as blessed at one time or another, when Vernon gave a speech or preached a sermon dedicated to some special event or idea? Is it my imagination, or was the structure of each one unfailingly similar?

Inevitably, in his introduction there would be the launching of a barrage of descriptions and quotations from classical literature, the contemporary media and the various sectors of society. Where, we preachers would ask ourselves, did he get all of this? Sometimes he would startle his audience with such vivid descriptions of events and thoughts of our time that we were convinced, even frightened, that there were no answers and no way out of the dilemma he was describing. On occasion he would take the thinking of a great philosopher, like Immanual Kant, and reduce it to three simple, but overarching questions. Or he would set forth the perspective on a contemporary scheme of ethics with five key words. Sometimes he would actually appear to build a case in favor of something or someone who was outspokenly anti-Christ.

One can see him squint his eyes, his face contorted in a kind of pain as he seemed to agonize as he spoke about the horror of the consequences of the issue. Arms folded and finger to the lips he would symbolize total concentration. "Can he pull this one out of the fire?" I found myself sometimes asking. "Has he finally pursued a question for which Scripture has no response?"

But then the speech would proceed to a ringing affirmation of some aspect of Scripture which spoke to the matter. We would all sit back not a bit comforted. "The Bible slashes across all of these claims," he would cry and then go on to explain his point. "Here," he would say, "are three ringing cries from the Word of God that speak to Kant...or to this issue...or to that event." We all learned to take notes furiously.

Then there was the conclusion we always came to expect: a poem, a dramatic story, a quotation from an outstanding mind or a simple peasant. It almost always came from a source that none of us would have ever read. But it was always the ribbon about the package. Together the pieces of the talk would be a look at our real world in the light of a great and magnificent God.

I write of these moments knowing that scores of others could have written of similar themes. Mine is not the only story which features Vernon Grounds as a prime mover and shaker in decision-making and personal growth. Others would merely fill in the blanks and describe different events. Being the possessive human being that I am, I would like to believe that all of these experiences with Vernon Grounds happened only to me. But they didn't. And that's all right, for the world is marked today with men and women who are better in life-quality, deeper in spirit, more effective in serving and leadership, because this man touched them, as he touched me. How many have faced a "junction-moment" in life and said, "I better call Vernon"?

I love Vernon Grounds because I see him every day somewhere in me. When I search for a penetrating question to ask someone who needs to be "drawn out," I hear a voice somewhere within saying, "Vernon would have used that question." When I instinctively reach out to give a friend an affirming embrace I quietly realize that Grounds taught me to touch people unashamedly.

When I am preaching a sermon and a string of words come forth that seem above and beyond the real me, I quietly reflect, "That sounds like something Vernon would have said." As I occasionally slouch in a breakfast nook, my head leaning on a hand looking across the table at a troubled young man anxious to tell his story, I give inner thanks for Vernon who taught me how to listen and ask questions.

I love him, because he has always willed for me to do things in which he then took enthusiastic satisfaction. Every young person has a desire to perform in some way in front of one's father or mentor and hear a "Well-done, son." I have heard that sort of affirmation, when Vernon sat in audiences where I was speaking and then met me at the conclusion with words and gestures which poured encouragement into me (even if it was undeserved). Each time he made it clear; he was rejoicing in whatever success God had mercifully given another. To delight in another's success is a remarkable quality.

Any article or book written is inevitably followed by a note from the Office of the President Emeritus saying how proud he is. A birthday is always recognized by a card, a special event by a gift of a book. (He has sustained the publishing business singlehandedly).

I love Vernon Grounds (today the seminary president emeritus, counselor, editor, sage), because he has not stopped growing when other men have retreated to sunny climates and shuffleboard courts. Rather he has traveled to the "Central Americas" of our world to see human suffering and injustice and returned to tell us about it. He has looked with horror at the scandal of nuclear proliferation and asked penetrating questions as to whether Christians are known for war-making or peace-making. He has called our attention to the broken person in this harsh world, the man or woman whose mind has snapped in the midst of stress or whose personality has been warped by an inhuman relational environment. I love him, because he asks me to think and act on these things, but, unlike some others, never out of self-righteous anger.

It has been many years since I sat in the front row of a church and listened to a complete sermon for the first time. Yet now I realize that I have been listening to a sermon that has gone on for years. This sermon has come not only from a pulpit, but from a life lived with dynamism and integrity, a performance that is Christ-like and Spirit-filled.

I have written of the public sermon of Vernon Grounds and how it has marked so many with its tenderness, its fertile and refreshing leadership in the discovery of new ideas, its light-hearted optimism when there was so much to be disappointed about. I've written about the personal things, the people-building aspects of Vernon Grounds. Others would have singled out the scholarship he has provided for readers, or the leadership he has given to the seminary community, or the theological contributions he has offered to the church. Some might even have suggested that he has been virtually a one-man placement agency for pastors and Christian workers. Obviously one can't mention everything.

But I can't ignore the private sermons that Vernon has always preached: his absolute faithfulness as a husband to his wife, Ann; his deep pride and satisfaction in his daughter, Barbara; his fresh delight in his granddaughter; his loyalty to working associates; his fidelity to friends.

I love the man, because in a world in which there are very few heroes, he opened his life to many of us as a model and taught us that there is a way to live that is healing, reconciling, hope-inspiring. And then, asking nothing in return, he released us to become what God had purposed us to be. We have seen the Lord Christ in him.

George Young, a novice missionary in the western deserts of China, was mentored by the great George Hunter. Of Hunter Young wrote:

> He taught me...that the man who will keep right to the end of the chapter is the man whose gaze is fixed on God, whose joy is in God's company, and whose heart is pure in its devotion to the will of God. My last sight of [George Hunter] was like Odells' last sight of Mallory and Irvine on Everest, battling against great odds and in the teeth of a raging blizzard, "going strong for the top." From the summit above and ahead of him nothing could turn him back.

I think of and visualize Vernon Grounds in words like those.

Have I embarrassed my friend, Vernon, with words and accolades that seem too lavish? Perhaps. But he himself has never been one to miss a chance to use an adjective or an adverb, if it would light up a description, or to praise someone in whom he believed. He has never shrinked away from larger-than-life phrases, when he thought they would serve the purpose of conveying unbridled love and admiration. Neither have I. It's a way of saying for myself and for thousands of others who have shared experiences such as these as they listened and watched Vernon Grounds preach his sermons: "We are very, very grateful. Thank you, dear friend."

Biographical Sketch

Vernon C. Grounds: A Gifted Man for Others

Gordon R. Lewis

During Vernon Grounds' childhood years, his family did not anticipate that he would later befriend hundreds of people while teaching, preaching, and lecturing on scores of subjects. His parents would not have predicted that he would become a caring counselor, stimulating professor, seminary president and influential author. Little did they know that some day their son would move on the cutting edge of theological thinking and help shape Conservative Baptist and evangelical thought and practice for nearly four decades.

Born July 19, 1914, in New Jersey to John and Bertha Grounds, Vernon Carl Grounds grew up the youngest of three children. Vernon's father, a train engineer for New York Central Railroad, frequently took Vernon and his older brother John to the railroad yards to climb into the cab of an engine. While John enjoyed this thoroughly, Vernon painfully endured the smell of smoke and the heat of the cab. Purchasing his first automobile as an adolescent, Vernon showed little interest in it mechanically. To get the jalopy started, his sister Mildred reported, he would frequently call for his father's help. Going to the rescue, his father often found that the car was only out of gas! Father despaired of Vernon's "ever amounting to anything."

Early in his education, however, Vernon distinguished himself as a student of many fields and an outstanding speaker. In high school at Clifton, New Jersey, he excelled on the debating team. At Rutgers University his growing interests and abilities were reflected in wide reading, love of poetry and singing in the glee club. His excellence in all the fields studied was recognized when in 1937 he received his Bachelor of Arts degree from Rutgers with Phi Beta Kappa honors.

As Vernon's intellectual horizons expanded in his first year of college, his childhood Christian faith (Lutheran) was shrinking almost to zero. While spending the summer of 1933 at home in Clifton he heard a gospel quartet made up of former high school friends. Following the service, some of the members of the quartet invited him to a home to discuss Christianity. Thinking that they offered an interesting opportunity for psychological observation, he went with them. But in conversation with them that evening he was struck by the fact that indisputably something had occurred in their lives. He found them "strangely different" from what he had previously known them to be.

How could he explain the difference? Later he testified, "Maybe, I thought to myself, God is for real. Maybe the Gospel is true after all. Maybe Jesus Christ is more than a myth; maybe He is a supernatural reality able to change people. Half skeptically, half seriously, therefore, as members of the group were praying out loud, one after the other, I too prayed, asking God, if he was real, to show me that Jesus Christ was his son and could be my Savior." And God did![1]

Trusting his new found Savior and Lord, Vernon found himself singing:

> My sin -- O the bliss of this glorious thought,
> My sin -- not in part but the whole,
> Is nailed to the cross and I bear it no more,
> Praise the Lord, praise the Lord, O my soul!

Later recalling this experience, Vernon wrote, "Suddenly I felt engulfed by God's love, so engulfed that I started to weep. A moving awareness of Presence gripped me." Forty years later, he could not dismiss that emotional evening as merely psychological. "As I interpret the experience," he said, "it was a psychological reaction no doubt, but a psychological reaction triggered by an encounter with God."[2]

Having experienced faith personally Vernon joined the gospel quartet as both singer and preacher. Later a pianist, Ann Barton, joined the group's ministry. On June 17, 1939, Ann and Vernon were married. In addition to Ann's dedication and faithfulness to the Lord and to Vernon through the years she is known for her ministries as a church organist and an instructor in piano for many who now serve the Lord in the field of music.

Vernon did not short-change profound thinking in his education. Two books especially helped strengthen his faith and enhanced his early teaching in apologetics. On the one hand, Thomas Mann's novel *The Magic Mountain* unfolded issues and options that confront people perennially. The author offered him no solutions, but "starkly revealed that without the gospel all culture and philosophy and experience reach a self-destructive impasse."[3]

On the other hand James Orr's *The Christian View of God and the World* gave Vernon positive help in reconciling faith and reason. This book, Grounds explained, "freed me from the haunting suspicion that belief in the gospel must be maintained by faith alone in defiance of learning and logic. It made me realize that the Christian has no rival when it comes to seeing life steadily and seeing it whole."[4]

As pastor of the Gospel Tabernacle in Paterson, New Jersey from 1934-1945 Vernon effectively communicated his faith. The congregation grew from 25 to 300. During this time, he also taught at neighboring schools: Hawthorne Evening Bible School, American Seminary of the Bible, and King's College.

While pastoring in Paterson Vernon earned his Bachelor of Divinity degree at Faith Theological Seminary in Wilmington, Delaware. At Faith his classmates included

Francis Schaeffer, Kenneth Kantzer, Art Glasser, Joseph Bayly and Jack Murray.

When about to graduate from Faith, a Presbyterian sponsored seminary, Grounds received a call as pastor of one of the largest independent Presbyterian churches at that time in St. Louis, Missouri. But having accepted their call, he became concerned about the sufficiency of the evidence for baptism of infants. After an agonizing struggle over the issues he concluded that he was not free to lead a Presbyterian church because of his underlying baptistic convictions. With the courage of those convictions he immediately withdrew his acceptance. Providentially, then, God led Vernon to an educational career in Baptist schools.

Vernon's full time teaching career began in 1945, when he became Dean and Professor of Theology and Apologetics at Baptist Bible Seminary in Johnson City, New York. There he was known for his thought-provoking lectures and outstanding preaching. His concerns for students soon led to many hours of counseling. In addition to strengthening Baptist Bible Seminary academically during those six years, Vernon helped to strengthen its constituency by speaking in many surrounding churches.

Vernon and Ann Grounds moved to Denver in 1951 to assume responsibilities as Academic Dean of the one year old Conservative Baptist Theological Seminary. In 1956 he was installed as president of that school. Finding himself suddenly thrust into the midst of the conflict of people trying to set different directions for the seminary, he sought some reassuring indication of God's guidance.

Reflecting on that period of testing in the early years at Denver Seminary, he has written, "What was I to do, a wholly innocent bystander who had been forced willy-nilly to become a participant in a distressing controversy? Should I resign, or should I stay and struggle to set right things that were, in my opinion, wretchedly wrong?" How thankful all the friends of Denver Seminary are for the answer that prayer received! "I distinctly remember," Vernon wrote, "the time of day and the very spot on the street where, as I was walking and subvocally praying, confusion abruptly clarified, uncertainty gave way to calm decisiveness and a sense of God's sustaining strength took possession of me."[5]

It is understandable that out of experiences like this, one of Vernon's favorite poetic prayers includes the lines,

> Lord, to my heart bring back the springtime,
> Take away the cold and dark of sin
> Fill me just now with your Holy Spirit,
> May I warm and tender be again.

God answered that prayer for Vernon Grounds in the seminary's early years. In the words of his late colleague, Raymond McLaughlin, "Vernon Grounds guided the seminary through struggle, deprivation and criticism into peaceful years." Later criticism would also be directed toward him, primarily for some of his writings, but he refrained from defending himself and defended the Christian faith and the seminary's commitment to it.

When Grounds became president of the seminary in 1956, funds for salaries were rarely adequate. In those days Vernon Grounds accepted his paycheck only after others received theirs. Grounds delegated many of the administrative details of finances, buildings and lands to Vice President Douglas Birk whose faithful attention to detail freed Grounds to pursue his academic, preaching and counseling interests. Within the faculty and staff, Grounds maintained an open and friendly spirit of collegiality.

Because Grounds put ministry to others first, it was not until May 12, 1960, that he completed and gained approval of his 470 page dissertation on "The Concept of Love in the Psychology of Sigmund Freud" (with its 1332 footnotes)! It was satisfactorily defended on May 28. So on June 6, 1960, twenty years after starting the program. Vernon interrupted a conference in Dedham, Massachusetts, to receive his well-earned Doctor of Philosophy degree from Drew University. He lists among the benefits of the "travail" of these protracted doctoral studies the frequent reading of Soren Kierkegaard's *Works of Love*, from which he "came to realize overwhelmingly the centrality and multidimensionality of love in biblical faith."[6]

Vernon Grounds was honored by Wheaton College with a Doctor of Divinity degree (D.D.) in 1954 and by Gordon College, with a Doctor of Humane Letters degree (L.H.D.) in 1977.

While seminary responsibilities often took Grounds away from his devoted wife Ann and daughter Barbara, they were regularly mentioned with appreciation in his annual Christmas letters. At the banquet honoring her father's retirement from the presidency of the seminary, Barbara reminisced, "Father was often away from home, so my encouragements, instructions and discipline were carried on by letters from him." One in particular stands out: "Now that you have shown what good discipline you have with regard to caring for your room, how about exercising that same discipline on the practice of the piano?" When Barbara faced religious doubts in college days, he noted that "intellectual problems strengthen us just as physical exercise strengthens us." A closing word could be, "Chin up, knees down."[7]

Barbara, now married to Robert Owen and mother of one daughter, Emily, serves as receptionist at the Vernon Grounds Counseling and Training Center (8000 E. Girard, Denver, CO 80231). Here Vernon continues to devote many hours to personal, marital and family counseling as well as student internship training. At her father's retirement dinner, Barbara mused "Although my father could not fix things around the house, his gifts seemed to be in fixing and mending broken hearts and helping hurting people."

With characteristic care for the psychological, ethical and spiritual problems of students preparing for ministry to others, Vernon established a major at Denver Seminary leading to the M.A. in counseling psychology. He has served as Cauwels Professor of Pastoral Care and Christian Ethics as well as chair of the philosophy of religion department.

Those who know of the countless burdens and pressures he shared wondered how Vernon could keep such a buoyant spirit himself. Similarly, he seemed not to covet the things of the wealthy he sometimes visited and served. One element in the answer came out in a Christmas letter, December 17, 1965: "I am learning viscerally...what Paul means in the 7th chapter of First Corinthians when he advises us to act 'as though not' -- to sit so loosely to the things of this world that they can be sloughed off without any keen sense of loss. Nonchalance -- is that the term for which I am groping? Maybe if I call it a sanctified nonchalance, you will dig me! At any rate, I experience an increasing objectivity regarding matters which once had an almost infinite significance. I am starting to perceive that their significance is an infinity short of infinity."

Given to hospitality, Vernon and Ann often entertained faculty, faculty wives, students, alumni and out of town guests. Far beyond the call of ordinary hospitality, at times they even invited people to live in their home (for weeks and months) until ready to face the world on their own again. Regularly Vernon would take students and others to breakfast and lunch for fellowship and counseling sessions.

With his exceptional breadth of interests and his ability to examine controversial issues objectively, Vernon has written numerous helpful articles on biblical, spiritual, psychological, historical and theological subjects. His timely resolution to seemingly irresolvable controversies has led the way for pastors and leaders in both the Conservative Baptist movement and in other evangelical denominations during the past four decades. As the listings in his extensive bibliography indicate, his writing has been as prodigious as his counseling.

During Vernon's deanship and presidency at the seminary the enrollment grew steadily from about 30 to 388 students. It gained accreditation with the North Central Association of Colleges and Schools and the Association of Theological Schools in the United States and Canada. Under Grounds' leadership the seminary campus moved from a more restricted area in Denver to the present eleven acre site of the former Kent School for Girls in Southeast Denver. And through the years of Vernon Grounds' presidency the seminary achieved national recognition as a graduate theological institution to be taken seriously.

Giving himself regularly to the Word and prayer, Vernon Grounds frequently stimulated prayer sessions among the faculty and the whole seminary family. Although usually in a position of praying for others, in 1963 he needed special intercession. While walking on Wednesday evening,

November 6, 1963, Vernon was hit by a car, tossed some distance and landed on the right side of his head and face. In answer to prayer after several days in the hospital, a week at home recuperating from the concussion and some subsequent dizziness, he was able again to resume his busy schedule in ministry to others. Sometime during that first foggy night in the hospital a promise came to him distinctly, "I will not die but live, and will proclaim what the Lord has done" (Psalm 118:17).

Those concerned for Vernon during his millions of miles of flights learned of another dramatic answer to prayer on Monday, November 18, 1968. After lecturing at San Diego State College, he flew to Los Angeles and waited there for an after midnight connection to Denver. Fog closed in, however, and the impatient traveler finally learned that the delayed flight had been cancelled. The next morning at 8:00 the replacement flight soared toward Denver. Suddenly Vernon was aroused by a jarring. A small explosion had occurred toward the tail of the plane. Smoke began filling the cabin. A composed stewardess, using a fire extinguisher, quickly put out the flames. Oxygen masks helped the breathing until the smoke cleared. When the plane landed safely in Denver the FBI arrested a saboteur who had unsuccessfully tried to explode a device to destroy himself and everyone on board. Reflecting on the mystery of divine providence, Vernon mused: suppose there had been no fog in Los Angeles the previous night when the suspect boarded the plane. Had passengers been asleep and the crew less alert, the fire might not have been put out in time. At any rate a tragedy of flaming horror and certain death was averted. Again Vernon put his testimony in the words of Scripture, "Be at rest once more, O my soul, for the Lord has been good to you. For you, O Lord, have delivered my soul from death, my eyes from tears, my feet from stumbling, that I may walk before the Lord in the land of the living" (Psalm 116:7-9).

About the first of October, 1970, a medical examination indicated that Mrs. Grounds had cancer. When they learned of her condition, Vernon and Ann claimed John 11:4, "This sickness will not end in death. No, it is for God's glory." As Vernon wrote in his Christmas letter that year, "we literally sensed the uplift and comfort which came from the fervent intercession of friends everywhere, known and unknown." The intercession availed. After five weeks of cobalt treatments, surgery completely removed the malignancy. To this day no evidence of recurrence has been found.

The public speaking ministry of Vernon Grounds has also been exceptional. Annually, in addition to addressing seminary chapels, convocations and graduations, he has included three regional and national Conservative Baptist meetings and visits to several college campuses to speak in chapel and talk with prospective seminary students. Often he would present a scholarly address to the Evangelical Theological Society. In week-long and shorter conferences he spoke at large and small churches and schools around the nation. Not infrequently his comfort would be sought by the bereaved in the preaching of funeral messages for his friends.

He has been invited to speak in other countries as well. Vernon participated in the World Conference on Evangelism in Berlin, Germany in December, 1966. He and Ann returned to Europe for a month in 1971 and again in 1984. His 25th wedding anniversary gift from friends was a trip to Hawaii where he could take complete rest. But he could not say no to numerous invitations to address groups there. Other trips took him to Central and South America.

With all of his administrative, speaking and writing responsibilities, he has carried a full load of teaching hours. Always desiring to take a personal interest in his students, he has shared his life as well as his thought with them. His breadth of reading and extensive vocabulary have stimulated his students' minds. Discerningly he takes elements of truth from writers whose systems of thought may have been non-Christian and unexemplary. Vernon does not leave major doctrinal issues unsettled, however. He quotes the writer who said that the purpose of opening the mind is like opening the mouth. It is to close it again upon something solid! Remarkably Vernon exemplifies the ability to integrate biblical studies, history, theology, philosophy, apologetics, literature, psychology, education and homiletics.

Although he retired from the seminary presidency in 1979, Vernon Grounds continues to carry a heavy schedule of teaching at the seminary as well as counseling and speaking. He has served on the boards of several evangelical agencies including the Young Life Institute, Jews for Jesus and the Spiritual Counterfeits Project. He was for several years the secretary-treasurer of the Evangelical Theological Society. He now serves as president of Evangelicals for Social Action, and edits the *Bulletin* of the Theological Students Fellowship of Inter-Versity Christian Fellowship. His administrative assistance to Evangelical Ministries to New Religions made possible its conference on "New Age Issues" at the seminary in March, 1985, and its widely circulated "Statement on the New Age Movement."

In recognition of Vernon Grounds' outstanding service to the seminary, the Vernon C. Grounds Learning Center, the newest chapel and classroom building, was named in his honor. In the Center are the twenty thousand books making up his personal library. With typical generosity he has donated this exceptional collection to the seminary library. The tribute in bronze in the entrance to the Learning Center summarizes the impact of his life on all who have known him:

> He taught us to temper
> truth with love,
> and love with truth.

Now into his eighth decade, Vernon maintains a schedule that would overwhelm others half his age. He has modeled a disciplined stewardship of his health through walking, weight-lifting and rope-jumping. Adding zest to his love for walking is his impressive collection of walking-sticks, most of them gifts from friends around the world who have known his touch upon their lives.

Vernon confessed that he is still learning a number of important lessons in the life of faith when asked to speak of his own spiritual pilgrimage at the Denver Seminary chapel in October, 1985. He included stubborn obedience to God's calling; a down to earth biblical realism; the value of walking by faith, the priorities of serving people; the importance of avoiding a judgmental attitude and retaining a measure of humility and humor about himself. In conclusion he did not claim fully to comprehend everything, but commended holding fast above everything else to Jesus Christ and to God's grace.

The influence of Vernon Grounds in my own life illustrates some of the ways he has helped many others. As my professor at Baptist Bible Seminary he stimulated my early interest in apologetics and theology and was God's primary instrument to guide me toward a teaching ministry. Through Vernon's counsel the Lord led me to study at Gordon College and Faith Theological Seminary. Though I had just graduated from seminary, his recommendation helped open my first teaching opportunity in 1951 as his successor in apologetics at Baptist Bible Seminary, Johnson City, New York. His encouragement was invaluable during my first years of teaching and through my graduate studies. During twenty-eight years as his colleague at Denver Seminary he has been a faithful friend, a stimulating colleague, an effective administrator and a fruitful minister of God's Word to me. By God's grace Vernon has exhibited his many-splendored love for God and others with remarkable self-discipline, integrity and intellectual vigor. And he has accomplished all of this with quiet humility, unstinting generosity and a gentle spirit.

In many exceptional ways Vernon Grounds has exhibited the freedom of a believer under the lordship of the biblically revealed Christ. Set free from sinful desires and personal concerns by his love for God, Vernon could freely serve the educated and uneducated, the churched and unchurched, the well and the ill, the wealthy and the poor. Christian liberty for Vernon Grounds has not meant a license to selfish acquisition, but by the grace of the Lord, the ability to give himself for others.

This gifted man has freely brought to many others the healing, comfort and cheer expressed in one of his favorite hymns,

Sometimes a light surprises
The Chrisitian while he sings;

It is the Lord who rises
With healing in His wings:
When comforts are declining,
He grants the soul again
A season of clear shining
To cheer it after rain.
(William Cowper)

Notes

1. Vernon Grounds, "Coincidence or Providence?" David Enlow, ed., *My Most Memorable Encounter with God* (Wheaton: Tyndale House, 1977), pp. 70-71.
2. Ibid., pp. 71-72.
3. Vernon Grounds, "Books That Helped Shape My Life," *Eternity*, 23/3 (March, 1972), p. 45.
4. Ibid.
5. "Coincidence or Providence?" Ibid., p. 72.
6. "Books That Helped Shape My Life," Ibid.
7. Retirement from Presidency Dinner, audio tape.

A Select Bibliography of the Works of Vernon C. Grounds

Compiled by Jeannette E. France

Books

The Reason for Our Hope. Chicago: Moody Press, 1945, pp. 128. (Also published in Japanese).

Evangelicalism and Social Responsibility. Scottdate, PA: Herald Press, 1969, pp. 38.

What a Church Owes Its Pastor; and, What a Pastor Owes His Church. Conservative Baptist Press, 197-?, pp. 23.

Revolution and the Christian Faith. Philadelphia: J. B. Lippincott, 1971, pp. 240.

Emotional Problems and the Gospel. Grand Rapids, MI: Zondervan Publishing House, 1976, pp. 111. (Also published in Spanish).

Radical Commitment: Getting Serious About Christian Growth. Portland, OR: Multnomah Press, 1984, pp. 124.

Articles and Contributions to Published Works

"Is Love in the Fundamentalist Creed?" *Eternity*, 5/6 (June, 1954), pp. 13, 14, 41.

"How Pursuit Becomes Possession," *Eternity*, 6/7 (July, 1955), pp. 8, 9, 46, 47.

"Modern Psychology and the Gospel," (Part I), *Eternity*, 6/4 (April, 1955), pp. 12, 13, 54-56.

"Modern Psychology and the Gospel," (Part II), *Eternity*, 6/5 (May, 1955), pp. 18, 19, 36-39.

"The Nature of Evangelicalism," *Eternity*, 7/2 (Feb., 1956), pp. 12, 13, 42, 43.

"Has Freud Anything for Christians?" *Eternity*, 7/7 (July, 1956), pp. 8, 9, 46-48.

"A Revolutionary Gospel," *Eternity*, 7/9 (Sept., 1956), pp. 12, 13, 40-43.

"If Man Ever Reaches Mars," *Eternity*, 7/11 (Nov., 1956), pp. 6, 7, 52-56.

"Making Jesus Master," *Eternity*, 7/12 (Dec., 1956), pp. 14, 15, 45-48.

"The Theologian and the Preacher," *Christianity Today*, 2/18 (June 9, 1958), pp. 15-18.

"Test Your Salvation," *Eternity*, 9/2 (Feb., 1958), pp. 20, 21, 46, 47.

"Do All Things Really Work Together for Good?" *Eternity*, 9/8 (August, 1958), pp. 15-17, 38.

"The Possible You," *Eternity*, 10/2 (Feb., 1959), pp. 13-15.

"Fellowship Is Not For Porcupines," *Eternity*, 10/8 (August, 1959), pp. 18-20, 46, 47.

"Incarnation," *Eternity*, 10/12 (Dec., 1959), pp. 9, 37.

"Atonement," "Miracle," "Suicide," in *Baker's Dictionary of Theology*, Everett F. Harrison, Editor-in-Chief, Geoffrey W. Bromiley, Assoc. Editor, Carl F. H. Henry, Consulting Editor. Grand Rapids, MI: Baker Book House, 1960.

"Check Up on Your Commitment," *Eternity*, 11/3 (April, 1960), pp. 22, 23.

"The Baptists and Religious Liberty," *Christian Heritage*, 22/6 (June, 1961), pp. 10-15, 32.

"Fundamentalism Needs a Reformation, *Eternity*, 12/12 (Dec., 1961), pp. 21-23.

"The Christian and Human Government," *Christian Heritage*, 23/6 (June, 1962), pp. 22-25.

"Is Christian Education Honest?" *Eternity*, 13/9 (Sept., 1962), pp. 29-31, 38.

"Commandments, Ten," "Prayer," "Resurrection of Jesus Christ," "Stoicism," "Temptation," "Virgin Birth," in *The Zondervan Pictorial Bible Dictionary*, Gen. Ed.: Merrill C. Tenney. Grand Rapids, MI: Zondervan Publishing House, 1963.

"We Deny the Charges!" *Christian Heritage*, 24/1 (Jan., 1963), pp. 6-9, 32.

"The Biblical Basis of Christian Unity, *United Evangelical Action*, 22/8 (Oct., 1963), pp. 20, 21, 24, 25.

"Building Walls Up or Breaking Walls Down," *Christian Heritage*, 25/3 (Mar., 1964), pp. 12-15, 31.

"Church and State: A Baptist Perspective," *Christian Heritage*, 25/4 (April, 1964), pp. 18, 19, 29-31.

"Miracle or Mirage," *Christian Heritage*, 25/7 (Sept., 1964), pp. 22-24.

"Roman Catholicism in the Sixties, *Christian Heritage*, 25/8 (Oct., 1964), pp. 8-11.

"Roman Catholicism in the Sixties," (Part II), *Christian Heritage*, 25/9 (Nov., 1964), pp. 14-18.

"The Biblical Renaissance in Roman Catholicism," *Christian Heritage*, 25/10 (Dec., 1964), pp. 10-13, 25.

"Love: Poetry or Power," *Eternity*, 15/9 (Sept., 1964), pp. 23-26.

"The Ghetto and the Trumpet Call," *United Evangelical Action*, 23/4 (June, 1964), pp. 8-10, 16.

"The Word of God and Protestant-Catholic Reunion," *Christian Heritage*, 26:1 (Jan., 1965), pp. 6-9, 28, 29, 32.

"Perspective on the Papacy at the Midpoint of the 1960," *Christian Heritage*, 26/2 (Feb., 1965), pp. 12-15.

"Have the Issues Really Changed?" *Christian Heritage*, 26/3 (Mar., 1965), pp. 14, 15, 25, 28.

"Rome's Tempest in Theology", *Christian Heritage*, 26/4 (April, 1965), pp. 6, 7, 13-15.

"The Ironical Paradox in Catholic Theology," *Christian Heritage*, 26:5 (May, 1965), pp. 6, 7, 31, 32.

"The Roman Catholic Church and Contraception," *Christian Heritage*, 26/6 (June, 1965), pp. 6-9.

"A Crisis in Authority," *Christian Heritage*, 26/7 (Sept., 1965), pp. 10-13, 31.

"A Ghost Haunts the Council," *Christian Heritage*, 26/8 (Oct., 1965), pp. 6-9, 25.

"The Conflict within Catholicism," *Christian Heritage*, 26/9 (Nov., 1965), pp. 12-15, 18.

"The Conflict within Catholicism," (Part II), *Christian Heritage*, 26/10 (Dec., 1965), pp. 6-9.

"The Graveyard Theology: A Brief Introduction to Brash Infidelity," in *Is God "Dead"* ? A Symposium with chapters contributed by Billy Graham, Bernard Ramm, Vernon C. Grounds, David Hubbard. Grand Rapids, MI: Zondervan Publishing House, 1966, pp. 9-56.

"The Essential Unity," *Christian Heritage*, 27/1 (Jan., 1966), pp. 16-18.

"Is Objective Analysis Possible?" *Christian Heritage*, 27/2 (Feb., 1966), pp. 8-10.

"Post-Conciliar Protestant-Catholic Relationships," *Christian Heritage*, 27/3 (Mar., 1966), pp. 6, 8, 32.

"The Ark and the Rowboat," *Christian Heritage*, 27/4 (April, 1966), pp. 16-19, 32.

"The Church or the Churches?" *Christian Heritage*, 27/5 (May, 1966), pp. 9-11, 21.

"The Crisis in Authority," *Christian Heritage*, 27/6 (June, 1966), pp. 10-12, 29-30.

"The Shaky Case for Missions," *Christian Heritage*, 27/8 (Oct. 1966), pp. 26-28.

"Seven Steps to Survival," *Christian Heritage*, 27/9 (Nov., 1966), pp. 22-24.

"Building on the Bible: A Seminary President's View of God's Infallible Word," *Christianity Today*, 11/4 (Nov. 25, 1966), pp. 9, 10, 12.

"The Peril of Pious Idolatry," *Eternity*, 17/6 (June, 1966), pp. 24-26, 34.

"Roadblocks to Ecumenicity," *Christian Heritage*, 28/1 (Jan. 1967), pp. 22-23, 26.

"The Predicament of Post-Conciliar Catholicism," *Christian Heritage*, 28/2 (Feb. 1967), pp. 22-25.

"Who Needs the Bible? A Protestant View," *Christian Heritage*, 28/3 (Mar., 1967), pp. 11, 12, 23-25, 32.

"Post-Biblical Means Post-Christian," *Christian Heritage*, 28/4 (April, 1967), pp. 10-12, 32.

"Post-Biblical Means Post-Christian," (Part II), *Christian Heritage*, 28/5 (May, 1967), pp. 24, 25, 29, 32.

"Rebaptism and Protestant Converts to Catholicism," *Christian Heritage*, 28/8 (Oct., 1967), pp. 26-28, 21.

"The Virgin's Place," *Christian Heritage*, 28/9 (Nov., 1967), pp. 10-12.

"Dogmas that Divide," *Christian Heritage* 28/10 (Dec., 1967, pp. 8-12.

"The New Morality: the Problem," *HIS*, 27/7 (April, 1967), pp. 14-16, 21, 22.

"The New Morality: What's Right With the New View of Wrong," *HIS*, 27/8 (May, 1967), pp. 6-10.

"The New Morality: What's Wrong With the New View of Right," (Part I), *HIS*, 28/1 (Oct., 1967), pp. 6-9.

"The New Morality: What's Wrong with the New View of Right," (Part II), *HIS*, 28/2 (Nov., 1967), pp. 15, 16, 23-27.

"The New Morality: The Right and Wrong of Sex, (Part I), *HIS*, 28/3 (Dec., 1967), pp. 12-16, 28-30.

"Sacramental Absurdities," *Christian Heritage*, 29/1 (Jan., 1968), pp. 22-25, 32.

"Roadblock: Mystery of the Mass," *Christian Heritage*, 29/2 (Feb., 1968), pp. 6-9.

"Dogmas That Divide: 'Sacramental Grace,'" *Christian Heritage*, 29/3 (Mar., 1968), pp. 26, 27, 30.

"Scandalized!" *Christian Heritage*, 29/4 (Apr., 1968), pp. 6, 7, 22, 23.

"How Deep the Chasm!" *Christian Heritage*, 29/5 (May, 1968), pp. 6, 7, 28, 29.

"We Are 'Other Christs,'" *Christian Heritage*, 29/6 (June, 1968), pp. 22, 23, 30, 31.

"Most Unusual Situation," *Christian Heritage*, 29/7 (Sept., 1968), pp. 26-28.

"A Gesture of Fellowship?" *Christian Heritage*, 29/8 (Oct., 1968), pp. 28, 29, 32.

"A Case of Miscarriage," *Christian Heritage*, 29/9 (Nov., 1968), pp. 22-25.

"The Issue is Infallibility," *Christian Heritage*, 29/10 (Dec., 1968), pp. 24, 25, 31.

"How Can We Face God?" *Eternity*, 18/9 (August, 1968), pp. 22, 23, 40.

"The New Morality: The Right and Wrong of Sex," (Part II), *HIS*, 28/6 (Mar., 1968), pp. 17, 18, 23-25.

"The New Morality: The Right and Wrong of Sex," (Part III), *HIS*, 28/7 (Apr., 1968), pp. 6-9.

"The New Morality: Why Wait for Marriage?" *HIS*, 28/8 (May 1968), pp. 31-35.

"The Achilles Heel," *Christian Heritage*, 30/1 (Jan., 1969), pp. 24-26.

"The Bishop's Blockbuster," *Christian Heritage*, 30/2 (Feb., 1969), pp. 30-32.

"A Papal Pandora," *Christian Heritage*, 30/3 (Mar., 1969), pp. 28-30.

"A Dishonest System?" *Christian Heritage*, 30/4 (Apr., 1969), pp. 10-12.

"The Fiction of Infallibility," *Christian Heritage* , 30/5 (May, 1969), pp. 8, 9, 26, 27.

"Infallibility: Fact or Fiction?" *Christian Heritage*, 30/6 (June, 1969), pp. 10-12.

"Reform or Revolt?" *Christian Heritage*, 30/7 (Sept., 1969), pp. 6-9

"Rome's Real Revolution," *Christian Heritage*, 30/8 (Oct., 1969), pp. 22, 25, 26.

"Faith and Doctrine: Contemporary or Contemptible?" *Christian Heritage*, 30/9 (Nov., 1969), pp. 30-32.

"Sophisticated Perversion," *Christian Heritage*, 30/10 (Dec., 1969), pp. 30-32.

"Evangelical Seminaries and Negro Students," *Freedom Now*, 5/2 (Mar.-Apr., 1969), pp. 22-25.

"Christian Education 2001: Ethics and Morality," *Teach*, 11/1 (Fall, 1969), pp. 31, 32.

"Holiness and Healthymindedness: (Piety and Psychology)," in *A Call to Christian Character*, edited by Bruce L. Shelley. Grand Rapids, MI: Zondervan Publishing House, 1970, pp. 123-132.

"Is the Church a Cultural Fossil?" *Christian Heritage*, 31/1 (Jan., 1970), pp. 6, 7, 32.

"The First Man: Real or Religious Myth?" *Christian Heritage*, 31/2 (Feb., 1970), pp. 24-27, 32.

"Scandalous Dishonesty," *Christian Heritage*, 31/3 (Mar., 1970), pp. 24-26.

"Turning Theology Topsy Turvy," *Christian Heritage*, 31/5 (May, 1970), pp. 28-30.

"The Anonymous Christian," *Christian Heritage*, 31/6 (June, 1970), pp. 6-9.

"Every Christian's Business--Theology," *Christian Heritage*, 31/7 (Sept., 1970), pp. 26-28.

"Spiritual Discernment Versus Scholarly Denial," *Christian Heritage*, 31/8 (Oct., 1970), pp. 10-12.

"Redefining the Doctrine of God," *Christian Heritage*, 31/9 (Nov., 1970), pp. 28-31.

"The Modern Idolatry," *Christian Heritage*, 31/10 (Dec., 1970), pp. 10-12.

"What Dare We Hope For?" *Eternity*, 21/1 (Jan., 1970), pp. 14, 15.

"The Future of Theology and the Theology of the Future," *Journal of the Evangelical Theological Society*, 13/3 (Summer, 1970), pp. 147-171.

"Mountain Manifesto," *Bibliotheca Sacra*, 128/510 (Apr.-June, 1971), pp. 135-141.

"Seer or Saboteur," *Christian Heritage*, 32/1 (Jan., 1971), pp. 10-12.

"A False Prophet," *Christian Heritage*, 32/3 (Mar., 1971), pp. 24-26.

"Revision or Perversion?" *Christian Heritage*, 32/4 (Apr., 1971), pp. 30-32.

"Mythomaniacs," *Christian Heritage*, 32/5 (May, 1971), pp. 22-25.

"The Gospel of Hope," *Christian Heritage*, 32/6 (June, 1971), pp. 6-9.

"Infallibility: An Insider's Inquiry," *Christian Heritage* , 32/7 (Sept., 1971), pp. 30-32.

"The Challenge Rome Faces Today!" *Christian Heritage*, 32/8 (Oct., 1971), pp. 30-32.

"Religious Toleration," *Christian Heritage*, 32/9 (Nov., 1971), pp. 8-11.

"Radically Protestantized?" *Christian Heritage*, 32/10 (Dec. 1971), pp. 24-27.

"Bombs or Bibles? Get Ready for Revolution!" *Christianity Today*, 15/8 (Jan. 15, 1971), pp. 4-6.

"Therapist and Theologian Look at Love," *Christianity Today*, 15/22 (Aug. 6, 1971), pp. 14-16.

"Revolution is Brewing," *Eternity*, 22/3 (Mar., 1971), pp. 12, 13, 44, 45.

"Existentialism: a Net to Catch a Fog," *Eternity*, 22/8 (Aug., 1971), pp. 16, 17, 36.

"Authority: Neither Authentic Nor Mature," *Christian Heritage*, 33/2 (Feb., 1972), pp. 22-25.

"The Continental Divide," *Christian Heritage*, 33/4 (Apr., 1972), pp. 26-29.

"The Not-So-Great Infallibility Machine," *Christian Heritage*, 33/5 (May, 1972), pp. 30-32.

"Infallibilty--A Dead Duck," *Christian Heritage*, 33/6 (June, 1972), pp. 30-32.

"Is There Any Immunity Against Apostasy?" *Christian Heritage*, 33/7 (Sept., 1972), pp. 22-24.

"Books That Helped Shape My Life," *Eternity*, 23/3 (Mar., 1972), p. 45.

"Genocide," "Murder," "Naturalistic Ethics," "Probabilism," "Satan," "Suicide," in *Baker's Dictionary of Christian Ethics*, edited by Carl F. H. Henry. Grand Rapids, MI: Baker Book House, 1973.

"Understanding the Neo-Mystical Movement," *Christian Heritage*, 34/1 (Jan., 1973), pp. 4-7.

"The Revolt Against Rationalism," *Christian Heritage*, 34/2 (Feb., 1973), pp. 26-28, 32.

"Neo-Mysticism Versus Supernaturalism," *Christian Heritage*, 34/3 (Mar., 1973), pp. 26-28.

"The Sad Story of Western Culture," *Christian Heritage*, 34/4 (Apr., 1973), pp. 26-29.

"Neo-Sacralism Versus Supernaturalism," *Christian Heritage*, 34/5 (May, 1973), pp. 4-7.

"Neo-Mysticism Versus True Supernaturalism," *Christian Heritage*, 34/6 (June, 1973), pp. 8-11.

"Neo-Mysticism Versus True Supernaturalism," *Christian Heritage*, 34/7 (Sept., 1973), pp. 26-28.

"Neo-Mysticism Versus True Supernaturalism," (Part VIII), *Christian Heritage*, 34/8 (Oct., 1973), pp. 26-29.

"Neo-Mysticism Versus True Supernaturalism; Poor Humpty-Dumpty or Blowing the Mind," (Part X), *Christian Heritage*, 34/10 (Dec., 1973), pp. 22-25, 32.

"How to Keep the Peace," *Eternity*, 24/4 (Apr., 1973), pp. 33, 34, 38.

"Hope Beyond Hopelessness," *The Other Side*, 9/5 (Sept.-Oct., 1973), pp. 12-15.

"Neo-Mysticism and the Nature of Man," *Christian Heritage*, 35/1 (Jan., 1974), pp. 30-32.

"Neo-Mysticism and the True Supernaturalism; Where Will It All End?" (Part XII), *Christian Heritage*, 35/2 (Feb., 1974), pp. 26-28, 32.

"Neo-Mysticism Versus True Supernaturalism; Are Mysticism and Christianity Enemies?" (Part XIII), *Christian Heritage*, 35/3 (Mar., 1974), pp. 10-12, 32.

"Neo-Mysticism and the True Supernaturalism; Evangelicalism Versus Neo-Mysticism," (Part XIV), *Christian Heritage*, 35/5 (May, 1974), pp. 4-7.

"Neo-Mysticism Versus True Supernatualism; New Testament Mysticism," (Part XV), *Christian Heritage*, 35/6 (June, 1974), pp. 24-27.

"Premillennialism and Social Pessismism (*sic*)," (Part I), *Christian Heritage*, 35/7 (Sept., 1974), pp. 24-27.

"Premillennialism and Social Pessimism," (Part II), *Christian Heritage*, 35/8 (Oct., 1974), pp. 22-25, 28, 29.

"The Bible and Emotional Problems; The Bible and Anxiety," (Part I), *Christian Heritage*, 35/10 (Dec., 1974), pp. 24-27.

"Why We Should Say 'Yes,'" *Eternity*, 25/8 (Aug., 1974), pp. 17, 44.

"Beatitudes, The," "Confession," "Humility," in *The Zondervan Pictorial Encyclopedia of the Bible*, 5 Vols. General Editor: Merrill C. Tenney, Associate Editor: Steven Barabas. Grand Rapids, MI: Zondervan Publishing House, 1975.

"Childbearing," "Children," "Faith, the Christian," "Faith, Rule of," "Faithfulness," in *Wycliffe Bible Encyclopedia*, Vol. 1, edited by Charles F. Pfeiffer, Howard F. Vox and John Rea. Chicago: Moody Press, 1975.

"The Bible and Emotional Problems; The Bible and Anxiety," (Part II), *Christian Heritage*, 36/1 (Jan., 1975), pp. 10-12, 21.

"The Bible and Emotional Problems; The Bible and Anxiety," (Part III), *Christian Heritage*, 36/2 (Feb., 1975), pp. 24-27.

"The Bible and Emotional Problems; The Bible and Anxiety, (Part IV), *Christian Heritage*, 36/3 (Mar., 1975), pp. 20-23.

"The Bible and Your Emotions; The Bible and Pride," (Part IV) (Part V), *Christian Heritage*, 36/4 (Apr., 1975), pp. 22-24.

"The Bible and Your Emotions; The Bible and Pride," (Part VI), *Christian Heritage*, 36/5 (May, 1975), pp. 26-29.

"The Bible and Your Emotions; The Bible and Anger," (Part VII), *Christian Heritage*, 36/6 (June, 1975), pp. 24-27.

"The Bible and Your Emotions; The Bible and Guilt," (Part VIII), *Christian Heritage*, 36/7 (Sept., 1975), pp. 28-31.

"The Bible and Your Emotions; The Bible and Guilt," (Part IX), *Christian Heritage*, 36/8 (Oct., 1975), pp. 22-25.

"The Bible and Your Emotions; The Bible and Guilt," (Part X), *Christian Heritage*, 36/9 (Nov., 1975), pp. 22-25.

"Christian Counseling: Who Has the Answer?" *Eternity*, 26/1 (Jan., 1975), pp. 16-19.

"Just Polishing Coffin Handles?" *Eternity*, 26/12 (Dec., 1975), p. 74.

"Pacesetters for the Radical Theologians of the 60s and 70s," (Part I), *Journal of the Evangelical Theological Society*, 18/3 (Summer, 1975), pp. 151-171. (From a forthcoming Moody Press book (1976) on *Tensions in Contemporary Theology* edited by S. Gundry and A. Johnson).

"Pacesetters for the Radical Theologians of the 60s and 70s," (Part II), *Journal of the Evangelical Theological Society*, 18/4 (Fall, 1975), pp. 255-283. (From a forthcoming Moody Press book (1976) on *Tensions in Contemporary Theology* edited by S. Gundry and A. Johnson).

"Pacesetters for the Radical Theologians of the Sixties and Seventies," in *Tensions in Contemporary Theology*, edited by Stanley N. Gundry and Alan F. Johnson. Chicago: Moody Press, 1976, pp. 45-101.

"The Hope of the Gospel/The Gospel of Hope," (Part I), *Christian Heritage*, 37/2 (Feb., 1976), pp. 22-25.

"The Hope of the Gospel/The Gospel of Hope," (Part II), *Christian Heritage*, 37/3 (Mar., 1976), pp. 30-32.

"The Hope of the Gospel/The Gospel of Hope," (Part III), *Christian Heritage*, 37/4 (Apr., 1976), pp. 26-29.

"The Buck Stops Here," *Christian Heritage*, 37/5 (May, 1976), pp. 26-29.

"Let Freedom Ring!" *Christian Heritage*, 37/7 (Sept., 1976), pp. 4-7.

"The Bible and the Modern Mind," (Part I), *Christian Heritage*, 37/10 (Dec., 1976), pp. 22-25.

"Sour With the Eagles, Sing with the Angels," *Christianity Today*, 20/23 (Aug., 27, 1976), pp. 9, 10.

"God's Perspective on Man," *Journal of the American Scientific Affiliation*, 28/4 (Dec., 1976), pp. 145-151.

"Coincidence or Providence?" in *My Most Memorable Encounter With God*, edited by David Enlow. Wheaton, IL: Tyndale House Publishers, 1977, pp. 67-78.

"The Bible and the Modern Mind," (Part II), *Christian Heritage*, 38/2 (Feb., 1977), pp. 10-12, 21.

"The Bible and the Modern Mind," (Part III), *Christian Heritage*, 38/3 (Mar., 1977), p. 8, 9, 27.

"The Bible and the Modern Mind," (Part IV), *Christian Heritage*, 38/5 (May, 1977), pp. 10-12.

"The Bible and the Modern Mind," (Part V), *Christian Heritage*, 38/6 (June, 1977), pp. 10-12, 27.

"The Bible and the Modern Mind," (Part VI), *Christian Heritage*, 38/7 (Sept., 1977), pp. 10-12.

"The Bible and the Modern Mind," (Part VII), *Christian Heritage*, 38/8 (Oct., 1977), pp. 12-14.

"The Dismal Consequences of Unbelief," *Christian Heritage*, 38/9 (Nov., 1977), pp. 22-24.

"The Intellect's Terminal Cancer," *Christian Heritage*, 38/10 (Dec., 1977), pp. 30-32.

"Faith to Face Failure, or What's So Great About Success?" *Christianity Today*, 22/5 (Dec. 9, 1977), pp. 12, 13.

"Hunger: Are Christians Hypocrites Concerning World Hunger?" *United Evangelical Action*, 36/2 (Spring, 1977), pp. 13, 14.

"Evangelical Views of Today's Moral Crisis," in *Evangelicals and Jews in Conversation on Scripture, Theology, and History*, edited by Marc H. Tanenbaum, Marvin R. Wilson, A. Jams Rudin. Grand Rapids: MI: Baker Book House, 1978, pp. 248-265.

"Lifeboat Banquet: Why Are Only a Select Few Invited?" *Eternity*, 28/1 (Jan., 1978), pp. 21, 23, 28, 30.

"Getting Into Shape Spirituality," *Christianity Today*, 23/9 (Feb. 2, 1979), pp. 24-27.

"Loving the World: Rightly or Wrongly," *Christianity Today*, 24/7 (Apr. 4, 1980), pp. 20-22.

"Church: An Indispensable Institution," *Decision*, 21/11 (Nov., 1980), p. 7.

"The Delicate Diplomacy of Jewish-Christian Dialogue," *Christianity Today*, 26/7 (25/8) (Apr. 24, 1981), pp. 26-29.

"Goodness: Reflections of the Incarnation," *Christianity Today*, 25/12 (June 26, 1981), pp. 28-29.

"Prevent the Postholiday Blues: How to Stay in the Saddle from Thanksgiving Through the New Year," *Christianity Today*, 25/19 (Nov. 6, 1981), p. 48.

"The Final State of the Wicked," *Journal of the Evangelical Theological Society*, 24/3 (Sept., 1981), pp. 211-220.

"What's So Great About Success?" *Leadership*, 2/1 (Winter, 1981), pp. 54-56.

"Physician, Heal Thyself," *Journal of Psychology and Christianity*, 1/2 (July, 1982), pp. 2-8.

"Caring for Teenagers: 8 Verbs That Speak Their Language," *Command*, 32/3 (Fall, 1983), pp. 26, 27.

"Challenge of Christlikeness," *Decision*, 24/2 (Feb., 1983), pp. 10. 11.

"Spiritual Weapons for Waging Peace: How Can We Denounce War Enough?" *The Other Side*, 19/4 (Apr., 1983), pp. 40, 41.

"The Problem of Proselytization: An Evangelical Perspective," in *Evangelicals and Jews in an Age of Pluralism*, edited by Marc H. Tanenbaum, Marvin R. Wilson, A. James Rudin. Grand Rapids, MI: Baker Book House, 1984, pp. 199-225.

"A Friend of Many Years Remembers Francis Schaeffer," *Christianity Today*, 28/9 (June 15, 1984), pp. 61-63, (News).

"A Call to Respect God's Image," *Christianity Today*, 29/6 (Apr. 5, 1985). pp. 14-16, (Editorial).

"Have We Learned Our Lesson? Three Books Talk About American Apathy in the Face of the Holocaust," *Christianity Today*, 29/12 (Sept. 6, 1985), pp. 40-43.

"The Price Love Paid," *Moody Monthly*, 85/8 (Apr., 1985), pp. 42, 43, 45.

"Truth and Tolerance," *Moody Monthly*, 85/11 (July/Aug., 1985), pp. 99-102.

"Pondering Our Christian Responsibility for the Poor," *Urban Advocate*, 1/4 (Summer, 1985), pp. 1, 6, 7.

"The Bible and the Modern Mind," in *Interpretation and History*, edited by R. Laird Harris, Swee-Hwa Quek, J. Robert Vannoy, Singapore: Christian Life Publishers, 1986, pp. 169-183.

"The Battle for Shalom," *Christianity Today*, 30/1 (Jan. 17, 1986), pp. 18, 20, (Editorial).

"Called to Be Saints--Not Well-Adjusted Sinners," *Christianity Today*, 30/1 (Jan. 17, 1986), p. 28.

Mimeographed Articles and Messages (Distributed to the Constituency of the Seminary in the "Conservative Baptist Today")

Biblical Separatists or Baptist Schismatics?, (Parts I-III), n.d.

Conservative Baptists at the Crossroads, n.d.

Correcting the Fundamentalist Corrective, n.d.

The New Testament Concept of the Church: Basic Baptist Beliefs, (Parts I-V), n.d.

Old-Line Conservatives vs. New-Style Separatists or is God's Word a Nose of Wax?, n.d.

Mimeographed Articles and Messages (Distributed to the Constituency of the Seminary in the "Seminary Study Series")

American Christians and America's Third Century, (This address was delivered by Dr. Vernon C. Grounds at the Seminary banquet held Wednesday night, June 30, in conjuction with the Annual Meeting of Conservtive Baptists at Valley Forge, Pennsylvania). (Published later in mimeographed form, n.d.).

Applied Christianity, 1/73.

The Atonement, Parts 1 and 2, n.d.

The Buck Stops Here, 9/75.

The Changing Years, Part 1, 5/70.

The Changing Years, Part 2, 6/70.

Christian Perspectives on Mental Illness, n.d.

Christianity and Psychotherapy: Two views of reality, 11/64.

The Communication of the Word, 1/73.

Contemporary Criticism of the Christmas Miracle, Parts 1 and 2, n.d.

Courtship and Early Marriage: The Changing Years, n.d.

Do All Things Really Work Together For Good?, n.d.

Doing the Good and Not Doing It, n.d.

Evangelicalism and Educaton, n.d.

The Fruit of Joy, n.d.

Fundamentalism and Evangelicalism, 1959.

The Future of Theology and the Theology of the Future, 3/70.

God's Perspective on Man, (This address was given by Dr. Gounds at the 1975 Conference of the American Scientific Affiliation in San Diego, California). (Published later in mimeographed form, n.d.).

Holy Worldliness and Worldly Holiness, n.d.

It's Still the World's Greatest Job!, n.d.

Love: Poetry or Power?, n.d.

Make Baptism Meaningful, n.d.

Management from a Biblical Perspective , (This address was delivered by Dr. Vernon C. Grounds at the Management Seminar sponsored by the Management Research Group in Los Angeles, California, on October 29, 1969). (Published later in mimeographed form, n.d.).

Middle and Old Age: The Changing Years, n.d.

The Postulate of Paradox, Parts 1 and 2, n.d.

Psychiatry and Christianity: Tension over therapy, n.d.

Psychiatry and Christianity: The mystery of man, n.d.

Psychiatry and Christianity: Tensions, n.d.

Psychology and the Gospel, n.d.

Reciprocal Responsibility, n.d.

The Role of Christian Higher Education in the Implementation of the Church's Mission, n.d.

A Study for Skeptics, n.d.

What is Evangelism?, 5/67.

When and Why the Psychiatrist Can't Help You, n.d.

Witness: What is it? (This address was prepared specifically for the banquet on Thursday evening, June 21, hosted by Conservative Baptist Seminary in conjunction with the 1973 Annual Meeting of Conservative Baptists in Portland, Oregon). (Published later in mimeographed form, 9/73).

Recorded Messages and Addresses

"Bail, Brother, Bail! And Keep on Bailing!" Denver Seminary Chapel, Nov. 9, 1983.

"Cardinal Tenets of Christianity," 9 tapes, Colorado Springs, CO: International Students, Inc.
1 - God's Purpose for Life.
2 - The Darkness of Life.
3 - What's Wrong in the World.
4 - Man's Spiritual Inabilities.
5 - Is Jesus Christ Really God?
6 - What Must I Do to Be Saved?
6a- Question and Answer Session.
7 - How Will I Change If I Accept Christ?
8 - What in the World Will Happen Next Year?

"Conservative Baptist Theological Seminary Orientation," Sept. 13, 1978.

"Change," Conservative Baptist Theological Seminary Senior Banquet '79.

"Charting a Course for Church Family Ministry. Panel/Question and Answer Time on the Family."

"Christian Concern About Peacemaking," April 20, 1982.

"Christian Perspective - Two Crises:" 3 tapes, Sacandaga Bible Conference.
1 - Male Mid-Life Problems.
2 - Male Mid-Life Problems.
3 - Problems of Aging.

"Christian Self-Esteem."

"Christianity and the Growth Process," 3 tapes, Colorado Springs: Young Life National Services.

"Divine Sovereignty: Hard Problem and/or Soft Pillow?" Sept. 28, 1982.

"Divorce and the Church," March 27, 1980, Conservative Baptist Theological Seminary Senior Colloquium.

"The Essence of Quality Theological Education," Pentagon Industries, 1972?.

"Ethic for a Troubled Age."

"Father and His Two Prodigal Sons" 2 tapes, Sacandaga Bible Conference
1 - The Prodigal Who Stayed Home/The Prodigal Who Left Home.
2 - Father Who Wouldn't Quit Loving.

"God's Will Reconsidered," Oct. 7, 1981.

"Gospel Tabernacle 50th Anniversary," Paterson, New Jersey, June 18, 1972.

"The Greatness of God."

"Hate Versus Love," Sacandaga Bible Conference.

"Heaven: Everlasting Dullness or Eternal Delight?" Sacandaga Bible Conference.

"How to Avoid Failure as a Father."

"How to Minister to One Another," Sept. 28, 1978.

"If God Let Me Start My Ministry All Over Again," May 24, 1979.

"The Impact of the New Age Movement on Psychology," Colorado Springs, CO: Inter-Mountain Media.

"It's Time to Think About Time," Denver Seminary Chapel, April 10, 1980.

"Jesus as Lord," Sacandaga Bible Conference.

"Jesus as Leader," Sacandaga Bible Conference.

"Late 20th Century Thought I."

"Late 20th Century Thought II."

"Life of Christ; Christ's Baptism," Wheaton College Chapel series, WETN Recording, 1974.

"Love One Another," Eastern CB Regional Meetings, Toms River, NJ: First Baptist Church, Oct. 2, 1979.

"Love: The World's Most Misunderstood Word."

"Memorial Service for Lew Gras," May 28, 1982.

"Mental Illness: Top of the Agenda Problem," Denver Seminary Chapel, Nov. 16, 1984.

"Neo-Orthodox Theology."

"Nicaragua," Denver Seminary Chapel, Jan. 18, 1983.

"Pilgrim's Progress," Denver Seminary Chapel, Oct 16, 1985.

"Politics, Piety, and Paranoia," Christian Open Forum, Rockmont College, Oct. 21, 1980.

"Radical Theologians I."

"Radical Theologians II."

"The Role of Emotions in Ministry."

"Simple Suggestions on Learning to Love," Denver Seminary Chapel, Feb. 28, 1984.

"The Sin of Idolizing the Familiy."

"Some Personal Observations on the Meaning of Success," A.T.S. Tape Library, Baccalaureate Address, Wilmore, KY: Asbury Theological Seminary, 1977.

"Spiritual Weapons for Peace: I Timothy 2:1-4," Preaching Today #9, Carol Stream, IL: Christianity Today and Leadership, 1984?.

"Staley Lectures (1983)," 4 tapes, "Developing Christian Maturity," Feb. 10-11, 1983.

"Theological Hope I."

"Theological Hope II."

"Theological Liberalism I."

"Theological Liberalism II."

"Three Levels of Living: License, Legalism, and Love," Sacandaga Bible Conference.

"Today's Theological Spectrum."

"What Difference Does the Church Really Make?" and "For Me to Live is Christ," Great Sermons Series ("GSS"), A

Division of Word Incorporated. 33 1/3 LP Sound Recording with "GSS" Study Guide.

"The Whys and Ways of Worship," Jan. 23, 1979.

"The Wonders and Worry of Marriage."

"Worship Service with Dr. and Mrs. Grounds," Denver Seminary Chapel, Feb. 18, 1986.

"You Can't Kid Your Kids."

Part I

Christian Freedom -- Theory

Freedom and Interpretation: An Ethical Approach

Kenneth W. M. Wozniak

The believer who reflects upon the meaning of freedom sooner or later will discover that one's conclusions on this subject, unlike those concerning other theological or biblical themes, are not easily categorized or unalterably established. This seeming imprecision will not affect all persons in the same way. To some such imprecision opens up a dangerous crevice in what appears to be an otherwise comfortable, well-defined faith. Others will see this imprecision as an unimportant or irrelevant curiosity. To them it has nothing to do with responsible Christian living in a world of spiritual and physical starvation. Such discussions are seen as fit only for the privileged few who enjoy the luxury of reflection. Still others will see this imprecision as the key to the expression of all that is central to the human relationship with God: liberty, joy, hope, release, individuality, meaning. But since freedom is the opposite of conformity, these differences in outlook should by no means be viewed as a threat either to freedom or to Christian unity.

In spite of the imprecision, there are a number of concepts which are fundamental to any understanding of Christian freedom. Certain expressions of the French sociologist Jacques Ellul in *The Ethics of Freedom* are particularly insightful in determining some of those concepts. Ellul's outlook focuses on freedom in terms of uniqueness, limits, function and implementation. A brief understanding of these four elements will serve as a helpful foundation on which to build a case for the use of Scripture in ethics.

If there exists a flavor of freedom which can be called distinctively Christian, as Paul seems to suggest,[1] then there must be something quite unique about Christian freedom. Ellul declares that only through the resurrection of Christ is freedom possible.[2] In this sense Christians alone are afforded the possibility of true freedom. In Christ's resurrection God's glory was made manifest,[3] and only through the hope given by that resurrection can the believer sense personal freedom. In experiencing the power of the resurrection, however, one realizes that the purpose of freedom lies in the pursuit of that divine glory which originally gave rise to the resurrection.

Ellul reminds us that in the attempt to express Christian freedom, one encounters the problem of limits.[4] In the resurrection Jesus was liberated from all earthly constraints. Since the one who is in Christ has been raised with him, to some extent the believer has been freed from the world. At the same time presence in the world necessitates limits. This conflict between release from the world and presence within it gives rise to one all-important question: "How do we know the limits of our freedom?"

In both word and deed Jesus taught how in a fallen world one's otherwise boundless freedom ought to be bridled. The bridle is love. Through love freedom can be expressed, particularly when one confronts the aggression of an enemy, for through love an other is freed from the shackles of *being* an enemy.[5] It is love that frees freedom, moving it from head and heart to hands and feet. Through the action of love the liberation of Jesus' resurrection is actualized in the world. This is a paradox: freedom is freed by that which also limits it -- love.

If freedom is to be of any practical value, it must serve some purpose and have some function. The function of freedom, according to Ellul, is dual: love and the glory of God.[6] Freedom in relation to presence in the world implies choice. For the Christian the choice is whether or not to love and thereby bring glory to God. Freedom, then, enables the believer to seek what is in the best interest of others, what will build them up. God has done this for all in the resurrection of Christ, and when we do it for others we reflect God to them, thus bringing glory to our maker. It is only when we know we are free, however, that we truly turn from self-interest to others.

Having understood something of freedom's uniqueness, limits, and function, it remains for us to see how freedom is implemented, that is, we need to think about how freedom is related to ethics. Ellul writes that "freedom is the ethical aspect of hope,"[7] and that hope is the human response to divine love and grace.[8] God is gracious and loving to us. We respond with hope, and God reciprocates with the gift of freedom so that we can concretize our hope by specific acts of obedience to God.[9]

At this point the importance of our subject becomes clear. Our task as God's free people is to live out that freedom in our daily actions. Yet the difficulty of knowing God's will increases as the world becomes more industrialized, computerized and urbanized, in contrast to the world of the Scriptures. We need to know how to use the Bible to address the perplexing ethical situations which our society thrusts upon us, particularly those concerning which Scripture offers no specific advice. What we need is a biblical hermeneutic, or interpretive schema, for modern-day ethics. It is only through the consistent application of the proper ethical hermeneutic that we can avoid turning freedom into license and present a unified, relevant Christianity to those who are not experiencing Christian freedom. The Christian who is living a free life of hope, love and selflessness, rooted in an understanding of Scripture which is consistent and personally relevant, will live out a world view which will not only glorify God, but also attract the modern, serious-minded individual. Developing the necessary ethical hermeneutic is therefore crucial.

Evangelical history does not have much to offer on the subject of ethical hermeneutic. It is clear that the evangelical heritage is rich with concern for social matters.[10] Yet there has never been a conscious effort to delineate a usable means of employing Scripture when treating social issues. The result has been irreconcilable social stances within an evangelicalism that claims to be directed by the authority of Scripture.

Prior to approaching the task of developing an ethical hermeneutic, however, it is necessary to understand the concepts of moral authority and theological authority. The work of Richard T. DeGeorge and Edward John Carnell can be helpful at this point. After laying this groundwork, the concept of "story" can be used to build the hermeneutic.

The Nature of Authority

DeGeorge defines moral authority as "the authority to act as one is morally required."[11] Basic to an understanding of moral authority, then, is the notion that the "authority of moral obligation is the right to act as [we] are morally obliged to act."[12] If we *must* act as duty demands, then we have the *right* so to act, for duty cannot demand what human freedom and dignity condemn. Yet how do we come to understand what duty demands and thus to understand what we have a right to do? In answer to this question DeGeorge distinguishes three types of moral authority.

First, he articulates what is rather obvious. There exists what he calls an executive moral authority, that is, an author of morality. Such an authority is a moral *legislator* and *enforcer*. The commands of this authority are obligatory, simply because they have been given, and are enforced through the use of power. The classic example of an executive moral authority at work is the giving of the decalogue. The fact that it was God as a moral legislator who gave the commandments makes them good. No other defense of them is necessary. When we break them we must answer to God for our actions, since God both enforces them and judges the violator.

Second, moral authority may be epistemic (i.e., related to knowledge). An epistemic moral authority is constituted by virtue of superior moral knowledge. The authority may be individual (such as DeGeorge), a group (such as a church), or a book (such as Soren Kierkegaard's *Works of Love*). For evangelicals the prime (and possibly exclusive in theory, but surely not in parctice) epistemic moral authority is Scripture. In I Corinthians 8, Paul gives a good example of this kind of moral authority. In his discussion of food offered to an idol, he declares that even though some people believe idols really exist, the strong *know* that there is only one God. Yet, he admits that not everyone knows this truth. When such persons eat food offered to an idol, their consciences are offended and they are thereby defiled. The knowledgable Christian, Paul concludes, is not to eat such meat in the presence of an unenlightened believer. Here Paul is offering superior moral knowledge (i.e., idols do not really exist, and eating meat offered to them does not in reality defile). It is by virtue of his *superior knowledge* that he becomes a moral authority for those who read his letter.

Third, exemplary moral authority is displayed through model behavior. Such behavior serves to inspire others to follow. Ironically, the most striking exemplary moral authority of the last half century was a negative one -- Adolf Hitler. More recently the lives of Dr. Martin Luther King, Jr. and Gandhi have served as positive exemplary moral authorities. Evangelicals clearly accept one life as supremely exemplary -- that of Jesus Christ. The lives of others can also function as models, whether negatively or positively. Noah's drunkenness, for example, serves as a negative exemplary authority (Genesis 9:20-27). Joseph, Moses, David and Daniel, on the other hand, are nearly always positive examples. Paul appeals to his exemplary authority in II Thessalonians 3:7, for he urges his readers to emulate his life.

Moral reasoning is usually best conveyed through epistemic moral authority, whereas values and attitudes most often are best conveyed through the exemplary variety. Since two kinds of authority involve interaction with and the approval of the *subjects* of that authority, they are closely related. Most good moral teachers are also good moral examples.[13] Executive moral authority, in contrast, allows for no interaction with or approval by its subjects. It merely demands their submission.

DeGeorge adds one observation that is particularly applicable to this article:

> Disagreements among authorities...tend to undermine the authority of all of them. This is clearly seen to be the case when within a given church or society formal epistemic moral

> authorities differ as to the morality of birth control or abortion or divorce; and it is also the case when differing sects or segments of the society hold varying views on the morality of an act or on moral values.[14]

Having analyzed the nature of moral authority, he warns that its Achilles' heel is lack of agreement among those who claim to convey or bear that authority. That is the problem which we as evangelicals face when it comes to the moral authority of the Bible. Many of us claim to understand and declare that authority. Yet the almost total lack of harmony in our declaration undermines, in the estimation of those who observe us, the moral authority of Scripture itself.

Before developing the desired ethical hermeneutic it is necessary to understand not only the nature of moral authority but also the way it compares with theological authority. That comparison can best take place through a discussion of the nature of truth. Edward John Carnell's thinking is helpful at this point.[15]

Carnell points out that we typically recognize two types of truth: ontological and propositional. The former has to do with what is. Something is true to the extent that it participates in what is. The latter concerns itself with the conceptual ordering of reality. It puts the mind in touch with the real. The former deals with the empirical, whereas the latter deals with the rational. Together these two kinds of truth make up the descriptive essence of human existence (i.e., they encompass the entire orbit of human reality and experience with regard to what *exists*), for they describe for us what exists.

There is, however, a third kind of truth which Carnell identifies, namely, truth as personal rectitude. This kind of truth comprehends all that we *ought* to be and do. It deals with the imperative essence of human existence (i.e., the entire orbit of human reality and experience with regard to what *ought to be*) and constitutes our moral experience. When we have personal convictions about what we *should* be and how we *ought* to act, then we are dealing with truth in the imperative essence.

The fact that the whole corpus of truth comes from two different essences, the descriptive and the imperative, suggests that the authority for one essence may not be the same as that for the other essence. Or, possibly, it may suggest that the same authority may function in more than one way when dealing with two different forms of human experience. We must realize that the affirmation, "the Bible is authoritative for faith and practice," refers largely to authority in theology and ethics. Theology concerns itself fundamentally with the descriptive essence. When we study theology we begin by inquiring concerning the way God is, the nature of salvation, the nature of the church, and so on. The Bible, we assert, is our authority in this task, for we use what it teaches concerning the nature of reality as the basis and support for our belief statements on particular themes as well as for the overarching theological structures we develop. In order to avoid improper biblical interpretation, we set as a goal the careful and consistent application of the rules of hermeneutics. Those rules include accurate translation and exegesis, consideration of the context and the author's intent, attention to the literary forms with which we are dealing, and so on. If we do not apply these rules properly we end up with erroneous theology. Properly applied, however, they theoretically keep us from gross warpage of spiritual realities.

As we move from the descriptive essence to the imperative one, that is, from theology to ethics, we encounter a major difficulty with biblical authority. Not only are we dealing with an essence different from the one with which theology was concerned, but also with subjects on which the Bible has little or nothing to say. Of course Scripture has direct teaching on subjects such as murder and adultery, and on these subjects the hermeneutic we use for theology is applicable. But on the whole the Bible is neither explicit nor complete in its teaching on the vast majority of social problems we encounter today. Where, for example, do we find clear direct Scriptural teaching on the subject of school bussing? Or where does Paul speak out on how to resolve the problem of the run-away arms race? To what chapter and verse can we turn to guide us in the selection of sites for nuclear power plants, presuming we can defend their existence at all? It is clear that on these issues and on many others like them we cannot apply the hermeneutic used for theology and hope to arrive at useful biblical answers, for in ethics we deal with a different essence from that of theology. Ethics deals with *prescription*; theology with *description.*

All of this is not to say that the Bible is not authoritative for ethics; on the contrary it is. This discussion serves to underscore that as evangelicals we have not yet developed a useful hermeneutic for ethics. As a result evangelicals apply different interpretive schemes to arrive at social prescription. Some appeal to biblical lists or commands and thus view executive moral authority as a primary tool of hermeneutics. Others focus on scriptural principles, parabolic illustrations, lifestyles, cultural and societal norms, or casuistry, and so employ some form or combination of epistemic and exemplary authority as the chief interpretive tool for moving from the biblical text to solutions for social difficulties. The result is conflicting position statements, most of which are not the product of a properly-applied, carefully-constructed hermeneutic for ethics, and many of which are influenced more by other factors than by the Bible.

Story as Moral Hermeneutic

The resolution to this problem requires a moral hermeneutic -- one which includes the useful elements of the theological hermeneutic with which we are familiar and functions in such a way that all of the forms of moral authority -- executive, epistemic, and exemplary -- may be included. This theological hermeneutic is what I choose to call a "micro-hermeneutic." It takes into account the details of the biblical text, such as grammar (i.e., tense, mood, voice, word order), logical argumentation, context of the writer and readers, literary form, occasion for the writing, relationship to passages dealing with the same subject or written by the same author, and the like. At the same time it seeks to understand the relationship of specific passages to the major themes of the Bible as a whole. Usually, however, it focuses on details rather than major themes.

The desired moral hermeneutic, I propose, must be a "macro-hermeneutic." It involves the applicable details as well as the overall biblical presentation, but focuses primarily on the major themes. The macro-hermeneutic does not deny the propriety or application of the micro-hermeneutic, but rather realizes that within the imperative essence, that is, the moral sphere, the micro-hermeneutic yields insufficient guidance and knowledge regarding those subjects on which the Bible has no explicit teaching. It is in the development, understanding and employment of this macro-hermeneutic that we can hope to resolve our prime difficulty, namely, the extent to which we are free to use the Bible in varying ways when addressing ethical subjects, and the way we are to come to an understanding of what duty demands.

We are confronted with the question, "What kind of overall interpretive framework *would* be sufficient to yield substantial moral guidance and thus serve as the required macro-hermeneutic, while remaining true to the biblical text?" As a possible answer to this question, I suggest the concept of "story." The story which for us is morally *authoritative*, in all senses of that word as I have described them, is the Christian story: that story which is impressed upon our minds as we read Scripture and which rings true in our spirits whenever we hear any part of it rehearsed in our presence. My suggestion, I realize, raises at least two questions: (1) why is the concept of story associated with morality? and (2) how might the Christian story serve as a macro-hermeneutic?

Story is more than the rehearsal of events as they occurred, either in history or fantasy; it is those events as placed within an interpretive framework of meaning and value. The storyteller *constructs* the framework, in the event of a new story, or *repeats* it, in the case of an old story. The members of the framework are the life purposes and values which the storyteller wishes the listeners to adopt and affirm as their own. Those purposes and values may be such things as wealth, power, honor and veracity. However, they could also be the glorification of God, servanthood, peace, justice and love. For the storyteller to relate the framework without the events is to rob the story of its power to convince the listener to affirm the framework as one's own. An ethicist lacks moral authority if an audience is told to pursue peace, honor or love without any basis for that imperative. But if the same ethicist supports an imperative with the authoritative narrative from which it is drawn, then the audience is more likely to internalize the elements of the imperative.

No story can be told value-free. If it is a historical story, that is, if it includes historical events, we learn what the storyteller sees as important to remember from the retold events. We do not learn *everything* which happened, but merely the events which the storyteller deems to be of value in achieving the purposes that called forth the narrative.

Even the most objective recounting of history, then, is filtered through an ethical grid. It couches facts within values; it places the descriptive essence of human experience within the imperative essence. In telling a story the ethicist draws values from seemingly objective events and thereby attempts to establish the goodness of the values themselves. The storyteller is thus confirmed as a moral authority in the minds of the audience, for an appeal has been made to a story the audience holds as morally authoritative.

Once a story has been established as morally authoritative, it becomes an archetype. In it the audience looks not only for what was, but also for what ought to be. The listeners see their personal histories, or stories, not an entities in themselves, but in relation to the archetypal story. The archetype is a goal to be achieved and a pattern to be lived, for in achieving and living the archetype the individual or group expresses personal values.

The archetype need not be limited to its own context, however, for it serves as a moral authority for other contexts as well. The issues involved in the original context of the archetype do not need to be the same as the issues being confronted by the audience, for an archetype, being more than mere events, is trans-situational. An archetype is primarily the expression of values in a context -- *any* context -- not just in one particular context. Charles Winquest conveys this idea when he writes,

> The novelist, the poet, the philosopher, or the theologian tells a story in order to find a story. This is an experiment in possibility. The stories are relative and are bound by the limits of their originating circumstances. But the movement of understanding reaches beyond the content of the story in the consciousness of new relationships.[16]

Without the archetypal story to guide us, our own personal stories would be full of inconsistencies, irrelevant action and dead-end plots. The archetype, however, gives to our individual stories a proper meaning and value framework on which to hang the events of our lives.

I have previously suggested that for evangelicals the Christian story can act as a moral authority. Likewise the concept of story can function as a moral macro-hermeneutic by which we can properly apply Scripture to moral situations concerning which the Bible offers no explicit teaching. An articulation of the content of the Christian story is beyond the immediate concern of this article. It is simply the content of Scripture viewed as a whole. More germane is the *functioning* of the story as a moral authority.

I mentioned that a major source of the crisis we now face in moral authority arises from the inability of many moral prescriptivists to find in the Bible all the forms of moral authority -- executive, epistemic and exemplary. The result is that some ethicists appeal to Paul's teachings, others to the example of Jesus, and still others to the way God commanded and guided Israel. All cite Scripture, to be sure, but their prescriptive statements are in conflict with each other. The beauty of the concept of story is that it includes *all* of the forms of moral authority. It integrates them into an interpretive whole which then serves as the moral archetype. Any passage of Scripture to which appeal is made, be it a command, a lifestyle example or a didactic section, should be seen not as an isolated authoritative unit, but rather as a part of the authoritative archetypal story. Any prescriptive statement made by an ethicist must conform first and foremost to the story, if it is to be considered Christian. If this conformity is lacking, the statement is not Christian. In fact it may even violate the moral authority of Scripture, even though proof-texts are offered as supporting evidence.

The story becomes the macro-hermeneutic through which any passage finds its proper *moral* application and thus may claim to function as a moral authority. As Stanley Hauerwas declares, "There is...an essential connection between authority, tradition, and change. Reasoning from tradition [or story] is thus the primary form and method of authority."[17] Such reasoning results in movement from where one is to where one ought to be. The personal story thereby approaches the archetypal story of Scripture, and the Bible's authority becomes realized in morality.

Let one illustrative example of the use of story in ethics suffice. At one point in his life Jesus was confronted with a moral question regarding the actions necessary in order to gain eternal life. His response was an appeal to the commandments to love God and neighbor. Yet the appeal did not satisfy his interrogator regarding the identity of a neighbor. (In itself the command to love one's neighbor does not convince us of its moral value.) In arguing for the correctness of his response Jesus did not quote more Scripture or try to reason from facts to values. Rather, he told a story.

That story, the Good Samaritan, remains today as one of the most powerful cases for viewing anyone in need as neighbor. Yet merely to distill from the story the principle of granting help according to need is to rob the Good Samaritan story of its power to convince the listener to internalize the value which the narrative pictures. Moral authority rests in the retelling of the story, and when the story is retold, no further moral argumentation is required.

The parable of the Good Samaritan is a part of the overall Christian story, which today can function as our moral authority. The church is a community whose moral identity is characterized by adherence to the story. Any member who offers a position-statement that is out of harmony with the story is offering a non-Christian statement, for it violates the church's moral identity. All statements that follow from the story, even though they may not totally agree with each other, are Christian statements.

The church's moral witness to the world certainly could be improved, if it would begin to apply the ethical hermeneutic of story in a consistent manner. If those outside the church could observe evangelicalism united around a morally authoritative story, then perhaps they could see in our approach to difficult moral situations a demonstration of Christian hope -- the ethical aspect of freedom.

Notes

1. See Galatians 2:4.
2. Jacques Ellul, *The Ethics of Freedom*, trans. and ed. by Geoffrey W. Bromiley (Grand Rapids: Wm. B. Eerdmans Pub. Co., 1976). p. 14.
3. Ibid.
4. Ibid., p. 185.
5. Ibid., p. 200.
6. Ibid., pp. 218-219.
7. Ibid., p. 12.
8. Ibid., p. 13.
9. Ibid., pp. 13, 62.
10. See, for example, Donald W. Dayton, *Discovering an Evangelical Heritage*, (New York: Harper and Row, 1976), Carl F. H. Henry, *The Uneasy Conscience of Modern Fundamentalism*, (Grand Rapids: Wm. B. Eerdmans Pub. Co., 1947), Norris Magnuson, *Salvation in the Slums: Evangelical Social Work, 1865-1920*, (Metuchen: Scarecrow, 1977), and Timothy L. Smith, *Revivalism and Social Reform*, (New York: Harper and Row, 1965).
11. Richard T. DeGeorge, "Authority and Morality," Frederich J. Adelmann, S.J., ed., *Authority* (The Hague, Netherlands: Martinus Nijhoff, 1974), p. 47.
12. Ibid., p. 46.
13. Ibid., pp. 38-42.
14. Ibid., p. 41.
15. See Edward John Carnell, *Christian Commitment: An Apologetic*, (New York: The Macmillan Co., 1957), pp. 14-30.

16. Charles Winquist, *Homecoming: Interpretation, Transformation and Individuation*, (Ann Arbor: Scholars Press, 1978), p. 10.

17. Stanley Hauerwas, "The Moral Authority of Scripture," *Interpretation*, Vol. 34, Oct. 1980, p. 359.

The Flight From God: Kierkegaard's *Fear and Trembling* And Universal Ethical Systems

Stanley J. Grenz

> When the woman saw that the fruit of the tree was good for food and pleasing to the eye, and also desirable for gaining wisdom, she took some and ate it. She also gave some to her husband, who was with her, and he ate it. Then the eyes of both of them were opened, and they realized they were naked; so they sewed fig leaves together and made coverings for themselves. Then the man and his wife heard the sound of the LORD God as he was walking in the garden in the cool of the day, and they hid from the LORD God among the trees of the garden (Genesis 3:6-8).

The third chapter of the Book of Genesis narrates in a simple, unassuming manner the fall of humanity and its results. According to the story, once Adam and Eve become cognizant of their disobedience any pretense of innocence in the presence of each other and Yahweh is impossible. Their subsequent reactions in this new situation are therefore predictable. To hide their sense of guilt in the face of each other they sew clothing of fig leaves. To hide their guilt from

Yahweh, when they hear him walking in the garden they scurry behind a tree. Adam and Eve apparently think the clothing and the trees can serve as a refuge from the fearful reality of standing immediately in the presence of God. They hope that these created objects -- the work of their hands and the work of God's hands -- can shield them from the awful position of being totally free, directly accountable to God. The couple fail to realize that being human entails an immediacy before God, which cannot be mitigated even in disobedience.

The response of the first human couple as narrated by the Genesis story depicts an action which the descendants of Adam have repeated throughout human history. Just as Adam and Eve in the story seek to mitigate their immediacy before God by hiding behind clothing and trees, their children have continually sought to deny personal, immediate accountability to God. Driven by a sense of guilt, all persons seek refuge in that which they create (personal efforts to obtain "righteousness") or in that which God creates (the divine moral absolute). Soren Kierkegaard, the melancholy Dane of the nineteenth century, however, insightfully points out the folly of this universal human tendency.

The Nineteenth Century Voice

The reigning ethical system in nineteenth century Denmark, which formed the background to Kierkegaard's writings, was that of G.W.F. Hegel, who to some extent was indebted to his predecessor, Immanuel Kant. Kant built his ethic on the premise that there is a plurality of moral norms which have their basis in the individual's sense of absolute duty. These norms are unconditional duties which persons ought always to perform and ought never to disobey. Since this sense of duty, and not empirical or hypothetical considerations, is the sole basis for ethical principles, ethics is unconditional. One cannot look for exceptions, since one's duty is categorical. One must do one's duty without fail, no matter what may be the consequences. Duty is a categorical imperative.

Lying at the heart of ethical decision making, in Kant's view, is the "categorical imperative," the central dictum of ethics. Although he phrased this universal rule in various ways, its basic formulation was stated in his work, *Fundamental Principles of the Metaphysics of Morals*: "Act only on that maxim whereby thou canst at the same time will that it should become a universal law."[1]

Seventeen years after Kant's death, Hegel utilized his predecessor's work to outline his own ethical position in *Philosophie des Rechts*. Hegel will not allow the entrusting of moral decisions to the fallible individual conscience. Rather he emphasizes "public morality," which in typical post-Enlightenment fashion centers on obedience to the law of the state. The state is the guardian of universal ethical law. If one disobeys the state, one sins against the whole body politic and becomes thereby an "individual," even though one seeks to appeal to individual conscience. The only remedy for such sin is a return to conformity to the general morality. To remain an individual is to lie "in temptation," since as an individual one calls into question the state as the upholder of the universal.[2]

The ethical systems of Kant and Hegel are significant. Kant's suggestion is clear and universally applicable, at least in theory. When faced by a moral decision, one ought to pose the question, "Which possible action would I desire as a universal law?" One's answer to that question then serves as the guiding principle of one's conduct in the situation. Hegel's outlook is likewise straightforward. The individual looks to the state for the proper course of action, since it is society that has the task of answering Kant's question.

Although the ethical systems of Kant and Hegel may be helpful, from a Kierkegaardian perspective they repeat the fallacy of the first couple in the Genesis narrative. Just as Adam and Eve try to hide behind loin coverings and trees, so their children seek to hide from their accountability to God through universal ethical laws or through the collective decrees of government. Rather than directing the individual to accept the burden of personal ethical decision-making, these systems become tempting facades, behind which the individual hides in the attempt to mitigate direct responsibility before God. This is Kierkegaard's attack on the ethics of Kant and Hegel, an attack of which his book *Fear and Trembling*, written under the pseudonym, Johannes de Silentio, is a significant part.

Kierkegaard's Book, *Fear and Trembling*

The plan of *Fear and Trembling* is straightforward. Johannes de Silentio begins with a preface in which he attacks the Danish Hegelians who seek to "go beyond" Hegel's system, just as Hegel "went beyond" Kant. In contrast to them, Johannes is content to remain with the subject of faith, which even Hegel, who "went beyond" faith, misunderstood. Then he proceeds to a prelude in which he recites four variants of the story of Abraham's sacrifice of Isaac. This is followed by a "panegyric" upon Abraham which includes some ramifications of that significant incident in the life of Abraham. In the fourth section, "Problemata: Preliminary Expectoration," the author discusses the paradoxical nature of faith. Three problems of deep ethical significance that arise out of Abraham's situation are then posed and discussed. The book closes with an epilogue in which the author again expresses the need for each generation to stop at faith.

That faith is the main topic of *Fear and Trembling* is obvious. Kierkegaard revealed this fact within the book:

> It is now my intention to draw out from the story of Abraham the dialectical consequences inherent in it, expressing them in the form of problemata, in order to see what a tremendous paradox faith is, a paradox which is capable of transforming a murder into a holy act well-pleasing to God, a paradox which gives Isaac back to Abraham, which no thought can master, because faith begins precisely there where thinking leaves off.[3]

But in addition to the theme of faith, interpreters have seen other purposes, themes and hidden meanings in this work. Many have pointed to the relation between the book and the author's broken engagement with Regina Olsen. Most understand Kierkegaard as identifying himself with the figure of Abraham: as Abraham has to sacrifice Isaac, so the author felt compelled to sacrifice his love.[4] But others, such as Gregor Malantschuk, see Kierkegaard as Isaac:

> Kierkegaard simply wanted to tell Regina that he himself was being sacrificed, and therefore he had to sacrifice her...We must think of Kierkegaard as an Isaac who, unlike the biblical Isaac, is aware that he is being sacrificed.[5]

Of greater interest than speculation concerning the role of Kierkegaard within the book is the concept of ethics which is reflected in it. The author raises a significant ethical question. In the words of Kierkegaard's biographer, Walter Lowrie, the book raises the question, is Abraham a "prerogative instance of an exception to the universal...can the universal maxims of morality be suspended by the pursuit of a particular end indicated directly by God?"[6] The great practical consequences of this question are profoundly stated by Ronald Grimsley:

> A sacrifice like Abraham's raises in a very acute form the question of putting aside the fulfillment of moral obligations for the sake of some higher ideal. With religious faith of this kind we move from the safe ground of universal values to the paradox and uncertainty of individual faith...the "knight of faith"...cannot relate his situation to the realm of universal values.[7]

Although all of Kierkegaard's writings have been subjected to various interpretations, perhaps no aspect of his thought has been more open to misunderstanding than his ethic. In this regard James Collins rightly declares,

> his teaching on the possibility of suspending ethical duties has been given a sensational twist, so that a Sartre can conclude that a consistent existentialist must strictly be the creator of his own moral values and obligations. This inference is possible only when Kierkegaard's ethical reflections are cut off from their context in this overall study of the various modes of existence.[8]

In actuality, Kierkegaard never set out to build a system of ethics, even an existential system. He considered himself a corrective, not a norm. He was content to let the Kantian-Hegelian system remain, but desired through his writings to pry his fellow Danes out of their habit of hiding behind this system and to help them realize that they must stand as individuals directly before God. To this end three questions are posed in *Fear and Trembling* by means of which the Hegelian claim to have surpassed Christian faith is examined. These questions form the basis of Kierkegaard's critique of the purely ethical way of life.

1. "Is there such a thing as a teleological suspension of the ethical?" Kant's ethical system makes conformity to the universal law the highest good. To Kierkegaard this is abhorrent, because it dethrones God from his status of being the chief end of the individual human being. For Kierkegaard, neither obedience to the law from a virtuous will nor universal moral laws can be ends in themselves. Laws are "good" only as they refer back to the Creator, and a person is "good" only as one searches for God alone. Thus, Kierkegaard opposes Kant's emphasis on absolute obedience to universal law on the ground that one's chief end, namely the search for God, must never be truncated by philosophical convictions concerning universal law. Kant directs the human will to universal laws, but Kierkegaard points out that God alone is the proper object of the will.

In the same way Kierkegaard finds Hegel's ethic, with its emphasis upon the subordination of the individual will to the will of the community, to be scandalous. In such a system, Abraham, who is willing to sacrifice Isaac, can only be seen as a murderer. But this is not the case -- Abraham is a hero of the Bible, and Abraham's act is hailed as an example of faith. Hence, Hegel's ethic cannot be correct, for as the Abraham story shows, the individual acting in faith is above universal ethical laws.

When God calls an individual, that person becomes responsible to one who is infinitely higher than all moral laws and customs of society. For this reason the demands made by the Lord are higher than personal responsibilities to family and community. The true Christian, then, must obey ethical norms only when they do not conflict with the call of God. Should the Lord so require, the norms of the community, which have only temporal goals, must be suspended for the higher goal of God. According to Kierkegaard this rejection of ethical norms in answering the call of God is the "teleological suspension of the ethical," which must be valid if Abraham is not to be lost.

2. "Is there such a thing as an absolute duty toward God?" In Kantian ethics God is approached through obedience to universal laws. For Kierkegaard this is a very dangerous doctrine. First, it renders God unimportant for ethical responsibility, ultimately leading to ethical atheism, since personal duty is directed toward the law and not toward God. Second, Kant's ethic causes persons to hide behind an ethical system. Rather than being a reminder of the direct responsibility of each person before God, Kantianism teaches that obedience to God is mediated by obedience to an ethical system. In this way one's relationship to God is seen as determined only indirectly, namely by one's relationship to the universal law.

In contrast to all such ethical teaching the faith of Abraham was not based on his relation to universal law. If that had been the case, he would have been a sinner -- a murderer. Rather, Abraham exemplifies an instance in which duty was founded directly and immediately on God. His action was right, not because it was in accordance with the law (it actually was not), but because it was directed toward

God. Therefore, there is an absolute duty toward God, Kierkegaard concludes, one which is not mediated by one's duty toward ethical laws.

3. "Was Abraham ethically defensible in keeping silent about his purpose before Sarah, before Eleazar, before Isaac?" According to Hegel and Kant being silent is indefensible, since an act is judged to be "right" in so far as it is in accordance with universal law. In the *Philosophie des Rechts* Hegel declares it is undesirable to leave moral decisions to the fallible individual conscience. Rather, the state must be the final authority. For Hegel, then, one's ethical task is to "reveal himself in the universal."

If Hegel is correct, Abraham's silence marks him as a sinner. But according to Kierkegaard Abraham had to remain silent. As one commentator rightly concludes: "Had Abraham tried to explain that he was not a murderer, who would believe him? So he was committed to a painful silence and concealment."[9] In contrast to the Hegelian ideal, Abraham, the hero of the biblical story, did not reveal his purpose, but sought to be justified in the presence of God alone.

The implication of Abraham's silence is clear. Once an individual comes into a relationship with the eternal God and acknowledges a higher obligation than that of the community, "he becomes isolated from the community and cannot make himself understood by it."[10] Universal laws can be discussed and explained by means of reference to the interests of the community. But God's command to an individual can be contrary to the interests of the community and therefore cannot be discussed, explained or understood. For this reason the true Christian may find it necessary to keep silent and with this silence be misunderstood, according to Kierkegaard.

At first one might be drawn to the life of the individual of faith as exemplified by Abraham. Such a life is rightly perceived as freeing the individual from bondage to legal systems. But Kierkegaard cautions against any hasty decision. Any would-be follower must understand that this life is one of "fear and trembling," for it is filled with dread. First, there is the dread of being wrong. As Thomas Croxall aptly states:

> Suppose after all Abraham was mistaken, suppose the whole thing was but a temptation of the devil. Who can save him then? Deftly Johannes depicts the horror of Abraham. A tragic hero one can understand, and he claims our tears. But one cannot weep over Abraham.[11]

If wrong, Abraham could not have received the honor and respect given even to a tragic hero, according to Kierkegaard. The tragic hero must make a great personal sacrifice for the sake of some ethical duty. Yet in spite of this sacrifice, his action is profitable for someone. But had Abraham been wrong concerning God's command to kill Isaac, his action would have benefited no one. Rather than being admired by others in spite of his tragedy, he would have been condemned by all as a murderer.

Secondly, there is the dread of silence. Johannes de Silentio suggests there are two possible types of silence. Demonic silence is that condition in which the individual is prevented from speaking only because of some psychological motive. But the silence of the person of faith is due solely to one's relationship with God. Because there are these two possibilities, the individual, who like Abraham cannot disclose the purpose of an action, must evaluate this silence in order to determine its quality: Is it truly the silence of faith, or is it demonic?

Finally, there is the dread caused by the individual's own commitments. Many would seek to join Abraham, the man of faith, solely with the motive of being free to practice lawlessness. In contrast, however, the genuine individual, according to Kierkegaard, is not blind to the importance of morality. Such a person is sincerely attached to universal moral laws. Nevertheless, this one knows that morality is not an end in itself. The moral life is pursued with the full realization that one may be called to suspend universal morality for the sake of God. This characteristic of the true individual of faith is shown by the nature of Abraham's faith. By faith he steadfastly expected to receive Isaac back, even if Isaac were to be sacrificed. In the same way, by faith the true individual of faith expects to receive what was given up in the act of obedience, namely virtue. At the same time, however, the individual of faith no longer sees morality or virtue as determining one's relationship to God.

In summary, Soren Kierkegaard sought to provide a corrective to the nineteenth century ethical ideal. As Adam and Eve desired to have their position before God mediated by some external creation, so also Kierkegaard's contemporaries attempted to mediate the position of the individual before God by an ethical system. Each individual must stand before God as one responsible directly to the Creator. This is the message of Kierkegaard to the Danish Kantians and Hegelians.

The Twentieth Century Echo

In recent years Kierkegaard's position has been assailed in various ways. Some critics suggest that he misunderstood the story of Abraham. Modern biblical criticism, it is claimed, treats the story "as a Midrash, designed to show that God abhors the then prevalent practice of offering the first-born son to the Deity," thus implying that "its ethical purpose is clear."[12] In other words, God's command to Abraham is not to be confused with some historical event in the life of a historical person, but rather is a vivid way of criticizing the ancient, widespread practice of human sacrifice. The biblical account is a story designed to caution Israel against the sin of religious infanticide.

Regardless of whether or not this interpretation is accurate, as a criticism of Kierkegaard it misses the point. The Genesis story depicts God as commanding the sacrifice of Isaac, so that *within the narrative* God appears to be commanding an action contrary to the divine moral law. The purpose of the story may be related to child sacrifices, but for the story's hero the personal, existential choice centers around obedience to God's rightful commands. Herein lie the dread, anxiety and forced silence.

Kierkegaard is also criticized for limiting ethics to the universal or normative. Disagreeing both with Kant and

Kierkegaard, some suggest that ethics includes everything that is right, even if it is abnormal. Croxall says,

> Admittedly faith has to leap *beyond* reasons, but not contrary to reasonableness. In other words, our reason has to tell us that good is likely to ensue from our act of faith, not evil; which is as much as to say that ethics will be reinstated.[13]

Croxall bases this criticism on the nature of God as rational. Through Abraham's faithful obedience, God "would show His ways to be ultimately right, reasonable, and therefore ultimately ethical. 'Shall not the Judge of all the earth do *right?'* is the confidence of the man of faith."[14]

In response, two things must be noted. First, Kierkegaard is not attempting to establish an ethical system. Rather, he is supplying a corrective for Kant, who taught that the proper course of action is determined by what one would will to be a universal, and for Hegel, who saw the State as the guardian of universal law. Thus, the modern rejection of Kant need not entail a rejection of Kierkegaard, but rather would include an acceptance of his corrective.

More important though, this criticism shows that its proponent has misunderstood the account of Abraham. In all likelihood Abraham's reason did *not* tell him that good would ensue from his act of murder. Rather, reason, as defined by Croxall, must have sided with the moral absolute and against all possibility of an ensuing good. He was to kill Isaac, the son of promise! What possible good could come of it? It was Abraham's faith in the greatness of God, not the reasonable nature of the request, which caused him trustingly to obey the command. Kierkegaard disagrees with the idea that God will always act according to human reason. He is the transcendent, incomprehensible God, who is often not understood by the human mind. As Paul wrote, "How unsearchable his judgments, and his paths beyond tracing out!" (Romans 11:33). For this reason Kierkegaard resists any attempt to limit God within the sphere of any ethical system.

The futile attempt to mediate the human position before God with ethical systems continues today. The Kantian tradition, for example, continues into the present in the form of what is called "non-conflicting absolutism." Some have altered Kant's system somewhat by seeking to base universals in the very nature of God or in "God's revealed Word." The central thrust, however, remains the same -- the attempt to discover universal norms which must not be disobeyed at any price. In this understanding, to break such a norm is to sin against God.

In addition to modern Kantianism there are several other systems which have received much attention in recent years. Joseph Fletcher's situationalism declares "love" to be the norm for ethical actions. Whatever is done from the motive of love for others is right, while whatever is not motivated by love is wrong. Another system is Norman Geisler's hierarchicalism, which declares that

> things are ordered on a scale of good, ranging from least to most good. Ethically speaking, some things are better than others. Values must be weighted, and one must act accordingly. Lesser goods must give way to greater goods.[15]

In the eyes of a hierarchicalist to break one norm while obeying a higher is ethically right.

While these two systems are advanced by persons who consider themselves Christians, there are other ethical orientations which are not built on a Christian base. Naturalistic empiricism, for example, has as its goal, in the words of James Collins,

> to place ethics upon a completely naturalistic basis, by providing an explanation of obligation and the other aspects of moral life, without making an appeal to a transcendent God.[16]

As an answer to naturalism, Kierkegaard alone is insufficient. Naturalism, however, tends to base standards of conduct on the goals, interests and actions of the community or of some specific group, reminiscent of nineteenth century Hegelianism. Therefore, Kierkegaard's attack on Hegel's system is indirectly applicable to naturalism. Kierkegaard decries any attempt to release oneself from accountability before God by hiding behind the ethics of a group, since the individual is thereby destroyed. Inasmuch as naturalism attempts to do just that, it falls under Kierkegaard's critique.

A similar response may be offered from a Kierkegaardian perspective to contemporary situationalism. It also seeks to mediate the human position before God by an ethical system, even though the system has but one norm. For Kierkegaard any norm that demands total allegiance can lead the individual from humanity's chief end, God. Further, even in situationalism Abraham stands condemned, since his willingness to sacrifice Isaac must be judged as unethical, when measured against the norm of love.

Norman Geisler claims that hierarchicalism is exempt from the critique which arises from the case of Abraham. According to Geisler this system

> takes issue with Kierkegaard's analysis, claiming that there was a higher ethical purpose or principle in view of which Abraham was ethically justified in his decision. The higher principle was his duty to obey God which always transcends one's duty to another man.[17]

In response to this claim several things must be observed. Geisler is in fundamental agreement with Kierkegaard, insofar as he admits that at times certain ethical norms must be suspended for the sake of a higher goal (for Geisler this goal is obedience to a higher norm). In other words, both agree that the story of Abraham, in which the injunction against murder was suspended for a higher *telos*, stands as a counter-example to any ethical system which posits a plurality of norms that are all equally absolute.

It is precisely at this point, however, that Geisler parts company with Kierkegaard. Kierkegaard accepts the Kantian understanding that norms are universally binding. Geisler, in contrast, speaks of the universal nature of norms, but then places a limitation on their universality: "each universal ethical norm is absolutely and universally binding in its own sphere unless it is transcended by a higher norm."[18] This limitation, Geisler admits, results in norms which are "not universal in the broadest sense of the word," since "not all absolutes are absolutely absolute. Some are only relatively absolute, i.e. relative to their particular area."[19]

In defining ethical terms in this non-traditional way Geisler appears to be playing a semantic game in which universals are not universally applicable and absolutes are relative. This game continues as he seeks to differentiate between an *exception to* a norm (which is always disallowed) and an *exemption from* a norm (which is granted each time a higher norm is obeyed at the cost of a lower one). In this same game the non-compliance with a lower norm for the sake of a higher one does not constitute a transgression, but rather a transcending of the lower norm.[20]

This relativising of absolutes calls hierarchicalism into question as an ethical system. One wonders how a law which is not universal can be called a law. If there are exemptions from a norm (which actually constitute exceptions to it), then that norm is not a norm in the usual sense of the term, but rather is either an empirical statement of what human beings do or a rule of thumb to guide conduct in "normal" situations.

Herein lies a glaring weakness of hierarchicalism. It claims to include a plurality of universal norms. But in actuality it contains only one norm, that which stands at the top of the hierarchy, for only that law must always be obeyed. In Geisler's thinking this single norm appears to be obedience to God. If this is indeed the case, he is in fundamental agreement with Kierkegaard. Ultimately, Abraham can be justified in Geisler's system only because Geisler agrees with Kierkegaard that the life of obedience to any plurality of universal laws must be abandoned whenever such a life conflicts with one's absolute duty toward God. In short, either the various norms in Geisler's hierarchy are all universals, and he is in basic agreement with Kant (which he claims is not the case), or there is only one norm, the individual's duty to God, which is not a norm in the usual sense of ethical laws, but transcends ethics. In the first alternative Abraham stands as a counter-example to Geisler's position, whereas in the second alternative his position is that of Kierkegaard, with whom he claims to disagree.

Since hierarchicalism cannot be hailed as a consistent ethical system replacing that of Kant, Kierkegaard's message, standing as it does within the Kantian-Hegelian framework, remains relevant. No norm (not even Norm Geisler) will ever be able to mediate one's position before God. The life of the individual must always be directed toward God alone, who may on occasion ask one to act in a seemingly unethical manner. Obedience to God's call, even when this entails disobedience to ethical norms, demands that the Christian suspend the norms for the sake of a higher goal.

Those who calculate obedience to God only in terms of obedience to a given ethical system will always find Kierkegaard's knight of faith an enigma. Nevertheless, the Christian must risk misunderstanding in the quest for knowing and doing God's will. Obedience to God entails a further risk, the risk of being mistaken. Therefore, the Christian must act with fear and trembling, with humility and repentance, yet acting as well in faith, for "faith begins...where reason leaves off." The life of faith is not easy, but it is the way to true freedom. This is the message of Soren Kierkegaard.

****

> When the woman saw that the fruit of the tree was good for food and pleasing to the eye, and also desirable for gaining wisdom, she took some and ate it. She also gave some to her husband, who was with her, and he ate it. Then the eyes of both of them were opened, and they realized they were naked;...Then the man and his wife heard the

> sound of the LORD God as he was walking in the garden in the cool of the day (Gen. 3:6,7a,8a).

The man and his wife repented of that which they had done and said to God, "Lord, we have sinned against heaven and in your sight; we are no longer worthy to be called your children."

> But the father said to his servants, 'Quick! Bring the best robe and put it on him. Put a ring on his finger and sandals on his feet. Bring the fattened calf and kill it. Let's have a feast and celebrate. For this son of mine was dead and is alive again; he was lost and is found.' So they began to celebrate (Luke 15:22-24).

Notes

1. Immanuel Kant, *Fundamental Principles of the Metaphysics of Morals*, in *Literary and Philosophical Essays* (The Harvard Classics), ed. Charles W. Eliot, (New York: P. F. Collier & Son, 1938), p. 332. For an alternate formulation, see Immanuel Kant, *Critique of Practical Reason*, trans. Lewis White Beck (New York: The Bobbs-Merrill Co., 1956), p. 30.
2. G. W. F. Hegel, *Philosophy of Right*, trans. T. M. Knox (New York: Oxford University Press, 1942). For a succinct summary of Hegel's book, see Thomas Henry Croxall, *Kierkegaard Commentary* (New York: Harper and Brothers, 1956), p. 152.
3. Soren Kierkgaard, *Fear and Trembling*, trans. Walter Lowrie (Princeton, New Jersey: Princeton University Press), p. 64.
4. See, for example, Ronald Grimsley, *Kierkegaard: A Biographical Introduction* (New York: Charles Scribner's Sons, 1973), p. 46.

5. Gregor Malantshcuk, *Kierkegaard's Thought*, trans. Howard V. and Edna H. Hong (Princeton, New Jersey: Princeton University Press, 1971), pp. 236, 238.

6. Walter Lowrie, *Kierkegaard*, 2 vols. (New York: Harper and Brothers, 1962), I/264.

7. Ronald Grimsley, *Kierkegaard: A Biographical Introduction* (New York: Charles Scribner's Sons, 1973), p. 47.

8. James Daniel Collins, *The Mind of Kierkegaard* (Chicago: Henry Regnery Company, 1965), p. 67.

9. Croxall, *Kierkegaard Commentary*, p. 150.

10. Gregor Malantschuk, *Kierkegaard's Way to the Truth*, trans. Mary Michelsen (Minneapolis: Augsburg Publishing House, 1963), p. 41.

11. Croxall, *Kierkegaard Commentary*, p. 157.

12. Idem, *Kierkegaard Studies* (London: Lutterworth Press, 1948), p. 126.

13. Ibid.

14. Ibid., p. 127.

15. Geisler, *Ethics*, p. 121.

16. Collins, *The Mind of Kierkegaard*, p. 69.

17. Geisler, *Ethics*, p. 121.

18. Ibid., p. 131.

19. Ibid., p. 132.

20. Ibid., p. 130.

Towards a Biblical Model of Counseling

John D. Carter

To attempt a full model of biblical counseling in a single article would be presumptuous. Therefore, this article has the more limited goal of defining specific components of a biblical model of counseling. It will begin with a description of the assumptions or perspectives which the author maintains are essential for a biblical theory of counseling. The next section will focus on the two biblical concepts, the Flesh and the Spirit, as they form the foundation for a biblical model of morality and immorality and, thus, a framework for counseling. The third section will show how responsibility and autonomy are part of a balanced biblical therapy and how they are related to the analysis of flesh and spirit. A conclusion and implication section will complete the article.

The Foundational Orientation

Unity of Truth

The assumptive foundation for the biblical model of counseling developed in this article is an expansion and clarification of what Carter (1977) has called a Christianity *Integrates* psychology model. This model begins with the assumption that "all truth is God's truth." Truth is understood as the New Testament concept of *alethia*, that is, something which is both voracious and real. Therefore, truth is more than its conceptualization or verbalization. It is something real. Reality in reference to God and the Scripture is also personal because God is personal and Scripture is the living voice of the Spirit

Relationship of Creation and Redemption

A second dimension which Carter outlined was that the Integrates model stresses equally providence and soteriology. God is the creator of the universe and humanity, and God is also the source of redemption. Mankind is created in God's image (Genesis 1:26, 27) but, as a result of the Fall, the image has become marred. In redemption, the image is being renewed (Ephesians 4:24; Colossians 3:10). Thus, God is at work in the world in two ways: through creation and through redemption. These two ways have historically been called general grace and special grace. Any view of counseling which calls itself biblical must recognize that God is at work in his world (which includes humankind) and also in redemption.

The larger impact of this issue is that God created psychology when he created humanity. Thus, there is a lawful psychology which operates in the human order. These laws are observable, like the rest of the lawfulness in the created order. The truths or laws of psychology are integrated with the truths of Scripture, because God is the author of both. Psychology, as just defined, is not the same as various systems or theories of psychology. Elsewhere, Carter (1977) has called the former "psychology with a small 'p'" and the latter "psychology with a capital 'P.'" The former refers to principles and concepts, while the latter refers to methods and theories with their implicit metaphysics.

The above two assumptions constitute the core or foundation on which an integrated model of counseling must be based. However, there are at least two additional issues which need to be emphasized as an adequate basis for a fully biblical model.

Network of Biblical Concepts

A third aspect of any biblical model of counseling is that it cannot be built on a single concept or even several biblical concepts alone. Rather, it must utilize the network of biblical concepts so as to maintain the balance, emphasis, and centrality of those concepts as they appear in the text (cf. 1 Thessalonians 5:14). There are several words in the New Testament which are frequently used to relate to what seems to be the counseling process: *noutheteo*, *parakaleo*, *paramutheomai* and some less frequently used words such as *hupodeiknumi*, *antechomai*, *paraineo* and *protrepo*. What does each of these concepts mean, how is it used, and in what way is each related to the others? Adams (1970) has analyzed *noutheteo* and its relationship to *didasko*. The other concepts which seem to relate to counseling have not been so analyzed nor have their interrelationships been clarified. However, Cerny (1976) has made a preliminary attempt to examine *parakaleo*, and Berry (1974) and Carter (1975) have noted the importance of this concept (frequently translated "comfort, console, or exhort"), because it is one of the spiritual gifts.

In addition to the issue of relationship among these concepts, there is the question of how each relates to specific problems or people. In 1 Thessalonians 5:14, the believers are encouraged (*parakaleo*) to admonish (*noutheteo*) the unruly, comfort (*paramutheomai*) the fainthearted, hold on to (*antechemai*) the weak, and be patient (*makrothumeo*) with everyone. This verse suggests widely varied helping styles to what seem to be three different problems, and a general style applicable to all people. Consequently, Minirth (1977) has argued that there is no single biblical model of counseling. Carlson (1976) has shown that Jesus used a wide variety of styles in relating to people. Hence, the question needs to be asked: "Is there a single model of counseling with a variety of techniques or is there more than one model in the Scripture?" (At the present stage of thinking, the author favors the former.)

Parameters of Counseling Models

The fourth issue, in many respects, involves aspects of the previous two issues. To speak of a biblical model or theory of counseling is to presume already the basic framework of the counseling model as it operates in our culture. A counseling model in this most general sense seems to have the following parameters, that is, it makes at least implicit assumptions about the following: human nature, the nature of pathology, the character and training of the counselor, the counselor's techniques, the counseling process (how change occurs), and the goal of counseling -- health. In relation to a biblical model, these parameters respectively become: humankind as created in God's image, that is, the aspects of substructure of human personality; the relationship of sin and psychopathology; who is qualified to counsel and how, that is, what is appropriate training and what are biblical intervention techniques; how change occurs as it relates to human nature; pathology and God's mediate or immediate involvement in the process; and finally, what is biblical normalcy or maturity.

As indicated above, the question "What is biblical counseling?" cannot be asked without facing the issue that counseling has a structure, function, meaning, and social location within the culture which is basically defined in psychological terms. This question is not problematic in terms of the assumption underlying the Integrates model since the basic principles of psychology are presumed to be both true and congruent with biblical truth.

Biblical Morality

Performance Morality as Distortion

Biblical morality, as defined in this section, is developed as a framework on which a biblical model of counseling may be built. Biblical morality must be distinguished from an approach that seems to be current in much of the Christian world but is, in fact, a distortion of biblical teaching. This distorted version will be called a "performance morality." It is characterized by doing, achieving, or performing. At its core is the notion "I am what I do." It is undergirded with "shoulds" and "should nots," for example: "I should read the Bible, pray, and love my neighbor; I should not lie, steal, or be involved in sex outside of marriage." In most Christian groups the list is much longer. However, the real problem is not in the length of the list or even in its content (which is often partly biblical), but with the principle of performance.

Conscience. Supporters of performance morality often appeal to two biblical concepts: conscience and guilt. The word "conscience (*suneideses*) appears 32 times in the New Testament, mainly in the epistles. Unfortunately, it is not used in a very systematic way, so it is difficult to think of it in a doctrinal sense. Rather, it appears as a *correlate* of the character of a particular person. The one exception is Romans 2:15, where conscience is defined as the feedback (the conscience bearing witness) from the "law...written on their hearts." In the two extended discussions of meat offered to idols (1 Corinthians 8 and 9), it is clear that there are two types of conscience -- the weaker brother's and the stronger brother's. Conscience seems to be a correlate of belief. In Hebrews 10:22, the believers in Christ are described as having their evil consciences purified. On the other hand, Paul, in 1 Timothy 1:5 and 1:19, ties faith in Christ and a good conscience together. But in Titus 1:15, the defiled and unbelieving have a defiled conscience. Thus, it becomes clear that conscience has the same character (good or evil) as the one possessing it. The New Testament, therefore, never appeals to conscience as a guide. There are appeals to Christ (Galatians 5;1), the Spirit (Galatians 3:3), love and affection for the Christian community (Philippians 2:12), the believer's great salvation (1 Peter 1:3-13), the believer's position in Christ (Colossians 2:20; 3:1) and the good (James 4:17), but never to conscience as such.

Guilt. The second concept often appealed to by the supporter of a performance morality is guilt. In the New Testament, there are three Greek words translated "guilt": *hupodikos*, *opheilo*, *enochos*. However, an examination indicates they are virtually always used in a legal sense, for example, "the whole world held accountable to God." (Romans 3:19). The appeal here is not to feelings or experiences, that is, not to psychological effect, but to one's legal status. There seem to be two exceptions: Hebrews 9:14 and 1 John 3:20. In the Hebrews passage, the potency of Christ and his sacrifice is contrasted to the impotence of the Old Testament sacrificial system. In verse 9:14, one of the powers of the blood of Christ is that it can "cleanse our consciences from acts that lead to death." The conscience makes people feel they ought to do, act, or atone, and feel guilty. Christ's blood has the power to purge the believer's conscience of the need to perform dead works -- works that are attempts at atonement.

The second passage, 1 John 3:20, does not use the term "guilt," but rather "condemn." However, guilt produces the feelings of condemnation. This verse says that "if our hearts condemn us, God is greater than our hearts and knows all things." The context is describing a believer's walk with God. In this context, a believer may feel condemned; however, God is not on the side of condemnation but on the believer's side. Thus, it becomes clear that the New Testament appeals neither to conscience as a guide nor to guilt as a motive for the believer living a Christian life.

Identity-Based Morality

Rather than a performance-based morality rooted in conscience and guilt (i.e., self-atonement), the New Testament describes an identity-based morality rooted in our position in Christ and our relationship to God as believers. It is only on this biblical foundation that a biblical model of counseling can be based. There are three aspects of biblical morality which build sequentially on each other: the believer's position, the believer's positional identity, and the renewal of the image.

Believer's position. The believer's position is variously described as *in* Christ, *in* the Spirit, *in* Him, and *in* the Light. Being *in* Christ is the basis for being a new creation (1 Corinthians 5:17). It is also the basis for resolving the fear of punishment which is produced in the believer by the moral conflict in our nature (Romans 8:1). The assertion that "there is now no condemnation for those who are *in* Christ

Jesus" means that the believer need not fear condemnation or punishment as a result of one's experienced moral conflict as described in Romans 7:14-29. In fact, the believer's position in Christ, with the accompanying loss or punishment, is used by Paul as a basis for dealing with the believer's experienced anguish in the personal effort to be morally good. *In* Christ means the believer stands as a son or daughter before God, having the righteousness of Christ, no longer dead in sin (separated from God) or subject to condemnation.

Believer's identity. The second aspect of biblical morality is the believer's positional identity. In the New Testament, morality is often described as Spirit in contrast to the Flesh, where Spirit and Flesh are principles. Flesh, as the sin principle, is described as contrary to the Spirit (Galatians 5:17) and appears to have a bipolar character. In appealing to believers to live morally, the New Testament contrasts believers' former positional deadness with their present positional life. That former deadness is the Flesh. Its bipolar character will be illustrated by two extended New Testament passages. Romans 6, begins with a rhetorical question: "Shall we go on sinning so that grace may increase?" In the next 10 verses Paul answers by describing the believer's positional identification with Christ in his death, burial, and resurrection. This discussion of positional identification ends in verse 11 with "Count yourselves dead to sin but alive to God." It is only after this culminating statement about believers' identity that Paul then addresses specific actions: "Do not let sin reign in your mortal body...Do not offer the parts of your body to sin, as instruments of wickedness" (verses 12 and 13). Thus, the appeal to specific action is based on our positional identity with Christ, that is, the believer's actions ought to flow consequently from one's identity. We act morally *out of* our identity, not *in order to have* an identity. The Pauline order is very close to Christ's statement "out of the overflow of the heart the mouth speaks" (Matthew 12:34). The actions in verses 12 and 13, described as lusts and unrighteousness, appear to have a behavioral or bodily quality. In current clinical terminology these actions appear to be impulsivity or acting out behavior.

In contrast to the bodily impulsive action side of the Flesh, Colossians 2:20-23 addresses the ascetic-legalistic side of the Flesh. The passage begins "Since you died with Christ...why, as though you still belonged to [the world], do you submit to its rules." These rules are described as "Do not handle! Do not taste! Do not touch!...based on human commands." These and any humanly-devised legalistic prohibitions appear to be wise (i.e., to the Flesh) in their rigor and ascetic devotion but are, in fact, humanly-devised religion (self-atonement), in that this humanly-devised ascetic-legalism is a fleshly attempt to control the Flesh. The appeal in this passage is for the believer to give up these legalistic prohibitions and ascetic practices because of the Christian's identity with Christ. Colossians 3:1 continues this line of argument: "Since, then, you have been raised with Christ, set your hearts on things above, where Christ is seated at the right hand of God." Again, the appeal is to the believer's identity with Christ. It is only after the believer's identity has been clearly defined that there is a basis for Paul to address specific action. Hence, the behaviorally oriented commands, the "put to death" of Colossians 3:5-9 and the "put on" of 3:10, are clearly grounded in the believer's positional identity with Christ, which Paul has just defined.

Consequently, the logic of Romans 6 and Colossians 2-3 is the same: Believers are commanded to act morally, because they have a new identity *in* and *with* Christ. However, the believer's positional identity in Christ is also an experiential identity, since each believer has a personal relationship with Christ. (Identity is always a product of a relationship, i.e., there is no identity without relationship.) Hence, the biblical morality is a being-congruent morality, rather than an achievement-performance morality, because the believer is commanded to act congruently with one's positional and personal identity with Christ instead of performing in order to obtain an identity. The importance of this point will be stressed later in the article.

Renewal of the image. The third aspect of New Testament morality is the renewal of the image. Believers' sanctification is described as a renewal of the image -- the image of him that created them (Ephesians 4:24; Colossians 3:10). The reference in these passages most clearly is to Genesis 1:26, where humankind is described as being created in God's image. As a result of disobedience, humanity fell into sin. Theology has understood this fall as a marring of the image (Berkhof, 1959). However, the image is never lost or destroyed. Rather, the passage cited above describes sanctification as a renewal. The Greek word for renewal (*anakainoo*) basically means continued change towards newness and, in context, a change back to being like the original creation. Thus, the sanctifying process, or living according to New Testament morality, is grounded not only in believers' identity with Christ through salvation but also in our identity with God in creation. Consequently, the being-congruent morality is also congruency with one's original and fundamental nature as the image of God.

Counseling from a Biblical Model

In this third section, both techniques and approaches to counseling will be examined as they relate to the biblical model described above and illustrated in Figure 1. The contrariness of the Flesh and the Spirit (Galatians 5:17) is illustrated by the perpendicularity of Spirit to Flesh in the upper half of the figure. Also, the bipolar character of the Flesh is labeled. Though it was not fully developed above, the Spirit is a separate dimension, and believers become more Christ-like as they are being sanctified. Christ is pictured as embodying Law and Grace, that is, moral authority and grace-given freedom. The lower half of the figure illustrates, via six dimensions, three broad styles or models of counseling. Two of the models follow fleshly distortions, and the third model is patterned after Christ's relationship to the believer. The ascetic-legalistic side is a distortion of law, and the impulsivity side is a distortion of grace-given freedom. This point will be reemphasized after the types of theories are described.

Legalistic Counseling Style

The three styles of therapy will be reviewed, summarizing the contribution of each dimension to each type of therapy. (In this article, counseling and therapy are used interchangeably.) The legalistically structured therapy sets goals defined by the particular theory in question; the therapist presumes, by virtue of this role, the primary responsibility to produce change in the client. Values are clear and well-defined, being dictated by the theory. Either cognitions or behavior are the basic focus, with the technique being to increase or reinforce behavior change. Therapy is directive and, therefore, tends to be relatively short term.

Implusive Counseling Style

In the impulsive-oriented style of counseling, therapy goals are a product of either the client's or therapist's unconscious, or some combination of both. Responsibility for the client is abdicated by the therapist and presumed to be only the client's. Values are, therefore, relative. Feelings are the focus, and they are either interpreted or reflected. Hence, therapy is not directed and tends to be long term.

Relational Counseling Style

The third type of counseling can be called relationship-based counseling, in that it stresses and assumes a balance between responsibility and autonomy in the client and between discipline and empathy in the therapist. This is in contrast to the legalistic emphasis on responsibility and discipline and the impulsivity emphasis on autonomy and empathy. Relationship-oriented therapy maintains a balanced orientation of the various dimensions listed in Figure 1, but it is a balance that is not mechanical. The balance is based on an ongoing relationship between a client who has needs and a counselor who reflects both empathy and discipline because of a commitment to both human autonomy and human responsibility and a personal embodiment of those principles in counseling relationships.

In relationship-oriented therapy, goals emerge and are determined in the tension between the client's conscious and unconscious needs and the therapist's theoretic understanding of relationship. Thus, the therapist presumes the client's responsibility and takes the responsibility to encourage the client to master what the client is responsible for; in other words, responsibility is shared. Values are discovered as the free application of the client's autonomy in that person's sphere of responsibility. Feeling, cognition, and behavior are all a part of therapy. The therapist is neither directive nor non-directive, but is responsive to the client's feelings, behavior, or thoughts in terms of the presenting and continuing client problems. Thus counseling may be short term or long term as the need dictates.

The key to relationship counseling is that the counselor responds to the client as a person and not as a director or as merely a reflector or interpreter. It is this personal quality which embodies the reality that life is lived in responsibility and autonomy. It means the counselor is present, but separate from the client. It is the counselor's concrete, personal presence which allows for the type of relationship in which the client can experience oneself. Thus, clients can begin to experience their own autonomy and their own presence to themselves and others.

As was indicated above, identity emerges from a relationship. So, the client gains a new identity -- a healthy one -- from this relationship. The maturity the client gains from relationship therapy is interdependence, that is, the client comes to prefer (choose) relationship, but is able to stand alone as the need arises. This is in contrast to the legalistic counseling which creates dependence by telling the client what to do, that is, by placing the client in the dependent position. Impulsivity counseling creates an isolated autonomy via the counselor's presence only in reflections or interpretation and the assumption that the client alone determines one's own values.

Though the counselor is less than perfect, relationship counseling incorporates, via the counselor (person and technique, i.e., in a human way), these two qualities of Law and Grace, which are central in Christ's relationship to the believer. In the legalistic or impulsivity styles of counseling this is not true. Both of these styles represent a fleshly distortion (not only in counseling, but also in human relationships in general), in that they distort by overemphasis one aspect of the Spirit and ignore the other. This results in a fleshly distortion of biblically based counseling.

Implications and Conclusion

The model for relationship counseling explicated in the second section of this article is grounded in the Christianity *Integrates* psychology orientation outlined by Carter (1977). This orientation assumes that "all truth is God's truth." Therefore, there is a counseling style (theory-model) which is congruent and integrated with biblical revelation, and there may be any number of counseling styles (theories-models) which are not. In the second section the foundation of the biblical counseling model was defined as the biblical relationship between the Flesh and Spirit as illustrated in Figure 1. Growth in the spirit is shown to be growth toward and identification with the Person of Christ, a person who embodies Law (as truth and authority) and Grace (as free-spontaneous life). The Flesh is defined as the bipolar dimension of Legalism-Impulsivity. These two aspects of the Flesh are defined and illustrated with Scripture which specifically describes both the believer's positional death to each of these aspects of Flesh and the Christian's life in Christ. The Bible's appeal for moral actions is based on the believer's ongoing life in and with Christ.

The bottom half of Figure 1 outlines six dimensions that relate to counseling: goals, responsibility, values, cognition/feeling/behavior, technique, and duration. Three approaches to counseling are then outlined. Two of these correspond in character with the two aspects of the Flesh. The third, relationship counseling, corresponds with the Spirit, that is, it is modeled after the relationship the believer has with Christ. Counselors act empathetically and with discipline (self-control); in so doing, they act autonomously and responsibly, incorporating and modeling Grace and Law in their relationships. Though any human counselor is less than perfect, relationship counseling incorporates, via the counselor (person and technique, i.e., in a human way), these two qualities of Law and Grace, which are central in Christ's relationship to the believer. In the legalistic or impulsivity styles of counseling, this is not true. Both of these styles represent a fleshly distortion not only in counseling, but also in human relationships in general; they distort by overemphasizing one aspect of the Spirit and ignoring the other. This produces a fleshly distortion of biblically based counseling. In conclusion it is interesting to note, as an aside, that the two fleshly distortions of counseling are mutually antagonistic to each other.

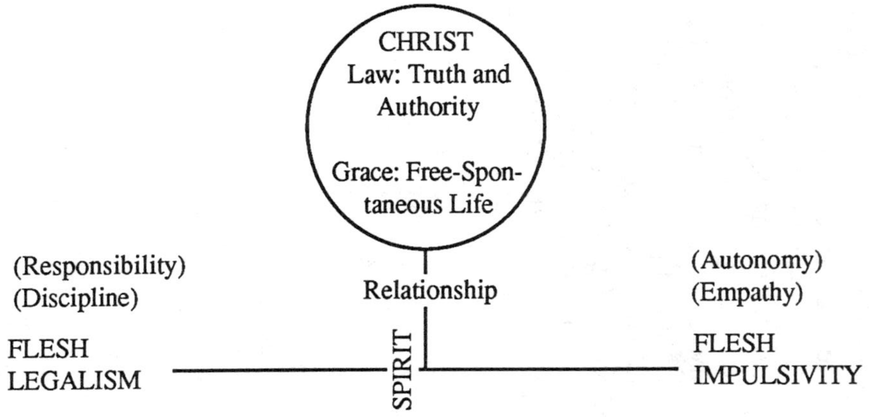

Dimensions	Legalistically Structured Therapy	Relationship Based Therapy	Impulsivity Oriented Therapy
1. Goals set by:	Theory	Individual/ Situational	Unconscious
2. Responsibility:	Therapist	Shared	Therapist Abdicates/ Presumes Client
3. Values:	Theory Dicatates	Discovered	Relative
4. Cognition Feeling/Behavior:	Cognitions/ Behaviors	All	Feelings
5. Style-Technique:	Directive	Personal	Reflective/Interpretive
6. Duration:	Short	Either	Long

Figure 1. A Biblical Model for Counseling

References

Adams, J. *Competent to Counsel.* Grand Rapids: Baker, 1970.

Berkhof, L. *Systematic Theology*. Grand Rapids: Eerdmans, 1959.

Berry, M. "Counseling in the Medical Office." *Journal of Psychology and Theology*, 1974, 2(3), pp. 174-181.

Carter, J.D. "Adams' Theory of Nouthetic Counseling." *Journal of Psychology and Theology* , 1975, 3(3), pp. 143-155.

Carter, J.D. "Secular and Sacred Models of Psychology and Religion." *Journal of Psychology and Theology*, 1977, 5(3), 197-208.

Carlson, D. "Jesus' Style of Relating: The Search For the Biblical View of Counseling." *Journal of Psychology and Theology*, 1976, 4(3), pp. 181-192.

Cerny, L.J. "A New Testament Counseling Model: *Parakaleo*." Unpublished manuscript. May, 1976.

Minirth, F. *Christian Psychiatry*. Old Tappan, NJ: Revell, 1977.

Human Freedom and Integration: Testing the Coherence of Theology and Psychology

Gerry Breshears

The Vision for Integration

Dr. Vernon Grounds taught my first seminary class. I had no idea of my privilege. The course title, Pastoral Care, gave ample freedom for his erudition. Our stubborn ignorance provided even more challenge for his skill as a teacher. We came to him, sure of God's call on our lives, sure of our skills as Bible interpreters, sure of our grasp on God's design of the world. Dr. Grounds encouraged our confidence, while challenging our ignorance. He lectured to help us know the facts, but more often he questioned to help us know our ignorance. Above all he transmitted a vision to us, a vision to see every part of our world, and to see it from a Christian vantage point.

His burden was the integration of a world view which would guide our actions and attitudes in this world.

He helped us to see that science (understood in the sense of the German, *Wissenschaft*, knowledge in the broad sense) can help us know *how* our world works. It can help us explain how the grass grows, how a brain functions, how the galaxies zoom through the vast emptiness of space.[1] Yet science alone cannot responsibly tell us where the world came from, why it is here or where it is going. Theology helps us know *why* our world exists, why humans exist, why we act in the baffling way we do. It focuses on God's unique actions, the human situation in general, and ultimate purposes. Yet theology alone cannot address the problems of specific times, specific societies, or specific humans.

Science without theology, the how without the why, reduces us to mere description. Theology without science, why without how, reduces us to mere abstraction. Integration marries the disciplines, helping us to see the world both as it is and as it ought to be.

Dr. Grounds would be satisfied with nothing less than a world view which begins from the theologian's "why" and takes full account of the scientist's "how." His questions constantly helped us to think again of our theology, to look again at our world, to bring the two disciplines to bear on one world.

We name this task integration. It is the organization of the various concepts, tasks, methods, purposes into a coherent whole. The possibility of integration comes from the conviction that one God is the Creator and Redeemer of the world, that all that is truth is from him. This unity behind reality assures us that constructing a coherent world view is possible.[2] Integration is a complex task, performed on at least six levels ranging from the world view level of presuppositions through the levels of general and specific propositions to the hypothesis and data levels.[3]

Dr. Grounds concentrated his efforts on the integration of theology and psychology. The possibility of integration of any two specific disciplines depends on overlap between the two fields. These two disciplines overlap in many areas: defining the nature of the person, describing the paradigmatic person, understanding the desperate effects of sin, overcoming sin's effects in individuals and society, to name a few. Each discipline informs the other. For example, the church, God's preeminent means of administering his grace today, ministers best when it utilizes the best psychological and sociological insights. Psychology heals psychopathology best when it takes account of the Bible's revelation of the nature of humans as the image of God, sin as affront to God and Jesus Christ as the paradigmatic human.

All Christians integrate their science and their theology. No psychologist could diagnose pathology, indeed could not even define pathology, without deciding what the ideal human ought to be. No theologian could be satisfied merely to manipulate Biblical propositions. Our Lord scourged the Pharisees for overlooking the needs of people in their devotion to their theology (Matt. 23:23; Mark 7:5-11). What troubles us is not *whether*, but *how* to integrate.

The Roadblock of Diverse Theological and Psychological Models

The integration of theology and psychology is impossible. Even a brief survey of different theological and psychological models illustrates the fundamental differences in such basic theological issues as sin, redemption and sanctification, and such psychological issues as personality, neurosis, therapy and wholeness. Successful integration must be between specific formulations of both theology and psychology.

Commitment to biblical authority helpfully reduces the bewildering diversity of theological options. Because every theological model must be tested against the Bible, possibilities for any such model cannot stray beyond that boundary. Even within bounds of evangelical Christianity the differences between theologies astounds anyone who holds to the perspicuity of Scripture. The spectrum between more Calvinistic and more Wesleyan formulations springs primarily from different understandings of the relationship between God's initiative and human responsibility in salvation.

Psychological models utilized by evangelicals are even more diverse than evangelical theologies. This diversity springs from the lack of commitment to any psychological authority source and from the relatively recent emergence of the models of psychology. Where the Bible serves to limit speculations by giving propositional truth about reality, psychology, apart from integration with theology, is limited only by the bewildering complexity of humanity. Theology has undergone centuries of refinement which have eliminated many false conceptions. Psychology has enjoyed no such extended analysis. Freud opened his office just a century ago. Most of the models have only been developed in the second half of this century. No wonder there is a lack of refinement in psychology.

The major formulations of psychology form not a spectrum, but a triangle. At one apex are the psychoanalytic descendants of Freud and Jung. At another apex are the many forms of behaviorism, beginning from the pioneering work of Watson, developed by the genius of Skinner emerging into pragmatic or functional psychology as well as the more recent cognitive models. The third apex of the triangular plane belongs to the humanistic, existential or "third force" models related to such psychologists as Allport, May, Maslow and Rogers.

There may be a fourth psychology school emerging. It has been termed transpersonal by Sutich, and has its first journal, *The Journal of Transpersonal Psychology*. It goes beyond the personalism of humanistic psychology, emphasizing mysticism and spiritualism. It incorporates many of the distinctives of Eastern religions and parapsychology. It is linked with what is being called "new age" thinking.

While theologians and psychologists wrestle with the diversities within their own fields of expertise, they usually fail to take account of the diversity on the other side of the integrative task. For example, Kotesky[4] seeks to achieve unity of psychological truth by looking at the data of psychology through a Christian perspective on humans as divinely-created beings. This allows him to see the truth in the various psychological models. But he completely overlooks the diversity within the Christian perspective, much of which appears in the very areas he examines.

Before launching into the integrative task, one must test the coherence of one's theological and psychological models. No one will ever successfully integrate a Calvinistic theology, with its denial of human autonomy, and a humanistic psychology, which presupposes that same autonomy.

Achieving coherence while wedding concepts from very different perspectives is the greatest area of difficulty for the integration of theology and psychology. They have very different beginning points: theology begins with God and His revelation; psychology begins with humanity in the world. They have very different primary foci: theology focuses first on God's glory and purposes in the world; psychology focuses first on humanity's pathologies and their care. They have different spheres: theology looks upward to God and outward to ministry in the world; psychology looks inward to understanding and renewing the human psyche. Even these simplistic categorizations indicate the difficulties.

Dr. Grounds' vision of an integrated world view is a noble one. I call on those who respond to this vision to do justice to both the unity and the diversity of theology and psychology as they proceed with their integrative work. Success in integration will come only for those who make the effort to be knowledgeable and specific in both their theology and their psychology.

Freedom As a Testing Point For Coherence

The concept of freedom will serve as an excellent testing point for the potential compatibility of a particular theology and a particular psychology. It can also eliminate many of the proposed combinations by showing them to be fundamentally incompatible. Because freedom approximates the essence of human nature, this fundamental concept gives us the criterion for testing compatibility between particular theological and scientific models of humanness.

Beginning to Define Freedom

Freedom. Few words are more widely used; few concepts are more elusive. It seems freedom must remain free even from definition. But the importance of the concept makes precise definition all the more important. We cannot move toward what we do not know. We cannot preserve or promote what we cannot define. We cannot use effectively what we do not fully understand.

Most definitions are negative. They say what freedom is not. For example, the dictionary defines it as "not under the control of some other person or some arbitrary power; able to act or think without compulsion or arbitrary restriction."[5] Antonyms help us see facets of what it is not: tyrannical, colonialist, chauvinistic, bigoted, censorsing, narrow minded, doctrinaire, authoritative, repressive, puritanical. But we must not make the mistake of transforming freedom into a negative concept. Freedom cannot be merely the absence of limitations. There must also be the reality of choice and action.

We will concern ourselves with personal freedom. While freedom can be ideological, political, religious or economic, the Christianization of the social sciences begins from the inner freedom of the person. Underlying all these other manifestations of freedom is the declaration that the human, as created by God, "is rational, conscientious, discriminating, responsible, capable of choice, decision and creativity."[6]

Inadequate Definitions

Popularly, freedom means the absolute absence of any limitation on one's personal choice of attitudes or actions. The shout, "Ain't nobody gonna tell me what to do!" expresses this attitude clearly. Freedom of speech often means the right to say absolutely whatever comes to mind. However, even a moment's thought shows that there can be no such thing as absolute freedom. "Human freedom is bound by historical, geographical, physical, psychological, intellectual, cultural and spiritual limitations."[7] Though I may choose to fly through the air with a flap of my arms, physical limitations make that wholly impossible in this world. Even the freedom to fly would be conditioned upon the presence of air. The continuing reality of depravity in humans and in the world makes it impossible fully to achieve human potential. Actions are never free from conditions. Finite, sinful persons in a finite, sin-marred world will never have the requisite abilities for every desired action.

Not all theologies or psychologies affirm personal freedom. The followers of Karl Marx, including many liberation theologians, deny the concept of personal freedom. They argue that human existence is essentially social. Humanity as a whole may be free in some sense, but individual humans are not. He taught the concept of economic determinism. Personal freedom is an illusion perpetrated by the oppressors in order to divert attention from the truth of economic determinism. True freedom comes only when one denies individual freedom and aligns oneself with the economic forces of history.

Sigmund Freud also denied individual freedom, stressing instinctual determinism, the unceasing battle between *eros* and *thanatos*. His therapy works to achieve inner freedom, strengthening the ego by delivering it from the damaging illusions picked up during the traumatic experiences of childhood. However, this freedom happens only in the individual's inner world. The boundaries of fate and necessity do not disappear. Inner freedom includes resignation and detachment in relation to the forces of fate and necessity.[8]

Some Calvinists[9] effectively deny freedom, stressing passages such as Ephesians 1:11. God works (*energountos*, from which comes the word "energy") *all* things according to the counsel of his will. All things are as necessarily worked by God as is the redemption of the elect. All events have their impetus in the sovereign counsel of the will of God as opposed to human will or initiative. According to this view, God is the supreme cause of every event in the world. Human acts merely follow the predetermined decision of God.

Despite this gallery of adherents, absolute determinism fares no better than absolute freedom. None of these views square with experience or the Bible. Experience informs us that ninety pound women can decide to lift cars off their babies, that people can decide to persevere in their self-chosen duties in spite of great hardship and difficulty, that humans decide to risk and sometimes give up their lives for strangers drowning in the Potomac river after a plane crash. Joshua challenged his people, "choose for yourselves this day whom you will serve" (Joshua 24:15), Jesus gave instructions for one who "refuses to listen" to exhortation (Matt. 18:17), and Paul scathingly rebuked Jews who chose to repudiate the Word of God (Acts 13:46).

Humans choose actions and are held responsible for them. Only moral responsibility can result in moral evil. People cannot be evil if they have not chosen their actions responsibly. The difference between murder and manslaughter rests on the element of choice within the one who causes death. Similarly, moral good comes only from self-decision to act. Heroism is heroic only if it is not compelled. Without the moral choice, there can be no personal good or evil. Empirical proof of freedom may elude us. But without it, both biblical psychology and responsible humanity fall. Freedom of choice is a presupposition of morality.

Even this simple analysis illustrates the power of the concept of freedom for evaluating models of psychology and theology. Any model which presumes absolute freedom from restraint or absolute determinism by denying self-determination collapses. This rules out all three apexes of our psychological triangle as well as the ends of the theological spectrum before we even begin to test coherence.

Developing a Definition of Freedom

We must continue to analyze the concept of freedom. A vast interior of the triangle and the spectrum still remain even if the apexes are gone. We will approach this task with a series of questions. Our task is not to find definitive answers for the questions. It is to provide a framework for outlining a personal view of freedom which in turn can test the coherence of specific theological and psychological models.

First, is freedom a nothing? Is it pure potentiality? Was there ever a time when God was more free than when he faced *nihil*, the total absence of created being, before he began to create? At that point his options were limited by nothing except his own volition and character. Freedom in this sense is the freedom of creativity. Most significant among the areas of creativity is the freedom to create humanity and human history. Of course humanity is not a nothing. However, humans (and humanity) have room for creativity, existing as unfinished products with the potential for shaping themselves and their world.

This concept of freedom relates closely to the philosophy of existentialism. One sees it in the philosophy of Sartre and Camus, the theology of Macquarrie and the psychology of Rogers. It is sharply different from the conception presented in our second question.

Second, is freedom a faculty? Is there something within the human which can be called the will? The concept of a faculty that God implanted in humans by which they choose between various courses of action runs very deep in Western philosophy and theology. One finds this "faculty psychology" in Plato, Aristotle, Augustine, Aquinas, Luther, Calvin and Descartes, to name only a few. In this conception, "will" is the source of the particular action. Just as a person has the faculty of thought and therefore is able to think, one has the faculty of will and therefore is able to choose.

Many contemporary thinkers reject faculty psychology in favor of an act-oriented psychology.[10] These thinkers would substitute "I do" for "I choose" or "I think." Part of the rationale for this rejection centers on the Cartesian dualism between mental things (*res cogitans*) and material things (*res extensa*). Behaviorists deride dualists for the dogma of the "ghost within the machine." Behaviorists undergo training so as to describe behavior without referring to mental states. David Hume and subsequent empiricists have rejected the concept of the inner self, because it cannot be objectified.

One must wonder if rejection of mental states, including the concept of will is not an unfounded reductionism. Although freedom and free will are not objectifiable, they are "subjectifiable." An empirically based investigation can be successful only when that which it is investigating can be objectified and spread out for scrutiny as an object. But the self stubbornly resists being made an object, remaining a subject. The investigator cannot be brought within the objectifying purview. "Empiricism provides a successful way of approach to the problems of nature, but it cannot give an adequate account of that being who has transcended nature, namely, the human being. The being who says 'I' is a breach in the texture of the merely natural."[11] Ian Ramsey maintained that the "I" is "logically odd,"[12] transcending the ordinary world. There always seems to be an undeniable self behind evident actions. Referring to the decision making powers of the self as the will need not entail all the details of Aristotelian metaphysics with its emphasis on unchanging, innate attributes. Denying the reality of the self in favor of acts alone is unbearably reductionistic.

Third, is freedom best defined in terms of contrary choice? Freedom in this sense is usually called libertarianism or voluntarism. A standard definition of freedom reads: "...an act is free if and only if the agent could have done otherwise, all other circumstances remaining the same."[13] A person is a free agent when there is at least one other action which could be substituted according to the agent's choice for the actual course of action.

There is necessarily an element of predictive indeterminacy in this definition.[14] No one, not even God, can predict my choice in advance with absolute accuracy. Past choices, habit patterns, character attributes and the like could make the prediction highly probable, but never absolutely certain. An alternative course of action must be kept open up to the instant of my choice. If my choice could be predicted, then prior internal or external causal conditions would be sufficient cause for the action and personal choice would be ruled out. While prior knowledge would not cause the event to occur, it would amount to a knowledge of the prior cause(s) which determined the choice.[15]

This conception does not require that there be an absence of causality. Causal conditions may well be present, but these conditions are insufficient to determine the action chosen by the person. The choice of the person must be added to the other causes in order to explain the action. Choice contains an element of self-causation. This explains why free choice need not reduce to arbitrary choice. There may be good reason for the action one chooses freely.

As inviting as this view of freedom is, one must realize that it invalidates truly scientific study of individuals, because science by definition is prediction based on knowledge of general laws pertaining to a state of affairs and the specific causes operating in the particular state of affairs.

Science, either social, psychological or physical, assumes that for any event there are antecedent causes. In psychology, the assumption is that if we knew all the laws and all the causes, we could predict behavior with 100 percent accuracy.[16]

Some contend that one may be able to predict the actions of a mass of individuals by hiding the small errors in prediction in the large number of people. For example sociology is compared to quantum physics and the laws covering gasses. This analogy fails precisely because of the difference between persons with free will and atoms without free will. Insurance companies predict death quite accurately by relying on natural laws, not on predictions of human behavior. Public relation experts try valiantly to predict human responses to their products (which are often people) and are conspicuous in their frequent failures. Human beings remain stubbornly unpredictable.

Fourth, is freedom best defined in terms of absence of restraint? Freedom in this sense is not absolute freedom from every limitation, but liberation from what binds, especially those bonds which are dehumanizing. Jesus was himself a paradigm of freedom. He was free from an overweening fear of death, from sin, greed and materialism, traditions of elders, legalism, conventional judgments, rigid content of Scripture, narrow nationalism, the law of violence, Jewish exclusivism, male chauvinism, religious austerity.[17] Christ's work was to deliver his followers from sin and its effects (Gal. 1:4; Matt. 1:21 and esp. Rom. 6) as well as from the elements of the world (Gal. 4:10; Col. 2:8-20; Rom. 14:1-23). Being free from the disabling bondage to sin would be freedom indeed.

This conception of freedom relates closely to a conception of autonomy as the basis of human worth and dignity. This idea springs directly from Immanuel Kant.[18] Humans are human if and only if they are able to make decisions autonomously, free from restraint or coercion. To the degree that they are limited they are less human.

Freedom *from* has much to commend it, for many factors bind humans, constricting their freedom. However, many dangers arise from this definition. The greatest limitation on human autonomy comes from human creatureliness.

Creatureliness means accountability to the Creator. Autonomy means freedom from external law, including the law of God. Thielicke makes the implications very clear:

> Briefly, what this word implies is that we cannot be told from outside, by God, who we are and what our end ought to be...The commands of God still apply, and thus live on, only if they can validate themselves before autonomous conscience as the final court.[19]

Once one takes up the idea of autonomy as a goal for human freedom, there can be no further use for the God of the Bible, God as the author of binding commands, as the author of righteousness.

If freedom *from* is taken in this sense of autonomy, then the human self must be defined before any relationship is initiated. Specifically, one must determine one's own value and dignity apart from God. But if the image of God means anything, it means that humans have their source and goal in God, the Creator. Defining one's self apart from God, as this conception entails, inevitably reduces human to subhuman.

This conception of freedom *from* also has the danger of turning liberty into license. When one throws off the shackles without thought for what one's goal or purpose is, distortion inevitably results.

Jesus' parable of the Prodigal Son graphically demonstrates the total bankruptcy of the contemporary quest for freedom from all restraint. The son leaves home to seek self fulfillment in the absence of all duty to family, enterprise, tradition, culture or values. He seeks to "find himself" in the freedom of the far country. But instead of finding freedom, he falls prey to the

> tyranny of the law of least resistance. The very lack of binding restraints that he willed leads him to the pigsty -- a highly symbolic term -- and makes it

> utterly clear that he has not exchanged his bondage to the father for freedom (which is what he really wanted), but rather for bondage to inferior powers.[20]

One may defend against these dangers by refusing to allow freedom *from* to depend on a conception of autonomy. Freedom *from* must be coupled with freedom *to*, the subject of the next questions.

Fifth, is freedom best defined in terms of consistency with purpose, character or nature? Thielicke argues, "He is not free who can do what he wills, but rather he who can become what he should."[21] This conception does not focus on freedom from restraint, for it posits the restraint of the nature or purpose of the person. Instead of seeking to free oneself from limitations, one enters into a genuine commitment to the obligations which come with purposeful life, especially life before God. Gaddy helps us understand:

> Jacques Maritain is said to have observed that no more penetrating question can be asked of a person than whether freedom is considered primarily as a throwing off or taking on of limitations. Christian freedom is never a motivation to retreat but always an invitation to service. A commitment to freedom is best demonstrated not through boisterous 'hurrahs' and bragadocious shouts of 'I am free,' but by means of persistent acts of service among those for whom freedom is not yet a firsthand experience.[22]

Freedom from bondage is an illusory goal. There is only false and true bondage. This understanding can range from the humanist's bondage to self-fulfillment to the bondage to Kant's categorical imperative to act as one would wish all humans to act, to the Christian's bondage to be a responsible child of God, predestined to be like Christ (cf. Romans 6:15-23; 8:29).

Jacques Ellul suggests freedom understood as making choices is very superficial. Not even Adam's freedom should be understood in this sense. He has only the divinely given possibility of being Adam living in fellowship with God. "Fellowship does not involve choice. Freedom is living in God's own freedom through this fellowship and in the unbroken unity of all creation in which there are no separate and incoherent bits and pieces between which to choose."[23] It is only after the fall that freedom is expressed as independence and consequently as freedom of choice between contradictory truths or attitudes. When the fragmentation of sin is overcome in Christ, independent choice will once again give way to the freedom of fellowship.

Jesus, the paradigmatic human, shows the measure of freedom in his responses to the temptation of the Devil.[24] When the Devil tempts him to choose for himself, Jesus shows that he is free to obey. He goes on to show that he is free to trust. He does not demand visible proof of God's faithfulness, but relies again on the word of God. Finally Jesus shows that he is free to serve. He developed the freedom of service as he spoke of all who would be great (Matt. 20:25-28). He shows this freedom on the Cross. Potter summarizes this well:

> Bearing the cross is the freest act we can do, because it was on the cross that God's freedom was manifest for us. And while we live in an unfree world, we are called to bear the cross so that others may be free. A Christian in the world today is thus one who, having received freedom, has been called to freedom -- not the freedom of self-indulgence, but freedom in Christ, which we express by being ourselves and being for others in love.[25]

Christ frees us *from* the domination of sin and the powers of darkness (Col. 1:13, 2:14-15). He also frees *to* enjoyment of fellowship with God (Rom. 8:14-17; Gal. 4:6-7) and to the enjoyment of the life of obedient righteousness and holiness for which we were created (Eph. 4:23-24). Freedom must include the freedom *to*. The freedom to be what one should be, the freedom to obey, the freedom to trust, the freedom to serve.

Sixth, is it meaningful to speak of freedom in degrees? We have already noted that freedom is never absolute for finite, sinful creatures in a finite, sin-marred world. Even given contrary choice, people have their range of choices restricted significantly by a small number of possibilities or by limited power. But the question goes beyond that. There are the limitations of one's genetic inheritance, including temperament, aptitudes, intelligence, one's place in the social and economic order and one's past choices, to name a few. Can we say that a prisoner on death row freely chooses his last meal? Is the choice of a drug addict between heroin and cocaine a free choice? Neither choice is made by a free person. The range of choices is severely restricted. However, they clearly meet the definition of free choice, since an alternative course of action is available.

Degrees of freedom are based on 1) the range and value of possibilities open to the agent and 2) the measure of power possessed by the agent. We judge humans more or less free depending on these two conditions. God may be said to be "maximally free," because he has all necessary power to perform all actions which are logically possible. Of course even God has some limitations on his range of choices since he can neither make a round square nor contradict his character (for example, by sinning) nor contradict his plan. Even God is not absolutely free.

One usually speaks of certain conditions which must be met for free agency, or self-determination to be meaningful. There must be the requisite abilities, information, sufficient time to deliberate and awareness of the decision at hand. Agents must be psychologically able to choose, and not overwhelmed by psychic compulsion. Also their agency must not be overcome by other agents. To the degree that these conditions are met, we speak of degrees of freedom, of self-determination.

It seems that degrees of freedom must be a part of any suitable definition. To deny freedom unless it be absolute is to deny freedom.

Seventh, is freedom compatible with any degree of determinism? Any scientific study depends on the predictability of result given a certain set of causes. If people act in an entirely undetermined manner, prediction of result would be wholly impossible. Therefore, if human freedom is mutually exclusive with any degree of determinism, then no one can study humans scientifically. Such a conception of freedom would end integration by ending science.

People who observe themselves or others quickly recognize how the inertia of patterns of habit and concept usually determine the range of choices. Thus defining freedom along with some level of determinism does not reduce freedom to an illusion. One chooses, even if habit or nature makes that choice certain.

Determinism troubles us when it rules out human choice entirely, rather than when it makes human actions predictable. Determinism troubles us, because we see it as meaning coercion, forcing the person against personal will, obliterating human initiative and responsibility.

Free choice commonly means that one can choose at least one alternative course of action. However, the precise meaning of "can" changes the sense of the sentence significantly.[26] For example, if "can" means ability, I cannot fly even though I may freely choose to do so. If "can" means opportunity, my son cannot pole vault a seven foot height while he is in his room, although he can do so easily at the track. If "can" is legal in nature, I cannot park in the bus stop in front of my house even though my car will fit there nicely.

For integrative purposes "can" is most often understood as "it is reasonable." "I can act in a certain way" translates "it is reasonable for me to act in that certain way, given my character and the specific circumstances." Following this line of thought, the common understanding of free choice (that one can choose among options without coercion) is not at all inconsistent with that fact that one's actions are predictable. Predictability depends on knowing the nature of the agent and the circumstances.

Following this idea, freedom means acting according to one's own desires, inclinations, habits, nature, etc. So long as one does not act out of coercion, so long as one makes a choice according to one's own desire, then the choice could be real and free, even if there was no possibility of alternate action. Freedom means being free to do what is reasonable, to follow one's desires, to be uncoerced.

Luther in his treatise, *The Bondage of the Will*, made a distinction between coercion and necessity. Coercion is external constraint which rules out the determining action of the individual. When an exasperated father grabs his son by the collar and drags him away from the mud puddle, the boy has no choice in the matter. But when human beings sin, even though fallen and alienated from God, without saving grace, and unable to do anything but go astray from God's righteousness, they still act responsibly. The guilt can be imputed to no one but the individual sinner. Each is the subject of one's sinful action even though one acts by necessity, bound by sinfulness. In this sense, a drug addict freely chooses cocaine, and a sinner freely chooses sin, even though they act under necessity of their own nature. Putting this in the positive, God freely chooses not to sin, Jesus freely chose not to sin, the glorified human in heaven freely chooses to obey God, not because they choose among the alternatives, but because they determine their own course of action. They are free to follow the dictates of their desires and character.

This understanding does not rule out choice among alternative courses of action. It broadens that conception to include self-determination, even when there may be no real alternative, even when actions are truly predictable. The central point is that if one's choice is reasonable and according to one's own inclinations, then it is free, even if it is necessary.

Unless one throws out all attempt to understand the actions of ourselves or others, it seems that freedom is compatible with some degree of determinism. The question of how much determinism it takes to eliminate any meaningful freedom is a question which must be answered for integration to be successful.[27]

Beginning the Task of Testing Coherence

The seven questions will help to formulate a basic definition of freedom. With that preliminary conception, models of theology and psychology can be tested for coherence. This testing can happen at the level of theory. For example, one can try to relate a Wesleyan theology to a psychoanalytic psychology. But the coherence goes beyond the abstract level. A definition of freedom will help establish limits for personality theory. It will likewise set a direction for a counseling model.

Most readers will have concluded that I am a moderately Calvinistic theologian. I hold that true freedom is the freedom to act consistently according to God's perfect will. It focuses on acts which are consistent with our origin as God's creation and our goal of Christlikeness, rather than choice between alternative courses of action (though alternatives do exist, I must hasten to add). I also see sinners freely choosing to act and think sinfully out of necessity. Their bondage to their sinful nature (e.g., Rom. 8:7; Eph. 2:3; Titus 3:3) gives them no consistent alternative. One has probably also recognized my rudimentary knowledge of psychology. Despite this lack of knowledge, for the sake of example I will briefly use my conception of freedom to illustrate how one would test coherence in integration.

Scripture makes it clear that unregenerate people will never achieve their destiny as humans apart from the grace of God. All evangelicals agree on this point. Humans are not free. Thus any psychology or counseling model which assumes innate goodness and thereby seeks to help clients to solve their problems by drawing on their own inner resources is bound to fail. Any model that defines the human in terms of a weakened growth instinct which will be solved by discovering one's inner resources and developing personal potential cannot hope to succeed. Unqualified respect for the client's perception of reality is inconsistent with the realization that one's view is marred by the binding effects of sin. Adopting the attitude of unconditional trust in the client's capacity for self-help, helping the client become more and more aware of the potential for helping oneself, ignores the reality of the bondage of sin. There is no possibility of self-recovery. People are simply not free in this respect.

Christians must realize that if we try help another person by teaching them to follow their instincts, trust their feelings, act according to their inclinations, then we have helped them become a more consistent sinner.

Letting clients set the goals for therapy may actually entail either helping them develop responsibility or reducing freedom to the sinfulness of autonomy. In all counseling situations, we must deal realistically with the deceptiveness of sin, sin-marred motives, the sinfulness of pride and self-reliance. "To ignore selfish motives and behavior in order to protect a person's ego is to do a disservice to the client in the long run if selfish life patterns adversely affect mental health."[28] Humans are not free to achieve their potential. Freedom is found not in self-reliance, but in obedience to God.

If freedom is understood in terms of freedom *to*, freedom to be what we ought to be, freedom to be Christlike, then we must view with suspicion counseling models which focus on growth. Growth must have its proper goal or it is merely change. Spontaneity sounds fulfilling until one realizes that a life of perpetual change would be a horrible fate. One would be set adrift from any integrity, any abiding structure and condemned to eternal restlessness. Freedom is found in consistency with our source, nature and goal as beings created for obedience to the will of God -- to glorify him and enjoy him forever.

Nondirective therapy is equally suspect if one sees freedom as freedom *to*. If one believes that Christlikeness is true freedom, then effective therapy can never be nondirective. That goal always directs our efforts.

Psychologies often gravitate toward a Wesleyan version of theology, because it emphasizes freedom as contrary choice and the human as a free agent (given the universalness of grace). However, I think it important to realize that an evangelical theology cannot overlook the reality of God's sovereignty over human actions. While Pharaoh acted according to his own desires in refusing to let the Israelite people go, he still fulfilled God's purpose

(Exodus 3-14; Romans 9). When the Jews and Romans crucified Jesus, they did so according to God's ordination, but remained fully responsible for their actions (Acts 2:22-23; 4:27-28). When God graciously intervenes in the lives of persons, he does not deny their freedom, but gives them their first taste of real freedom. The only source of this freedom is abiding in God's Word, becoming a disciple, letting the truth make one free (John 8:31-32). It is the Son who makes free (John 8:36), but this is not the freedom of spontaneity, but the freedom of obedience (I John 3:22-24).

Conclusion

Dr. Grounds' vision of integration of a fully biblical theology and a truly scientific psychology commends itself to all. Dismissing psychology as hopelessly humanistic or viewing theology as hopelessly religious destroys a truly Christian world view. However, integration does not happen automatically. One must examine the foundations of both theology and psychology. It is my contention that this can be done only if one takes into account the diversity in both theology and psychology. Overlooking this diversity destines one to an unsatisfactory result, because the starting point is reductionistic.

Because of the diversity, the integrative task overwhelms many who should pursue it. Beginning integration by looking at a foundational concept such as freedom eases the task immensely by eliminating many impossible combinations from consideration. However, this requires an appropriate definition of freedom. The seven questions raised in this essay are intended to assist the reader in making such a definition. Moving into the theological and psychological aspects of a developing world view will help one refine one's definition. This will in turn enable the next step -- refinement of the world view. It is a process of a lifetime.

Dr. Grounds' "pastoral care" in my life has challenged me to interact with the contemporary world from the foundation of the truth once for all delivered to the saints (Jude 3). That, too, is the process of a lifetime.

Notes

1. Vernon Grounds, "God's Perspective on Man," *Journal of the American Scientific Affiliation*, 1976, 28(4), p. 145.

2. C.F.H. Henry, *God Revelation and Authority* (Waco: Word, 1976), Vol. I(165-180) is a good introduction both to the tasks and the literature of integration.

3. Ignorance of the different levels is seen when someone tries to integrate science and the Bible. Science is at least at the hypothesis level, while the Bible is at the data level. For further reading on levels of integration see Robert Larzelere, "The Task Ahead: Six Levels of Integration of Christianity and Psychology," *Journal of Psychology and Theology*, 1980, 8(1), pp. 3-11 and Gary Collins, *Psychology and Theology: Prospects for Integration* (Nashville: Abingdon, 1981), pp. 22-38.

4. Ronald Kotesky, *Psychology from a Christian Perspective* (Nashville: Abingdon, 1980), p. 44.

5. *Webster's New World Dictionary*. Second College Edition, 1980, s.v. "free."

6. John Macquarrie, *In Search of Humanity* (New York: Crossroad, 1982), p. 11.

7. C. Welton Gaddy, "A Christian Understanding of Human Freedom," *Review and Expositor*, 1976, vol. 73, p. 298.

8. It is significant that Sigmund Freud and Karl Marx both drew their basic concepts of religion from Ludwig Feuerbach. It is not surprising that both were determinists and overtly hostile to religion.

9. Despite perceptions to the contrary, very few Calvinists argue that there is no personal freedom.

10. One of the most influential philosophers making this argument is Gilbert Rule, *The Concept of Mind* (London: Hutchinson House, 1949).

11. Macquarrie, p. 41.

12. Noted by Macquarrie, p. 41.

13. D.J. O'Connor, *Free Will* (Garden City: Doubleday, 1971), p. 82.

14. For example, Stephen Davis argues, that a genuine conception of freedom commits one to "a concept of genuine possibilities that implies real indeterminism" in his "A Defence of the Free Will Defence," *Religious Studies* , 1971, vol. 8, p. 335. See also Alvin Plantinga, *God, Freedom and Evil* (Grand Rapids: Wm. B. Eerdmans, 1974).

15. A seminal essay arguing that divine foreknowledge precludes human freedom is Nelson Pike, "Divine Omniscience and Voluntary Action," *Philosophical Review*, 1965, vol. LXXIV, pp. 27-46. The position goes back at least to Cicero. The assumption that genuine foreknowledge rules out genuine freedom is sometimes denied. For a compact summary of the debate see Basinger and Basinger (eds.), *Predestination and Free Will* (Downer's Grove: Inter-Varsity Press, 1985) and the literature cited there.

16. James R. Dolby, "Determinism, Degrees of Freedom, and the Christian: A Heuristic Approach," *Journal of the American Scientific Affiliation*, 1968, vol. 20(2), pp. 33-36.

17. Peter Rhea Jones, "The Liberating and Liberated Lord," *Review and Expositor*, 1976, vol. 73(3), p. 284.

18. See for example his study *The Doctrine of Virtue* (New York: Torchbooks, 1964), p. 99.

19. Helmut Thielicke, *Being Human ... Becoming Human*, trans. Geoffrey Bromiley (Garden City: Doubleday, 1984), p. 214.

20. Helmut Thielicke, *Freedom of the Christian Man*, trans. by John W. Doberstein, (New York: Harper & Row, 1963), p. 28.

21. Ibid., p. 10. This phrase is quoted from Paul de Lagarde.

22. Gaddy, C. Welton, "A Christian Understanding of Human Freedom," *Review and Expositor*, 1976, vol. 73(3), p. 301.

23. Jacques Ellul, *The Ethics of Freedom*, trans. by Geoffrey Bromiley (Grand Rapids: Wm. B. Eerdmans Pub. Co., 1976), p. 114.

24. Peter Toon develops this idea in his little book *Freed to Obey* (Wheaton: Tyndale House, 1979), pp. 25-34.

25. Philip Potter, "Turning to Freedom and Fullness," *International Review of Mission*, 1983, vol. 72(287), p.

320. Potter is the former General Secretary of the World Council of Churches.

26. I am indebted to John Feinberg "God Ordains All Things," in Basinger and Basinger, pp. 27-28, for helping me clarify this vital point.

27. Richard Taylor, "Determinism," in *Encyclopedia of Philosophy*, ed. Paul Edwards, (New York: Macmillan, 1967), vol. I(359-373) is an excellent introduction to the question of determinism and freedom. See also John Feinberg "And the Calvinist Shall Lie Down with the Atheist," *Trinity Journal* , n.s., Fall, 1980, vol. 1, pp. 142-152 and the literature cited there as well as the article in Basinger & Basinger.

28. Mark P. Cosgrove, *Psychology Gone Awry* (Grand Rapids: Zondervan Pub. House, 1979), p. 87.

From Slaveholder to American Abolitionist: Charles Hodge and the Slavery Issue

David Murchie

For nineteenth-century American Christianity, the concept of freedom was profoundly conditioned by the presence of legalized slavery in American society. Theoretical emphasis on "inward" freedom in Christ too often became the comfortable justification whereby pro-slavery Christians could maintain oppressive social class distinctions while simultaneously professing faith in the Christian God and his revealed Word in Scripture.

A central figure in the slavery debate was Charles Hodge, Princeton Theological Seminary professor, long-time editor of the *Princeton Review*, and staunch apologist for conservative orthodoxy. Hodge's pro-slavery stance early in the nineteenth century has been widely recognized and amply documented. He found no sin in the institution of slavery, as he defined that institution in narrow, abstract terms. But his support of slavery must be judged against his equally forthright disapproval of American slavery, a disapproval which intensified throughout Hodge's career. Hodge's 1836 "biblical" defense of slavery[1] and his firm opposition in 1844 to abolitionism[2] spoke clearly of his convictions on the legitimacy of slavery as an institution and the deprivation of natural rights which it entailed. From a biographical perspective, belief in the inferiority of slaves led Hodge into service as an officer in the New Jersey Colonization Society, demonstrating an interest he shared with his brother, Hugh Hodge, a Philadelphia physician.[3] Personal correspondence between the two brothers revealed Charles' serious concern regarding even the logistics of the colonization effort: "I think your Colonization Plan is (likely?) But if you are to found a Black United States on the Coast of Africa -- the states should be larger that (sic) the squares of a chequer board -- therefore get as far off as you can from Liberia."[4]

In fairness, one must recognize that though he firmly supported the institution of slavery, Hodge did, however patronizingly, call for proper treatment of slaves and for their "gradual emancipation," though the latter was, unfortunately, viewed as a "natural" process best left to its own inevitable development, or, more cynically stated, to the good will and judgment of the slaveholders. Hodge contended that "the right to hold slaves, (did) not involve the acknowledgment of the right to adopt measures adapted and intended to perpetuate their present mental and physical degradation."[5] Nevertheless, his call for proper treatment of slaves did not diminish his early belief in the legitimacy of slavery, and by the mid-1840s, as the cynosure of Old School Presbyterians, he became the chief adversary of the abolitionist position that all slavery was sin. He continued to define slavery narrowly as "involuntary servitude,"[6] claiming that the morality of the institution was to be determined by the attendant circumstances.

Critical appraisals of Hodge's pro-slavery views have most often called attention to his earlier works, e.g., "Slavery" (1836) and "Abolitionism" (1844). Dependence on these sources alone, however, fails to recognize that a significant shift in Hodge's thought on the subject of slavery began to occur during the years 1846-49. During this period, increased cotton production had made slavery increasingly profitable for the South, exacerbating the ill will that already existed between North and South. Hodge had come to believe that dissolution of the institution of slavery was favored by "the great body of enlightened and disinterested men even in the slave states."[7] The naive optimism, regarding the nature of man (slaveholder), which had earlier characterized Hodge's theoretical defense of slavery, began to yield to an increasing opposition to "perpetual slavery" and to a stronger advocacy of the proper treatment of slaves. According to Hodge, both conscience and Scripture witnessed against the legitimacy of perpetuating slavery, and such perpetuation portended a "fearful retribution for the descendants of those by whom such attempt (was) made."[8] Hodge reacted strongly against the contention that "since there must always be a labouring class of society, it is best in an economical, social and moral point of view, that they should be in a state of slavery." The condition of "ignorance and degradation" necessary for perpetuating the enslavement of one class by another could not be justified.[9] Emancipation was a moral duty, and conscience was "the only principle capable of competing with self-interest.[10] Furthermore, Hodge emphasized that the legitimacy of slavery, per se, did not necessarily extend to American practices of slaveholding:

> It is, therefore, no fair inference from the doctrine that slaveholding is not in itself sinful, that the Bible sanctions the actual system of slavery, or the slave laws now in force in this country. Much less can it be fairly inferred from the abstract lawfulness of slavery, that laws may be enacted and enforced to extend and perpetuate it.[11]

An increasing concern for the welfare of the slaves further served as a practical corrective for what might otherwise have been a wholesale advocacy of slavery with all its unjust extensions. All men were obligated "to promote the improvement of (their) fellow men," and this involved recognition of the right of all men "to intellectual culture and moral and religious education." To deprive anyone of this right in order to perpetuate his bondage was a great sin.[12] Even the church was involved in assuring that slaves were treated properly by their masters:

> If the Bible recognises the relation of master and slave as one which may exist in the church, it is a

> relation with regard to which the church has a right to teach, to exhort, and to exercise her watch and care. If the Bible tells believing masters what is their duty with respect to their slaves, the church is as much bound to see that her members perform those duties, as that they conform in any other respect to the law of Christ. Her duty here, is just what it is in relation to parents and children, subjects and rulers. She is bound to teach parents what their obligations are, to exhort them to act agreeably to them, and to visit their neglect of duty with her spiritual admonitions and censures.[13]

Hodge himself was quite favorably disposed to the employment of slaves by the Choctaw mission, since such employment supposedly helped legitimately to improve their condition:

> The slaves often earnestly desire to be employed by the mission, their condition is thereby improved, their privileges increased, and they are thus brought into the way of religious instruction, and perhaps of salvation. Unless slaveholding is a sin, it is hard to see how the force of these considerations is to be resisted.[14]

Hodge's increasing resistance to American slavery was accompanied by a developing interest in the specific political realities of emancipation. Although he still feared the communal impact of "the immediate and indiscrimate liberation of millions of slaves of a different and inferior race,"[15] and felt that the eradication of slavery was still best accomplished through "the gospel method of emancipation,"[16] by the end of the 1840s, he was convinced of the inevitable decline of slavery for reasons of political economy as well as morality. Demographic realities augured ominously against the continuation of slaveholding:

> One reason, then, why slavery cannot be perpetual is that the slaves increase in a more rapid ratio than the whites, and by the mere force of numbers must occupy the land...They will be too numerous to be profitable, and the time predicted by John Randolph (as we believe), must come, when the masters will run away from the slaves.[17]

Hodge offered the interesting and rather astute political observation that northern arguments for abolition could have been realized, if their advocates had themselves been willing to forego the economic benefits of slave labor. The following perceptive remarks by Hodge are reminiscent of the eighteenth century Quaker, John Woolman (1720-72), who refused to use sugar or dyes because they had been produced with slave labor;[18]

> Every use we make of the products of slave labour, is an encouragement to slavery. If all men were to agree not to use anything in the production of which slaves have been employed, slavery must instantly cease. This is not done here at the North. We presume it is not done by the committee (Prudential Committee of the American Board of Commissioners for Foreign Mission). It is not done by the missionaries. They doubtless consume the wheat, the beef, the corn which slaves have assisted in raising. It therefore seems very strange, that the committee should say, they will give up their schools rather than sanction slavery, when they will not give up the sugar for their coffee for the same reason.[19]

The political dimension of emancipation necessarily included reparations to slaveowners who would otherwise suffer at the hands of a society which had chosen to declare illegal an institution it had previously sanctioned: "If therefore the state has authorized the holding of slaves, the state must bear the expense of rectifying its own mistakes, when it comes to see that slavery is a public burden."[20] At this point, Hodge's frequently expressed individualism yielded to his sense of the organic, interdependent nature of large social and political realities.

Regarding the detailed formulation of an emancipation plan, Hodge was particularly impressed with the Spanish plan whereby a certain value was placed upon a slave, the slave then being allowed to accumulate his own money, eventually paying off his "value" to the owner. The slave could pay for his freedom in six equal installments, receiving one "free" day for each one-sixth reimbursement, with manumission following payment of the final sixth of the "value." The plan was attractive to Hodge in virtue of its gradual preparation of the slave for living in civilized society:

> In this way he (the slave) is trained to habits of industry and self-control, and prepared to provide for himself. If with this system could be connected some provision for liberating the wives and children of those who had worked out their own freedom, the plan of progressive emancipation would be relieved of much of its apparent injustice.[21]

In the latter half of the 1850s, Hodge continued to be concerned with themes developed earlier. Clear in his opposition to the perpetuation of slavery, he nevertheless persevered in his argument from silence for the lawfulness of slavery, per se, remarking in his Ephesians commentary (1856):

> It (slavery) is neither enjoined nor forbidden. It is simply assumed to be lawful, so that a Christian may consistently be an autocrat in the State, or a master of slaves. In this view the scriptural doctrine on this subject, differs on the one hand,

> from the doctrine that slave-holding is in itself sinful, on the ground that one man cannot lawfully possess or exercise the rights and authority over his fellow-men, which are involved in the relation of a master to his slaves. This of necessity leads to setting up a rule of faith and practice higher than the Scriptures, and thus tends to destroy their authority. It leads to uncharitable feelings and to unrighteous judgments, as well as to unwarrantable measures for abating the evil.[22]

Still assuming the biblical compatibility of concepts of human equality and social inferiority, Hodge maintained that the principle of equality among men was to apply in the treatment of slaves, though this equality was not to be understood in terms of social station:

> Paul requires for slaves not only what is strictly just, but *ten isoteta*. What is that? Literally, it is *equality*. This is not only its signification, but its meaning. Slaves are to be treated by their masters on the principles of equality. Not that they are to be equal with their masters in authority, or station, or circumstances; but they are to be treated as having, as men, as husbands, and as parents, equal rights with their masters. It is just as great a sin to deprive a slave of the just recompense for his labour, or to keep him in ignorance, or to take from him his wife or child, as it is to act thus towards a free man. This is the equality which the law of God demands, and on this principle the final judgment is to be administered. Christ will punish the master for defrauding the slave as severely as he will punish the slave for robbing his master. The same penalty will be inflicted for the violation of the conjugal or parental rights of the one as of the other. For, as the apostle adds, there is no respect of persons with him. At his bar the question will be, "What was done," not "who did it?"[23]

As this statement indicates, the overwhelming emphasis of Hodge's understanding of biblical equality involved the insidious establishment of a dichotomy between the slaves' personal lives and their lives as organic members of a larger society. This dichotomy revealed a tragically unrealistic aspect of Hodge's "equality," viz., its naive underestimation of social and institutional power, and its optimistic sentiment that human beings would not use that power for their own sinful purposes. The evil and abusive tendencies implicit within social and institutional power were recognized more explicitly by the U.S. Constitution with its system of checks and balances.

Hodge's concern for the orderly functioning of slavery and a charitable relationship between master and slave included instructive counsel for slaves as well as masters. In general, this counsel dealt with the spiritual responsibility and hopes of the slave, offering spiritual interpretation of present realities as an ameliorative replacement for the harsh realities of social inferiority and subordination. Hodge stressed the religious nature of the slave's obedience to the master, an understanding which, in Hodge's view, gave slave obedience an element of "spiritual freedom":

> Slaves were to regard their obedience to their masters as part of their obedience to Christ. This would give it the character of a religious service, because the motive is regard to divine authority, and its object is a divine person. It thus ceases to be servile, and becomes consistent with the highest mental elevation and spiritual freedom.[24]

In the increasingly materialistic and acquisitive society of mid-nineteenth century America, Hodge encouraged slaves to be content with their position by his stress on the distinct insignificance of the "external relations" of society in comparison to the "inward" freedom associated with liberty in Christ. The blessings of Christian liberty far outweighed the hardships of slavery:

> The possession of that liberty with which Christ makes his people free, is so great a blessing, that all other things, even the condition of slavery, are comparatively of no account...A man need care little about his external condition in this world, who is freed from the bondage of Satan, the curse of the law, the dominion of sin, and who is made a child and heir of God; that is, who is conformed to the image of his Son, and made a partaker of his exaltation and kingdom.[25]

Since the "external relations" of life were, comparatively speaking, of such minimal value, everyone was to "be contented with the station which God (had) assigned him in this life." Communion with God offered "contentment and happiness"; God's favor was life, "and his lovingkindness...better than life." Peace and holiness came through communion with God.[26] Service to God transformed the earthly servitude of a slave into a consolable spiritual freedom from bondage:

> Our obedience terminates on him; and this gives, as the apostle teaches, the sublimity of spiritual freedom even to service of a slave to his master, or of subjects to a despot. It is not in the power of man to reduce to bondage those who serve God in all the service they render their fellow men.[27]

Hodge's counsel to the slave included reference to the eschatological hope of a future life of blessedness. Hodge enjoined obedience on the part of the slave, for "'whatsoever good thing any man doeth, the same shall he receive of the Lord, whether he be bond or free.'" The present world distinguished between masters and slaves, but the next world would not.[28] Though such counsel undoubtedly had a hollow ring to it as far as most nineteenth century slaves were concerned, one must allow that Hodge was not without a sincere element of concern regarding the adverse circumstances in which others lived. Writing in a context other than slavery, a younger Hodge had offered the following interpretive comments on the "afflictive dispensations" or sufferings provided men by God:

> [Sufferings] give us the opportunity of practicing some of the highest virtues, and are eminently adapted to make us feel, that there is too much uncertainty with regard to things of this world to allow of our choosing it as a portion. Whatever renders the present unpleasant leads to the contemplation of the future. And if this contemplation should result in such a perception of the importance of what lies beyond the limits of the present life as to lead us to place our treasure there, we should soon find the spirit of quietness coming over our agitated and anxious feelings, and the anticipation of future good abundantly compensating for the want of present happiness.[29]

Less than a year before the beginning of the Civil War, Hodge remained pertinaciously critical of the abolitionists. He felt certain that his position represented the majority of northerners, and did his best to convince southern Christian leaders that most northerners were not abolitionists and were interested primarily in national unity. Hodge expressed his understanding of northern feeling in a personal letter to Robert L. Dabney, Southern Presbyterian and one of the most powerful and articulate proslavery advocates in the South:

> I am persuaded that the great majority of the North condemn 1. The language, spirit, and conduct of the abolitionists. 2. All attempts to promote dissatisfaction among the slaves or to induce them to escape from their master. 3. They condemn all laws designed to interfere with the restoration of

> fugitive slaves. They hold that such is a constitutional obligation and a moral duty... 4. [?] the Territories the people of the North admit that they are common property; and that the people of the South have exactly the same rights in them as the people of the North. They however, I presume generally hold that slavery is a creation of local law, and therefore can exist only within the sphere of the operation of that law... 5. I believe that if the proposition were submitted to the North to pay the full value of any fugitive slave, and to restore the Missouri compromise and thus divide the Territories, it would be sustained by an overwhelming majority of the Northern people. I believe further that the North would agree to any concessions or compromise, consistent with a good conscience, to avoid a dissolution of the Union.[30]

At the beginning of the war, however, Hodge roused the ire of Christian leaders in the South by his legal opinion that slavery was a "municipal" institution, whose existence depended on local, rather than natural, laws:

> In asserting, therefore, that slavery is a municipal institution, we say nothing as to its origin. We do not say that it is created by statute law. We only say that it rests on the *lex loci*, and that it has no legal existence beyond the operation of that law. In this respect it is on the same foundation with polygamy, orders of nobility, serfdom, and other local institutions, for which no natural or Divine law universally obligatory can be pleaded.[31]

Opposition to Hodge's legal position was typified by William J. Grayson's response to Hodge's "State of the Country" (1861) article. Grayson disagreed with Hodge's contention (in Grayson's words) "that slavery (was) a municipal regulation, and therefore (could) exist only where there (was) some law to create and enforce it."[32] Quite to the contrary, Grayson argued:

> The truth is just the reverse of the Republican dogma. The common custom, which is all that is meant by the common law of the world, has made slaves property from the beginning; it is municipal law which has enacted, from time to time, in one or another country, that slaves shall not be held as property. We need go no further than our own continent to establish the certainty of this fact. In North America, under the common law of common custom, before the Revolution, slavery existed everywhere. Since the Revolution, by the municipal or local laws of this or that State, of Massachusetts or New York, slavery exists no longer. It continues in those States where no such laws have been passed... Slavery then prevails under the general law; it is limited under particular or municipal law.[33]

In another rebuttal of Hodge's "State of the Country" position, John H. Rice argued in *The Southern Presbyterian Review* (1861) that slavery was a "domestic institution" outside of the federal government's sphere of concern. The problem was social and not political, for the relation between master and servant was a "family relation":

> The Federal Government has, therefore, no more right to abolish slavery, by direct or indirect legislation, either in the States or Territories, than it has to divorce, by general law, every husband and wife in New York or Pennsylvania.[34]

The editor of the *Southern Presbyterian* described Hodge's "State of the Country" article as an unfair attack on the

South, and Hodge responded with a letter to the editor, assuring him that his purpose in writing the article was to convince southerners that the abolitionists did not constitute a majority in the North:

> It [the "State of the Country" article] was intended to produce two effects, within the limited range of its influence, first, to convince the South that the mass of northern people are not abolitionists or hostile to the rights and interests of the South; and Second, to convince the North that the course adopted by the abolitionists is unjust and unscriptural.
>
> ...So far as the North is concerned the design of the article was to convince its readers, that the condemnation of slaveholding as a crime, and the denunciation of slave-holders as such as wicked, is anti-Scriptural and immoral -- that all attempts to render slaves disobedient or rebellious are criminal -- that all opposition to the restoration of fugitive slaves is contrary to the constitution, and to the moral law; that the north ought to do everything to conciliate the south, by making full compensation for fugitive slaves and by a division of the common territory.[35]

However, the earlier hints of Hodge's dissociation from proslavery advocates were confirmed, as Hodge put less and less emphasis on the legitimacy of social inferiority, and more on the abnormality of the condition. The relative subordination of one race to another was a legitimate worldwide phenomenon; but this subordination could not be justified on the basis of the weakness of one race, and it was not to be considered perpetual:

> The strong, physically or mentally, are not entitled to enslave the weak. Unless the inferiority be such as to render the less gifted race for ever incapable

> of freedom, it can form no justification in the sight of God or man for their perpetual bondage.[36]

The inferiority of the Negro did not mean that slavery was a "normal condition," nor was the inferiority "inherent and unalterable."[37] No one who believed the Bible as God's word could suggest that God had "doomed the black race to be the perpetual slaves of the white."[38] Hodge had come realistically to recognize the existence of a southern "slaveocracy," with its ever-present potential for concentrating wealth and power in the hands of a few. He expressed his abhorrence of the idea that a significant body of Presbyterians could tolerate the severe class discrimination engendered by slaveholding:

> That any large class of Presbyterians hold either of these views, that they believe it to be consistent with the word of God, with the spirit of the gospel, with the laws of human nature, that the few should be masters, and the many slaves; that all power, property, and every post of emolument and honour should by law be confined to one small class of the people, and the mass of mankind should be held as property, we are very loth to admit.[39]

Hodge's opposition to slavery was perhaps most poignantly revealed in his responses, during the initial stages of the war, to the legal matter of territorial slavery. His increasing commitment to the dissolution of slavery was apparent in his interest in restoring the Missouri Compromise. Hodge was worried that restoration of the compromise had been undermined by the Dred Scott decision, which effectively barred congressional prohibition of territorial slavery:

> The only way in which the Missouri compromise, or anything of a like nature, can be restored, is by altering the constitution, or reversing the Dred Scott decision. While that decision remains in force, it effectually prevents Congress from prohibiting the introduction of slavery into any of the common territories of the Union.[40]

Hodge's dissatisfaction with the Supreme Court's decision in Dred Scott included his criticism of the discontinuity and impermanence of the Court's decision:

> The law principles laid down by judges enlighten the intelligence, but they do not seem to bind the conscience of their successors. Otherwise [errors?] would be perpetuated. Every judge seems to feel bound to follow his own convictions as to what the law is. I do not think therefore the law as laid down by the majority of the Judges in the Dred Scott case has any binding force at all. Indeed it is said to be in direct contravention of all the previous rulings of that court.[41]

Hodge had expressed his support of the fugitive slave law, suggesting that the North should reimburse the South for slaves lost by the South to the North.[42] But this sympathy did not detract from his condemnation of the attempt to make slavery legal in the territories:

> It is probable, therefore, that the actual extension of slavery would not be greatly promoted by the adoption of the principle that it is entitled to legal protection in all the territories of the Union. The principle itself, however, we believe to be false and revolutionary.[43]

Hodge continued to argue in favor of a gradual emancipation to be effected through "a system of moral, intellectual, and social culture of the blacks, as would render their transition from slavery to freedom as certain and as healthful as the transition of man from childhood to manhood."[44] Slaves were like children, and their liberty could legitimately be restricted only as long as they were "unfit to use it aright."[45]

Hodge's 1838 argument against forcing the South to abolish slavery[46] had yielded to a defense of the right of Congress "to prohibit slavery in the territories,"[47] (a prohibition possible under the old Missouri Compromise of 1820), and by the end of the war, Hodge had opened a formidable assault on the unjust southern slave laws. In the providence of God, he proclaimed, the time had arrived for all people to address themselves earnestly to the eradication of slavery. The injustice of southern slave laws had been manifestly exhibited in the continued degradation of slaves resulting from a century of persistent effort to perpetuate slavery and prevent the progress of the slaves:

> One of the saddest proofs of the injustice of Southern laws, is, that after more than a century, the vast body of the slaves of the extreme southern states are in a condition of the greatest degradation. That this is not to be attributed to their inferiority as a race, but to the systematic effort to prevent their improvement, is clear, because it is only the "field hands" who are thus degraded. Household servants, and those living in cities, where they have the opportunity of learning mechanic arts, are as much improved, as intelligent and moral, as any other class of men of no higher advantages.[48]

By this time, Hodge had apparently lost confidence in the optimistic view that the institution of slavery could help to raise the slave from barbarism to Christianity and civilization. The southern perpetuation of slavery had been intentional, and no Christian could justify laws that served perpetually to degrade other human beings:

> It is self-evident that only an inferior race can permanently be held in slavery, and it is therefore unavoidable that the effort to perpetuate slavery involves the necessity of the perpetual degradation of a class of our fellow-men. Such was the design and effect of the laws which forbade slaves to be taught to read or write; which prohibited their holding property; which made it a legal axiom that slaves cannot marry; which authorized the separation of parents and children, and of those living as husbands and wives.[49]

From justifying slavery on the basis of the slave's incompetence, Hodge had come to emphasize that the perpetuation of the institution was artificial and directly connected with perpetuation of the slave's incompetence. American slavery could no longer be justified, and the perpetuators of it had no justifiable basis for its toleration. The illegal rebellion of the southern states threatened not only the existence of the nation, but "the annihilation of the principles of free Christian government" as well.[50] Though adversity might attend the final overthrow of slavery, Providence demanded its elimination: "The inevitable difficulties and sufferings consequent on such an abrupt change in the institutions and social organization of a great people, must be submitted to, as comprehended in the design of God in these events."[51] Even Hodge's strong commitment to preserving the established order had now been preempted by the imperative need to free the slaves.

The process of emancipation had been carried providentially past many "insurmountable barriers, the one remaining barrier being the charitable acceptance by all persons of those removed from their condition of bondage:

> The difficulties which formerly seemed insurmountable, in the providence of God, appear now to be almost removed. The most formidable remaining obstacle, we think, will be found to be the unwillingness of the human heart to see and accept the truth against the prejudices of habit and of interest; and to act towards those who have heretofore been degraded as slaves, with the charity of Christian principle in the necessary efforts to improve and elevate them.[52]

Hodge responded favorably to Lincoln's slavery policy, which recognized the unity of human origin and species and the illegitimacy of permanently distinguishing between classes of persons.[53] In concert with Lincoln, he commented:

> If all men are by nature one, if all have the same essential elements of humanity, there can be no just reason why any one class should be for ever condemned to inferiority and bondage. It was the great scriptural truth of the unity of the human race as to origin and species, which lay at the foundation of all President Lincoln's opinions and policy in regard to slavery... This being the case, neither the colour of the skin, nor unessential differences in the varieties of men, is any just ground for a permanent distinction between one class and another.[54]

After the Civil War, Hodge spoke sparingly on the issues of race and slavery, though a few remarks made in 1872 bear mention. He soundly condemned the sinful nature and "piracy" of the slave-trade: "Why have our own and other Christian nations pronounced the slave-trade piracy and punishable with death? Not because it interferes with the rights or liberty of their citizens but because it is wicked."[55] He also reiterated his former emphasis upon the need for proper treatment of slaves, though with a strangely inconsistent twist, viz., that the treatment of slaves was governed by the biblical principle that a laborer was worthy of his hire. Justice demanded that slaves receive proper payment for their work:

> Even on the theory of slavery, where the labourer himself, his time, and strength, and all he has, are assumed to belong to his master, the servant has a claim to a proper recompense, which it would be unjust to withhold from him. And in every department of life it is recognized as a simple matter of justice, that the man who performs a stipulated work, earns his wages.[56]

It is not clear what Hodge meant here by "proper recompense" or "wages," since the very essence of slavery involved involuntary servitude without compensation. The only consistent understanding of this statement would involve interpreting "wages" as the provision of the necessities of the slave, which, of course, the master was obligated to provide.

An interesting comparison may be made between Hodge's persistent defense of the involuntary servitude forced upon certain persons by others, and Hodge's contention, within the context of an 1872 argument against monasticism, that one had no right to relinquish one's own liberty through monastic vows:

> No man has the right to swear away his liberty; to reduce himself to a state of absolute subjection to a fellow-mortal. To his own master he must stand or fall. The vow of obedience made by every monk or nun was a violation of the apostolic injunction, "Be not ye the servants of men." The same remark is applicable to the vow of celibacy. No one has a right to take that vow; because celibacy is right or wrong according to circumstances. It may be a sin,

> and therefore no such vow can bind the conscience.[57]

It is true that Hodge was speaking here primarily of a spiritual liberty; but the bondage submitted to was nevertheless that of an enforced servitude to other persons. One might derive the interesting conclusion from this comparison that, according to Hodge, the voluntary relinquishing of individual liberty was evil, while the involuntary servitude forced upon the inferior classes of society was not.

This chronological discussion has attempted to indicate that Hodge was not the static and immovable, arch-defender of slavery that many have described him to have been. For example, in 1878 the *Evangelical Repository and United Presbyterian Worker* remarked:

> In his life he [Hodge] made mistakes, and sometimes threw his great influence on the wrong side. Notable instances of this were his advocacy of human slavery in our nation, and his position during the rebellion. Probably no other man did so much as he to produce the conviction that American slavery was not sinful. The Presbyterian Church in the United States assumed and held for years a false attitude respecting human bondage. Dr. Charles Hodge had his full share in leading his church into that position and retaining her in it. And when the slaveholder's rebellion came he did what he could to have his church stand in a doubtful, if not in a disloyal attitude. He was defeated, and the truth and right triumphed.[58]

Since charging Hodge with disloyalty could refer only to his opposition to the Gardiner Spring Resolution committing the 1861 General Assembly to an endorsement of the federal government, this statement exhibits a marked bias and superficiality. Furthermore, Hodge never varied in his support of the Northern cause during the Civil War.

A similar superficiality is apparent in a twentieth-century dissertation by Penrose St. Amant, though the nature of the author's criticism is biblical rather than ecclesiological. St. Amant comments on the inconsistency exhibited by Hodge in maintaining that slavery, per se, was not sinful, and that proper treatment of slaves would lead to the abolition of slavery:

> Thus ran the tortuous argument of Hodge and the Princeton school on the subject of slavery. An institution supported by proof-texts from the Bible could be abrogated by the inculcaton of a Biblical attitude toward the slaves![59]

St. Amant claims further that

> Hodge's effort to reconcile what he regarded as a Biblical teaching, namely, that the existence of slavery was a morally neutral condition, with the monstrous evils with which the actual practice of slaveholding were characterized is a nice example of the extent to which his Biblicism could drive him. The psychology of this and other similar efforts is clear. Since he believed whatever he thought the Bible taught to be true, regardless of the intellectual or moral difficulties engendered, it was possible for him to rationalize the problems his view sometimes posed, no matter how ridiculous the rationalization might appear to those who rejected his presupposition of Biblical infallibility.[60]

The main problem with Hodge's biblical defense of slavery, however, was not so much psychological as hermeneutical. One certainly does not doubt his personal commitment to the infallibility of the Bible; but this latter belief need not have deterred him from a condemnation of the institution of slavery, had he considered Scripture from a broad theological perspective. For the most part, Hodge built his early doctrine of slavery on acts of Christ interpreted without sufficient context, or, even more tenuously, on the failure of Christ to act in certain situations. It would be a sad principle indeed, which held that what Christ did not actively resist with teaching is not sinful, and therefore must be permitted. Christ's instructions to slaves did not imply that he condoned their condition of bondage any more than his favorable treatment of Zacchaeus condoned the tax collector's past history of extortion. From a more properly systematic perspective, in his defense of the institution of slavery, Hodge failed sufficiently to recognize that even if slavery were an institution necessary to the preservation of the present society, it was not a "divinely ordained institution," a designation which, biblically, has been reserved for the family, the church, and the state.

The characterization of Hodge as an advocate of slavery, then, is not altogether inaccurate. He found no sin in the institution of slavery, as he narrowly defined it, and even once bought a slave himself.[61] But his theoretical support of slavery, as defined in these narrowly abstract terms, must be judged against his outspoken and increasingly intense disapproval of American slavery.

Notes

1. Charles Hodge, "Slavery," *The Biblical Repertory and Theological Review* (1836).

2. Charles Hodge, "Abolitionism," *The Biblical Repertory and Princeton Review* (1844), periodical hereafter cited as *BRPR*.

3. Charles Hodge to Hugh Hodge, 23 October 1833, Hodge Family Letters and Papers, Princeton University Library, Princeton, New Jersey (collection hereafter cited as HLP).

4. Charles Hodge to Hugh Hodge, 23 November 1833, HLP.

5. Ibid., p. 297
6. Charles Hodge, "American Board, Special Report of the Prudential Committee," *BRPR* (1849): 37.
7. Charles Hodge, "Emancipation," *BRPR* (1849): 590.
8. Ibid., p. 606.
9. Charles Hodge, "General Assembly," *BRPR* (1846): 424.
10. Hodge, "Emancipation," p. 603.
11. Ibid., p. 602.
12. Ibid., p. 603.
13. Hodge, "General Assembly," *BRPR* (1846): 426-427.
14. Hodge, "American Board, Special Report of the Prudential Committee," p. 25.
15. Charles Hodge (with Dr. Hope), "The General Assembly," *BRPR* (1847): 429.
16. Ibid.
17. Hodge, "Emancipation," pp. 604-605.
18. H. Shelton Smith, Robert T. Handy, and Lefferts A. Loetscher, *American Christianity*, 2 vols. (New York, 1960-63), 1:293.
19. Hodge, "American Board, Special Report of the Prudential Committee," p. 26.
20. Hodge, "Emancipation," p. 593.
21. Ibid., p. 592.
22. Charles Hodge, *A Commentary on the Epistle to the Ephesians* (Wilmington, Delaware, 1972, reprint edition), p. 125. This edition is bound with Charles Hodge, *An Exposition of 1 and 2 Corinthians*
23. Ibid., p. 127.
24. Ibid., p. 126.
25. Hodge, *Corinthians*, p. 76.
26. Ibid.
27. Charles Hodge, Sermon -- Romans 13.1, Princeton Theological Seminary Library, n.p., n.d.
28. Hodge, *Ephesians*, p. 127.
29. Charles Hodge to Mary Hodge, ? March 1826, HLP. In another letter, Hodge expressed his concern for the poor and the consolation they had in regard to the future life. Speaking in anticipation of a bitter winter, Hodge wrote,

> There will be but few in any class of society who will not feel its bitterness most sensibly, but the thousands of poor through the country, will by their sufferings attest, that, if this world is the only home of man, and this life to afford all his blessedness, it would be better for many that they never were born (Charles Hodge to Mary Hodge, 29 December [1810-1891], HLP).

30. Charles Hodge to Robert L. Dabney, 15 December 1860, HLP.
31. Charles Hodge, "The Church and the Country," *BRPR* (1861): 357.
32. William J. Grayson, "Reply to Professor Hodge, on the 'State of the Country'" (Charleston: Steam-Power Presses of Evans & Cogwell, 1861), p. 20, in Sprague Collections, Collection 112; Political (sic) of the Rebellion, v. 2, 1861, Princeton Theological Seminary Library.
33. Ibid., pp. 20-21.
34. John H. Rice, "The Princeton Review on the State of the Country," *The Southern Presbyterian Review* 14 (1861): 34-35.
35. Charles Hodge to the editor of the *Southern Presbyterian*, 3 January 1861, HLP.
36. Hodge, "The Church and the Country," p. 360.
37. Charles Hodge, "England and America," *BRPR* (1862): 168-169.
38. Hodge, "The Church and the Country," p. 347.
39. Ibid.
40. Ibid., p. 374.
41. Charles Hodge to H. W. Green, 4 February 1861, HLP.
42. Charles Hodge, "The State of the Country," *BRPR* (1861): 36.
43. Hodge, "The Church and the Country," p. 354.
44. Charles Hodge, "The General Assembly," *BRPR* (1862): 521.
45. Charles Hodge, "The General Assembly," *BRPR* (1864): 548.

46. Charles Hodge, "West India Emancipation," *BRPR* (1838): 606.
47. Hodge, "The Church and the Country," p. 369.
48. Ibid., p. 548.
49. Charles Hodge, "President Lincoln,: *BRPR* (1865): 438.
50. Hodge, "The General Assembly," *BRPR* (1864): 542.
51. Hodge, "President Lincoln," p. 440.
52. Hodge, "The General Assembly," *BRPR* (1864): 543.
53. Hodge, "President Lincoln, pp. 456-457.
54. Charles Hodge, "*The Princeton Review* and the State of the Country and the Church," *BRPR* (1865): 641.
55. Charles Hodge, *Systematic Theology*, 3 vols. (Grand Rapids: Wm. B. Eerdmans Publishing Company, 1977, reprint edition), 3:341.
56. Ibid., p. 244.
57. Ibid., p. 320.
58. "Death of Dr. Charles Hodge," *The Evangelical Repository and United Presbyterian Worker* 55 (1878): 124.
59. Penrose St. Amant, "The Rise and Early Development of the Princeton School of Theology" (Ph.D. thesis, University of Edinburgh, 1952), p. 190.
60. Ibid., p. 196.
61. Hodge made reference to his purchase of a slave boy in an 1834 letter to brother Hugh:

> I was induced by various sufficient and weighty considerations to purchase the time of a boy 13 years old who has 12 years to serve -- and was to give $75. A very cheap purchase. He is the son of our [Lena ?] -- of an excellent family -- well brought up -- has been taught to read -- knows his catechism and is as neat and genteel a little boy as you could readily meet with. He belongs to the Rev. Mr. Rice of Spotswood -- brother in law to Dr. Carnahan. And as Mrs. Rice a Dutch a [sic] lady has no children she paid great attention to this boy. -- But the poor little fellow is I am persuaded

in consumption and I fear will not live 6 months! This is a great disappointment, for we felt we had gotten a prize and were rejoiced to see his mother so happy in having her son near her. I sent yesterday for Dr. Howell to examine him and he confirms all my apprehensions. I must therefore return him -- Mr. Rice, as is so apt to be the case with those who are constantly with consumptive patients, was and is deceived as to the nature of the disease. He was perfectly candid I have no doubt in saying he thought the boy -- merely slightly [asmatich ?] (Charles Hodge to Hugh Hodge, 9 January 1834, HLP).

The Sermon at Nazareth

(Luke 4:14-22)

William W. Klein

There are many things that have characterized Dr. Grounds in his career, but, it seems to me, this text captures some of his major concerns, the issues that have occupied much of his time and energies through the years. He has helped many of us see what the message in this sermon of Jesus means when lived out in today's world.

The Setting - Luke 4:14-15

Following the temptation narrative Luke tells about the character of Jesus' ministry at its next venue -- Galilee. Jesus himself was empowered by the Spirit; the Spirit was with or upon him. Mention of "news" about Jesus circulating in the region points to a period of ministry in Galilee, although Luke has not yet described any such ministry. This suggestion, however, is confirmed by the plural, "synagogues," and the fact that "everyone" praised him. For what might they praise him? Doubtless his mighty works are evidence that he is Spirit-filled; this accounts for his growing reputation. Just as elsewhere for Luke the presence of the Spirit accounts for the effectiveness of apostolic teaching, so with Jesus, the Spirit energizes both his works and words.

Luke's Placing Of This Incident

Whereas in vv. 14ff Luke presents Jesus' Galilean ministry in a favorable light, in vv. 16-30 we find a total rejection by his fellow Nazarenes. The significance of what Luke has done in including this example of Jesus' ministry is heightened, if Luke is responsible for locating this incident here at the outset of his Galilean narrative. Indeed many factors confirm that this is precisely what Luke has done. In Matthew (13:53-58) and Mark (6:1-6a) a remarkably similar story appears much later in Jesus' ministry. The essential parts of the Markan story appear in Luke 4, though there are divergences. It is extremely unlikely that what Mark records (6:1-6) could take place after the people of Nazareth had reacted as they did in Luke 4. As we noted above, 4:14ff point to a period of activity in Galilee that Luke has not described in any detail. As well in 4:23 the mention of prior activity in Capernaum suggests that in fact this incident is not the first in Jesus' Galilean ministry.

Lane,[1] among others, suggests that the gospels record two separate visits (and rejections) of Jesus at Nazareth. Though this is possible, it appears highly improbable. It is more likely that Luke is recording the same incident that Matthew and Mark record later and that Luke's version is based not on Mark's rendition, but on another source. Luke chose to employ this other source[2] rather than the Markan one, and for his own reasons he decided to include it at the outset, rather than where Mark and Matthew have it. If Luke did not view the incidents as one and the same, then it becomes more difficult to explain why he did not record the second visit to Nazareth where Mark and Matthew have it.[3]

Quite likely, then, this pericope performs for Luke what Mark 1:14ff does in the Second Gospel. Mark gives the following introduction to Jesus' ministry, particularly the content of his message: "The time has come...The kingdom of God is near. Repent and believe the good news." Luke accomplishes this function by telling of a specific occasion in Nazareth. As Marshall puts it, "The narrative is placed here, then, for its programmatic significance, and it contains many of the main themes of Lk.-Acts *in nuce*."[4]

That Day In The Nazareth Synagogue - Luke 4:16-17

Luke identifies the location of this incident as Nazareth. He also identifies Nazareth as Jesus' home town: it is where he was brought up, i.e., "from a very small child."[5] Although the gospels record many visits of Jesus to synagogues, this is the sole mention that synagogue attendance on the Sabbath was Jesus' custom. But Marshall[6] suggests that the parallel in Acts 17:2 may indicate that the reference is to Jesus' regular use of the synagogue for teaching (cf. 4:15).

Morris makes the point that "this is the earliest description of a synagogue service we have."[7] Without purporting to tell all that transpired during that synagogue service, Luke begins by saying that Jesus "stood up to read." Presumably this implies that he went up to the front or up onto the platform where the scroll was located. Luke does not explain why Jesus should be invited to read and then "preach." But the Acts chronology gives other accounts of distinguished visitors being invited to preach (Acts 13:15ff; 14:1; 16:13; 17:2, 10, 17; 18:4; 19:8). Schweizer provides this description of a typical first century synagogue worship service:

> Synagogue worship begins and ends with prayers and benedictions; its core is the reading of the law, as a rule by several lectors. This reading was probably fixed by the time of Jesus, while the reading from the prophets was still chosen freely. The Hebrew text was translated into the Aramaic vernacular and usually explained by one or more individuals. Any man -- women were excluded -- could announce his intention to read by standing up (cf. also I Cor. 14:30); as a rule, however, there was generally prior agreement on who would be asked to perform this function (Acts 13:15). The reader would sit to begin his explanation (vs. 20).[8]

Luke seems to indicate that Jesus did not make the choice of books to read. He was handed the book of the prophet Isaiah. At the same time it does appear that Jesus chose the specific passage(s) in Isaiah from which to read. But we cannot be sure about this; perhaps he was handed the scroll opened to this specific place. Morris notes: "This does not mean, as some think, that he read from a fixed lectionary. We cannot authenticate a lectionary as early as this."[9] Schweizer thinks that neither the scroll nor the specific reading was the prerogative of Jesus. Marshall assumes that Jesus was given the book he requested.[10]

The Reading From Isaiah - Luke 4:18-19

The texts Luke quotes are from Isaiah 61:1f and 58:6. The prophet speaks of the ministry of the Servant to people who are devastated; in fact, it is the "Servant of the Lord" who is speaking. The entire sixty-first chapter of Isaiah promises that God's anointed one will bring a healing balm to his people. In some ways Luke's quotation is very close to the wording of the LXX, yet he departs from it at several points.[11] Has Luke forgotten the text, not having it before him, so that he merely quotes it from memory?[12] This is unlikely. Likewise it would seem unlikely that Luke has intentionally altered the LXX to suit his purposes. Why would he excise the healing phrase from Isa 61:1, when this motif is so important for him and when he quotes the proverb in 4:23? In addition it is characteristic of Luke to preserve the wording of the LXX, not alter it. For Luke the text of the LXX was normative.[13] The far more likely explanation is that Luke records the incident, and especially the quotation, as it came to him in his source; the source could go back to Jesus himself. There is no inherent reason why this is not precisely how Jesus expressed himself.[14] In support of this possibility Chilton states: "Jesus availed himself of various phrases then associated with Isaiah 61 to bring out the meaning of the passage in a manner generally reminiscent of Targumic practice."[15]

Schweizer argues that an eschatological and messianic interpretation of Isaiah 61:1ff was current in the first century, citing, especially, 11QMelch. Stanton asserts, "There is now clear evidence that at the time of Jesus Isa. 61:1 was being interpreted in a quite specific way as referring to *the* eschatological prophet."[16] Dead Sea scrolls also connect Isa 61:1f to the jubilee years of Lev 25:10 and Deut 15:2, but there are no compelling reasons to posit that A.D. 26/27 was in fact observed as a jubilee year.

With that initial introduction we will proceed to consider Jesus' quotation from Isaiah line by line, attempting to understand its significance both for Jesus and for Luke.

"The Spirit of the Lord is on me,"[17]

Would Jesus identify himself as the Spirit-anointed one? Jeremias answers:

> Luke 4:18-21; Matt. 5:3 par. and 11:5 par. indicate that he [Jesus] applied the promise of the spirit in Isa. 61:1 to himself; in view of the remarkable statements made by the Teacher of Righteousness about himself, this no longer seems as inconceivable as it did a short time ago.[18]

Jesus adopts what amounts to a title: he is the one on whom rests the Spirit of the Lord. Coupled with the following title, the Anointed One, it links Jesus to the messianic tradition in Old Testament theology.[19]

"because he has anointed me"

In Isaiah 61 the Prophet is anointed. This Spirit-anointed One appears as the eschatological Prophet whom the prophets of Israel recognize as the Servant of the Lord (see, e.g., Isa 42:1, 4, 6f; 49:3, 6). Jesus' "official" anointing occurred at his baptism (Luke 3:22). Marshall says,

"Ultimately, the concepts of the echatological prophet and the Messiah merge."[20] Doubtless Jesus is claiming messiahship in quoting from this text as he does.

"to preach good news to the poor"

This is in harmony with 6:20 and is what we would expect of the ministry of a prophet. "Jesus brings redemption through a message, not a social or political reform; through a word, not a war."[21] The "poor" are those whose circumstances are dire; they are desperate and hopeless; they need a rescuer.[22]

Good news for the "poor" is a pervasive theme in Isaiah (e.g., 42:1, 6f; 29:18f). In Isaiah 61 the meaning of "the poor" is explained by the following expressions: brokenhearted, captives, prisoners, mourners and those who grieve.[23] Speaking of the Hebrew word for "poor" Jeremias notes, "in the prophets the word embraces the oppressed and the poor who know that they are thrown completely on God's help. Jesus used 'the poor' in this wide sense."[24] The only permanent answer to the needs of the poor is the coming of God's new order -- the dawning of the age of salvation. Jesus' ministry consistently demonstrated his concern for the outcasts and poor; his condemnations were often directed at the rich and proud.

Luke's gospel shows his concern for those who are literally "poor" (e.g., 6:20-26; cf. Mt 5:3; 7:22; 14:12f, 21; 18:22). We may not merely spiritualize "poor" here.

The LXX phrase "to heal the broken-hearted" (*iasasthai tous suntetrimmenous te kardia*), based on the next Hebrew phrase, is omitted in Luke's account. This omission is perplexing unless the phrase was absent from the source that Luke employed. Apparently he did not "check out" the LXX and quote it directly; he faithfully reproduced the source as it came to him.

"he has sent me to proclaim freedom (aphesin; also means "forgiveness") for the prisoners"

For Isaiah the sense was probably both literal and metaphorical (spiritual). However, as we will suggest below, the dominant sense must be spiritual: Jesus releases people from their imprisonment to sin. He offers salvation through the forgiveness (*en aphesei*) of sins (Lk 1:77).

"and recovery of sight for the blind,"

Blindness, for Isaiah, was mainly the spiritual blindness of the people (e.g., 42:18-20; 43:8; 56:10; 59:9-14), though Isaiah also prophesied of a time when even physical infirmities like blindness, deafness and lameness would be eradicated (35:5-10). Though Jesus did literally restore sight to the blind on several occasions recorded in the Gospels (bringing a foretaste of the age to come), the essential significance of this is probably metaphorical. Spiritual blindness characterized the unsaved (Luke 8:10b, 23f; cf. Matt. 13:14-17; John 9:39).

"to release the oppressed,"

This clause is not found in Isa. 61, but is from Isa. 58:6. Did Jesus interpolate, was there an Isaiah scroll with this addition already, or did Luke provide it? Many scholars argue that Jesus would never have made such an insertion in the course of a public reading, and therefore it was made at some point by the church. But there is no inherent reason to exclude the possibility that Jesus combined the Isa. 58:6 phrase with the text he was reading. Indeed Reicke argues that Jesus could easily have made such an insertion, being the prophet that he was.[25]

In this phrase the word *aphesis* occurs again. No doubt the Isaiah reference implied literal *release* for prisoners and the oppressed. But Luke employs the expression *aphesis hamartion* frequently in the Acts sermons (e.g., 2:38; 5:31; 10:43; 13:38; 26:18). This further confirms the suggestion made above; we may legitimately see a reference to forgiveness. Freedom is provided for those who are broken or bruised by sin. Luke's (and Jesus') use here of *aphesis*, so important for his theology, cannot be overlooked.[26] This is not merely a kind of physical relief; the shackles of sin are broken. God's salvation alone can effect this relief.

"to proclaim the year of the Lord's favor."

What does it mean to proclaim, literally, the year acceptable to the Lord? The verb *keryxai* replaces the LXX *kalesai*, stressing the public posture of proclamation.[27] What year is acceptable to the Lord? What year expresses his favor? Though it is possible that Jesus had the jubilee year (Lev 25:10) in mind, this seems to be extremely unlikely. Rather, it is a "favorable" year, because it is the year that God has chosen; it is a year of God's active blessing. Surely it confirms Jesus as the anointed one, the one who ushers in the messianic age, the year or age in which God displays his salvation.

There is an interesting linguistic confirmation of the tie between this *acceptable* year and Jesus who proclaims its arrival. The word "acceptable," *dektos*, describes "year" here in v. 19 and a "prophet" in v. 24. Tannehill observes, individuals "can only share in 'the Lord's acceptable year' if they accept the one who announces and brings it."[28]

The citation in Luke terminates prior to the complementary "day of vengeance of our God" which follows in Isa. 61:2. If this is the day of salvation, is the day of vengeance still future? Jesus intentionally omitted this final phrase, but for what purpose? Martin[29] argues that this omission serves to extend the scope of God's favor to the Gentiles, but this is not at all certain. Vengeance is not limited to the Gentiles. It is better to see this paralleling Paul's statement that "...now is the time of God's favor, now is the day of salvation" (2 Cor. 6:2). Salvation is now available to all; one day comes the judgment when God's favor will be available no longer.

The Aftermath - Luke 4:20-22

After finishing his reading Jesus "sat down," the Jewish (not Greco-Roman) posture for preaching (cf. Matt. 26:55). Luke says that *all* the people waited expectantly for Jesus' words (all eyes were fixed intently -- continuous action -- on him). Clearly they were expecting what we could call a sermon. Luke is specific about how Jesus began, *erxato*, his sermon to them: "Today this Scripture (*he graphe aute*) is fulfilled in your hearing." Jesus claims that in his ministry the prophecy of Isaiah is *today* fulfilled. He was inaugurating the era of salvation prophesied in the Old Testament writings. Jesus claims, according to Hill, that the "time of divine election, acceptance and presence is realised in the prophetic affirmation they have heard."[30] Now is the time of good news, for blindness and the bonds of oppression to be broken. What Isaiah foretold is now happening.[31] The prophecy is fulfilled "in your hearing," implying that the very listeners had the opportunity to experience the salvation Jesus proffered. In effect Jesus informed his listeners that he was the Messiah. The messianic age had dawned. The future "day" about which the Scriptures spoke had now arrived in the ministry of Jesus. Marshall says:

> ...Scriptures have come to fulfilment and the last days have begun. The era of salvation has arrived; it is the year of the Lord's favour, characterised by the preaching of good news to the needy and the performance of mighty works.[32]

Jesus did not simply announce that the day had arrived, as a messenger might do. His uses of *keryssein* in vv. 18 and 19 have performative functions. Jesus was not merely giving information; his proclamation accomplished the action it announced. In his spirit-energized works he demonstrated what this new age was to be like. It would be an age when the poor, exploited, oppressed and needy would find relief and God's favor. Salvation would be available to the spiritually-disadvantaged.

Luke records the reaction of his listeners at this point: "All spoke well (*emartyroun*) of him and were amazed (*ethaumazon*) at the gracious words that came from his lips". With imperfect tenses Luke conveys how the Nazarenes reacted to what Jesus said. The word *martyreo* usually has the sense of "to bear witness (to)" or "to be a witness." The Bauer-Arndt and Gingrich Dictionary cites occurrences of the sense of "to testify favorably, speak well (of)," which most versions and commentators prefer here in Luke 4. However, Marshall[33] and Jeremias[34] also note the sense "to bear witness against, condemn" (cf. Matt. 23:31), and offer a kind of negative sense for *thaumazein*, "to be shocked at." They prefer these latter senses, arguing that negative nuances for both verbs provide a smoother transition to the indignant surprise that the townspeople express in v. 22b and to the hostility that follows later in the account. Marshall argues as well that the parallel account in Matthew is one of uniform hostility, rather than initial approval that sours to murderous animosity.

How then can the phrase "the gracious words that came from his lips" be construed on this negative reading? Jeremias suggests this: "the people of Nazareth are shocked that Jesus quotes only the words of grace from Isaiah 61 to preach about, and omits the mention of vengeance, although it also occurred in the text."[35]

Several objections to this position arise. First, to construe *martyrein* negatively is problematic when its dominant sense in the New Testament is positive: to witness *for*. Is there sufficient evidence in the context to overturn this basic sense and see it negatively? This position also puts a severe strain on the meaning of "gracious words," *oi logoi tes charitos*. The most natural reading suggests taking this positively, as outlined in the entire Isaiah quotation. Jesus has announced great news -- the era of God's favor has dawned. With both verbs Luke conveys an outward reaction: the listeners are impressed, even amazed that Joseph's son should speak in these terms. Perhaps they are skeptical that this local boy should make such extravagant claims. Schweizer suggests that the audience saw only Jesus' rhetorical skill, but failed to understand the significance of what he said. But there's simply no hard evidence that the Nazarenes were incensed because Jesus neglected to finish the quotation and pronounce the requisite judgment upon the Gentiles. The natural sense of "grace" relates it to salvation, to God's *charis*; the day of salvation is here.

Hill has an alternative for explaining how the affirmation of the Nazarene audience turned to anger. He suggests,

> ...Jesus, by refusing to do miracles for his own people and by his words, is affirming that his acceptability to God, his place in God's purpose, requires him to bring relief and release to these outside Israel, and it was this that really created the resentment and antagonism.[36]

This is a better explanation. Luke's account is abbreviated; the transition from 4:22 to 4:23 is admittedly tortuous, but the citations concerning Elijah and Elisha confirm the parameters of the discussion that day. Jesus' acceptability as a prophet of God required him to go beyond the confines of the Jews, the respectable and religious Jews at that. Such a mission for the Prophet was contrary to their expectations and irritated them immensely. This suggestion also fits Luke's theology better. Because the Jews reject Jesus (and later, the apostolic gospel), the message goes to the Gentiles with whom it often finds greater success. This conforms to Luke's presentation of *Heilsgeschichte*.

Significance

Though an exegesis of the remaining verses in this pericope would prove interesting, we will stop at 4:22. What remains is to reflect on the implications of what Jesus and Luke have done in this incident. We will confine our discussion to what appear to be the larger issues.

1. We can profitably begin by asking why Luke includes this incident here, rather than in its more

chronologically correct position? The obvious reason is its programmatic nature. The incident displays several of Luke's key themes: the Holy Spirit, salvation, the poor and needy, fulfilment of prophecy and the authority of the Old Testament, the universal dimensions of the gospel,[37] the Jews' rejection of God's offer of salvation, and eschatology.[38] These points merit individual discussion:

a. The Holy Spirit. Lk. 4:18 establishes a unique identification of Jesus with the Holy Spirit. Jesus, the one anointed by the Spirit, is also rejected by Israel. Luke is sensitive to the crucial role the Spirit plays in the ministry of Jesus (cf. 3:22; 4:1, 14).[39] The presence of the Spirit is not incidental nor superfluous.

b. Salvation. Jesus inaugurates the way of salvation; in fact, he is the sole way, the entre to God's favor. The use of the word *euangelizomai* shows Luke's concern for salvation. Whereas it occurs only once in Matthew and never in Mark, Luke employs the term ten times in the Third Gospel and frequently in the Acts. On several occasions he uses it to summarize the character of Jesus' ministry (e.g., Luke 4:43; 8:1; 20:1; cf. Acts 10:36; Luke 3:18).

c. Healing and helping the poor and needy. Luke characterizes Jesus in Acts 10:38 as anointed by the Holy Spirit and as going about "doing good and healing all who were under the power of the devil..." We have noted Jesus' and Luke's emphasis upon ministry to the poor. This quotation places Jesus on the side of the outcasts rather than the powerful. His ministry proved him to be a friend of the rejected and hopeless.

If we evaluate these two objectives -- to bring salvation to sinners and help for the helpless -- we discover a two-pronged thrust to Jesus' ministry. For Jesus these two were inseparable. This fact is amply evident in the following pericopes in Luke 4. In vv. 31-37 Luke describes Jesus' ministry in terms of authoritative teaching *and* the power to exorcise demons. Then in vv. 38-44 Jesus again ministers through healing, exorcism *and* preaching the good news of the kingdom of God. The two prongs are inseparable; Jesus moves on both fronts to provide divine help to those who are in need.

d. The Old Testament. The fact that Jesus reads from the Old Testament serves Luke's purposes. The Hebrew scriptures continue to possess divine authority. Christianity is not divorced from the religion of the Old Testament. In fact Christ is the fulfilment of Old Testament Messianic prophecy (cf. Luke 24:44). The Prophet whom Isaiah envisioned has come in the person of Jesus of Nazareth.

e. Eschatology. Luke reflects a "realized eschatology": the age of fulfillment had arrived in the ministry of Jesus. His gospel shows how Jesus brought freedom, release and forgiveness to the poor, oppressed and exploited. And because Jesus' words inaugurated an era,[40] that "day" continues, right up to the present. The readers of Luke's Gospel could be sure that they were living in the year of the Lord's favor; so can we.

This is not to say that this pericope covers the full scope of Luke's testimony to Christ; many key themes may be missing. But it served Luke as a particularly appropriate illustration of many significant facets of Jesus' ministry as well as Luke's theology.

2. The synagogue incident, both in what Jesus does and in how the Nazarenes react to him, becomes a paradigm for the future mission of the church. Chilton goes so far as to say, "By his every action in the synagogue, Jesus is the *heilsgeschichtliche* cornerstone of a mission theology."[41] He continues, "It is perhaps not too much to say that Luke's Jesus is a proto-missionary of the apostolic church."[42]

But this does not imply that Luke has created this situation to find justification for the apostolic mission. It is best to see that the elements of the apostolic mission, with which Luke has been so involved in association with Paul, has sensitized him to look for precisely these elements in Jesus' ministry. After his thorough redaction critical, tradition critical and historical analyses, Chilton is quite positive that we have here the historical Jesus announcing his own divine commission. Luke turned this historical tradition into a "paradigm for mission by making it the inaugural scene in Jesus' public ministry and by describing the scene in language redolent of the situation of Acts."[43]

3. Jesus' mission and that taken up by the apostolic church then become paradigms for the church throughout its

history. As we too are "in Christ" we must implement his mission and expect a similar reaction from the "Nazarenes" around us. What would it mean for us if we accepted the mission of Jesus as we find it in this Lukan pericope?

It means, first, that we affirm and implement Jesus' two-pronged approach to ministry. Jesus did not view evangelism and physical healing as two separate agenda-items. He did not avoid or neglect the needy and oppressed. The anointing he received by God's Spirit was to proclaim good news for the poor, freedom for prisoners, sight for the blind and release for the oppressed. People are "poor" both physically and spiritually; they need the blessing and reward that only God can bring. God has chosen to offer the blessings of his kingdom through his kingdom subjects. It is our task to preach and heal as Jesus did. We must be on the side of the poor and oppressed as was Jesus. Where people are hurting, there Jesus' disciples ought to bring help -- spiritual *and* physical. Under the inspiration of the Holy Spirit Luke viewed this Nazareth incident as paradigmatic for the church. It explains the scope of Christian ministry as it was for Jesus. We short-change the power of the Christian message when we minimize or neglect either of these thrusts of the gospel.

Second, we must affirm that we possess the same Spirit-endowment for our mission of preaching and healing that Jesus did. Following his resurrection Jesus instructed his disciples about the significance of the passion events. Among the words Luke records are these:

> ...and repentance and forgiveness of sins will be preached in his [i.e., Christ's] name to all nations, beginning at Jerusalem. You are witnesses of these things. I am going to send you what my Father promised; but stay in the city until you have been clothed with power from on high. (Luke 24:47-49)

Jesus did not expect them to carry out their mission without the capacity to succeed. They required the *power from on high*. In Acts 2 Luke records the fulfillment of Jesus' promise. The frightened, cowardly disciples were transformed into bold witnesses who preached (2:14-40) and healed (3:1-10). We are their successors in every sense; we have the same commission and spiritual power they had. Jesus' disciples were not "super-Christians" possessing special powers not available to us. We must confidently proclaim to hurting people the good news of salvation in Christ while attending to their physical needs. We have every reason to expect that we will be as successful as they were. As the result of our ministry, people will be liberated, healed, released and, above all, *forgiven*. Hurting people ought to be the objects of our loving concern, just as much as they were of Jesus', for the Spirit who anointed Jesus to his ministry has anointed every member of Christ's church (cf. 1 Cor. 12:13; 6:19ff; Rom. 8:9-11, 14-17). Whatever we can do to provide help for suffering people is an extension of the ministry of Jesus. And, like Jesus, we ought to help physically and spiritually.

Perhaps we might also suggest here that some members of Christ's church sense a greater calling (and possibly giftedness) to ministry in one area rather than the other. I suspect that will be true. In the church we ought to give freedom and affirmation to people to express Christ's love in keeping with their calling. Likewise we must not minimize any Christian's gifts and call. If some are especially gifted in evangelism, they ought to be freed to concentrate on using those gifts. Some will be specially called to other means of witness/ministry. They ought to be encouraged and affirmed in their work in the kingdom of God. No Christian ought to denigrate either evangelism or physical healing; both are necessary expressions of Christ's love to hurting people. People need to be helped physically and spiritually. Some might specialize more in one or the other, but all Christians ought to be involved in this full-orbed "Good News."

Third, if this Nazareth incident is paradigmatic in Luke's eyes, then he is implying that rejection is to be expected when the gospel is proclaimed, even though this is the best message anyone could hear and alone provides hope for salvation. Acts such as clothing, feeding and finding jobs for people in the name of Jesus will not necessarily secure their repentance and faith in Jesus. Many people simply will not believe the Christian gospel, even when it is "tailored" exactly to their needs. The Jews as a whole rejected Jesus' messianic claims; even his native Nazarenes deemed preposterous the idea that this local carpenter could be the Prophet spoken of by Isaiah. How often did Peter and then Paul encounter this same response from the Jews.

In this account Luke reminds his readers that even the best of news may not find an eager reception. Doing good -- whether tending the sick or teaching the gospel -- can be discouraging when there is little response. It can be particularly disheartening when, in our efforts to show Christ's love, we are met with rejection and even hostility. The natural reaction is to toss in the towel and confess defeat. "Why bother?" we may be tempted to ask. Luke reminds his readers that Jesus faced similar responses from some of those to whom he ministered. Are we better than our Lord? Surely he was the master evangelist and teacher. Can we expect to have a better success rate than he? The point of ministry, then, cannot be framed in terms of results. Nor can its success. It is valid and imperative to evangelize and provide physical help to those in need apart from their response to our love. Jesus was anointed by God for ministry, and so he served others through the power of the Holy Spirit. That commission is ours as well.

Notes

1. W. Lane, *Commentary on Mark*, New International Commentary (Grand Rapids: Wm. B. Eerdmans Publishing Co., 1974), p. 201, n.2.

2. This is not to say that Luke merely includes this from his source intact. Throughout our section there is convincing evidence of Lukan style and vocabulary (See e.g., I. H. Marshall, *The Gospel of Luke*, New International Greek Testament Commentary (Grand Rapids: Wm. B. Eerdmans Publishing Co., 1978); and Tannehill, "The Mission of Jesus According to Luke IV 16-30," in *Jesus in Nazareth*, E. Grasser, et al. (Berlin: Walter de Gruyter & Co., 1972, pp. 64f).

3. Stonehouse admits it is possible that there were two Nazareth rejections reported in the synoptics, but concludes in favor of a single incident that occurred later and which Luke relocated. Luke reports the Nazareth incident as an instance of Jesus' ministry. "In effect, therefore, he does not say more than that, *in the course of Jesus' ministry in the synagogues of Galilee. He also preached in the synagogue at Nazareth*," *The Witness of Luke to Christ* (Grand Rapids: Wm. B. Eerdmans Publishing Co., 1953), p. 72 (his emphasis).

4. Marshall, *The Gospel of Luke*, pp. 177f.

5. E. E. Ellis, *The Gospel of Luke*, New Century Bible (London: Thomas Nelson and Sons, 1966), p. 96

6. Marshall, *The Gospel of Luke*, p. 181.

7. L. Morris, *The Gospel According to St. Luke*, Tyndale New Testament Commentaries (London: InterVarsity Press, 1974), p. 105.

8. E. Schweizer, *Good News According to Luke*, trans. D. E. Green (Atlanta: John Knox Press, 1984), p. 88; see also Marshall, *The Gospel of Luke*, p. 181.

9. Morris, *Luke*, p. 106.

10. Marshall, *The Gospel of Luke*, p. 182.

11. The LXX differs from the Hebrew text in several ways. First, *'adonay yhwh* is rendered by *kyrios*. Second, the next occurrence of *yhwh* is omitted. Third, the LXX substitutes the word "blind" in place of the Hebrew "imprisoned," thereby altering the sense of the phrase "and release from darkness for the *prisoners*."

12. So A. Plummer, *Gospel According to St. Luke*, International Critical Commentary (Edinburgh: T. & T. Clark, 1901), p. 121, and D. Hill, "The Rejection of Jesus at Nazareth (Luke IV 16-30)," *Novem Testamentum* 13 (1971), p. 177. Hill says that "Luke may be quoting freely or from memory."

13. On this point see B. Chilton, "Announcement in *Nazara*: An Analysis of Luke 4:16-21," *Gospel Perspectives*, Vol. 2, ed. R. J. France and D. Wenham (Sheffield: JSOT Press, 1981), pp. 163-166.

14. *Pace* R. C. Tannehill, "The Mission of Jesus According to Luke IV 16-30," p. 66, who thinks that Jesus could never have done this. Likewise the *heilsgeschichtliche*

pattern that Hill ("The Rejection of Jesus," p. 178) discovers in the pericope moves him to reject any historical basis for this incident. Hill admits that some incident like this could conceivably have happened sometime in Nazareth and that certainly Jesus might have at some time applied to himself the words of Isa. 61:1ff, but this is as much as Hill allows. Surely this anti-historical stance is too extreme. The presence of Lukan style and vocabulary need only show that Luke has reworked his source, not that he has created this incident. See, for a defense of historicity, the thorough work of Chilton ("Announcement in *Nazara*") and Marshall's work on this pericope in *The Gospel of Luke*, pp. 177-190.

15. Chilton, "Announcement in *Nazara*," p. 166.

16. G. N. Stanton, "On the christology of Q," in *Christ and Spirit in the New Testament* (C. F. D. Moule *Festschrift*), ed. B. Lindars and S. S. Smalley (Cambridge: University Press, 1973), p. 30.

17. For similar wording, cf. 1:35; 2:25; and Acts 1:8.

18. J. Jeremias, *New Testament Theology* (New York: Charles Scribner's Sons, 1971), p. 79.

19. This can be seen, e.g., in 2 Sam. 23:1f, where David is described as "the man anointed by the God of Jacob." Further, the text affirms, "The Spirit of the LORD spoke through me." In a patently messianic text the prophet proclaims, "A shoot will come up from the stump of Jesse; from his roots a Branch will bear fruit. The Spirit of the LORD will rest on him..." (Isa. 11:1ff). God will accomplish his purposes for the world through his "anointed one" (see Psa. 89:20ff; 132:10ff).

20. Marshall, *The Gospel of Luke*, p. 183.

21. E. E. Ellis, *Gospel of Luke*, p. 97.

22. We must insist upon the historical basis of Jesus' reference to the poor here. No doubt Karris is right in reminding us that Luke intended to speak to his readers in writing his Gospel. But it will not do simply to look for the content of "poor" on the redactional level and ignore any meaning this might have in the *Leben Jesu*. R. J. Karris, "Poor and Rich: The Lukan *Sitz im Leben*," in *Perspectives on Luke-Acts*, ed. C. H. Talbot (Danville, VA: National Association of Baptist Professors of Religion, 1978), p. 118, concludes that for Luke "poor" refers to the Christian

community of Luke's day, those who were suffering poverty, deprivation and persecution for their faith. Though Jesus does bring good news for suffering Christians, this hardly justifies denying any historical basis for this pericope.

23. For a discussion of the "Prophets and the Poor" see L. Sabourin, "Evangelize the Poor" (Lk 4:18), *Religious Studies Bulletin* 1/4 (1981), especially pp. 104-106. He finds that though poverty is basically an economic issue, it came to express an attitude of the soul. He says, "The 'poor' became the 'client' of God, receptive to his grace and disposed to accomplish his will" (pp. 104f). Eventually "poor" became, like "servant," a title of honor.

24. J. Jeremias, *New Testament Theology*, p. 113.

25. B. Reicke, "Jesus in Nazareth--Lk 4:14-30," in *Das Wort und die Woerter* (*Festschrift* fur G. Friedrich) ed. H. Balz and S. Shulz (Stuttgart, 1973), p. 49.

26. Tannehill notes, "in the light of the importance to Luke of the 'release of sins,' this must be an important aspect of what he had in mind..." ("The Mission of Jesus...", p. 71).

27. The Hebrew verb is *liqro*.

28. Tannehill, "The Mission of Jesus," p. 58.

29. R. P. Martin, "Salvation and Discipleship in Luke's Gospel," in *Interpreting the Gospels*, ed. J. L. Mays (Philadelphia: Fortress Press, 1981), p. 217.

30. D. Hill, "The Rejection of Jesus," p. 168.

31. Jeremias puts it this way: " 'the text of scripture is being fulfilled before your ears,' i.e. you are ear-witness that the promise that the time of God's grace is dawning, is being fulfilled *today*" (*New Testament Theology*, p. 105).

32. Marshall, *The Gospel of Luke*, p. 178.

33. Marshall, *The Gospel of Luke*, p. 185.

34. Jeremias, *New Testament Theology*, pp. 206ff.

35. Ibid., p. 207.

36. D. Hill, "The Rejection of Jesus," p. 170.

37. Though vv. 25-27 are not a part of our direct concern in this study, they provide a kind of Old Testament precedent of kindness to Gentiles. God displays his miracles among foreigners in the face of the unbelief of the Jews and, here, the Nazarenes' jealousy.

38. That this is a fitting way of summarizing Jesus' ministry is confirmed in the reply of Jesus recorded by Luke in 7:22.

39. Cf. Acts 10:38: "God anointed Jesus of Nazareth with the Holy Spirit and power."

40. This explains Peter's words recorded in Acts 2:17, where the prophecy of Joel is applied to the Pentecost phenomena. Joel's ambiguous "And afterward ..." (Joel 2:28) becomes Peter's "In the last days..." Also see, e.g., 2 Tim. 3:1 and 1 Jn. 3:18.

41. Chilton, "Announcement in *Nazara*," p. 158.

42. Ibid., 161. Chilton observes in the diction of 4:20, evidence of a mission theology. Both the term "attendant" (*uperetes*) and "to sit" (*kathizo*) are used elsewhere in synagogue contexts and preaching in particular (cf. Acts 13:5, 14, 16; 16:13; cf. Mt. 5:1; Mk. 9:35; Lk. 5:3).

43. Ibid., 168.

Part II

Christian Freedom -- Practice

A Non-Legalistic Approach to Lifestyle -- I John 2

A.W. Parmenter II

Scripture can come at us from several different directions at once. While we are informed that "God so loved the world" (John 3:16a), we are also given this simple prohibition, "Do not love the world or anything in the world" (I John 2:15). Are we forbidden to do what God himself does? While Paul in one place enjoins us not to be partners with immoral, impure and greedy people (Eph. 5:5-6), elsewhere he reasons that to avoid associating with immoral people we "would have to leave this world" (I Cor. 5:9-10).

How do we piece all of this together? How are we supposed to relate to the world? Do we love it? hate it? Are we "just a-passing through," or should we empty out our suitcases and make ourselves at home? The tension is more than theoretical: the real difficulty is in living. We want to be distinctively Christian, i.e., free from worldly values, but without living in an underground, hermetically-sealed shelter with our food brought in and our reading material censored.

Furthermore, some of us have reacted to the legalistic excesses of American fundamentalism. We appreciate the obvious devotion to holiness we have observed in our heritage but have come to enjoy the freedom of a "less severe" evangelicalism.[1] Have we lost something? Are we guilty of an incipient antinomianism, by encouraging a reckless exercise of "Christian freedom" and a lack of appreciation for the concerns our fundamentalist forebears were addressing?

I propose an examination of a *locus classicus*, I John 2:15-17, from a non-lcgalistic perspective. Legalism is a definite hazard to be avoided. It can rob us of the freedom Christ won for us (Gal 5:12), encourage an unspiritual pride (Col. 2:16-19) and cause us to become bogged down in secondary matters to the exclusion of what Jesus called "the more important matters of the law" (Mt. 23:23,24).[2] Perhaps if we could see more clearly just what is forbidden, we could maintain a finely-tuned balance between freedom and a godly caution regarding worldly attitudes. Our study will focus on John's command, the two reasons for his command, and a sobering warning.

The Command

The command not to love the world comes abruptly in the text. After speaking reassuringly to various groups among his readers[3] (I Jn. 2:12-14), John flatly prohibits them from loving the world (2:15a). It is something of a surprise to see love as a vice, not a virtue. Ordinarily, John uses *agape* favorably to refer to the highest sort of love, the love the Father demonstrated when he sent Hhs Son into the world on our behalf.[4] However, love for the "world" in this discussion is absolutely the wrong kind of love.

It is crucial to nail down what John has in mind when he speaks of the world. The term, *kosmos*, so important for the writer, occurs six times in the verses we are considering. Usually *kosmos* functions in a favorable sense. When we read that Jesus is the "atoning sacrifice for...the sins of the whole world" (2:2), we realize that God loves men and women in the world and has acted to secure their salvation.

However, John also develops the notion of *kosmos* in a more negative sense. The *kosmos* is under Satan's control (I Jn 5:19; Jn. 12:31), hates Jesus and his disciples (Jn 15:18-19), but is the object of God's saving purposes (Jn. 3:19). We are not forbidden to love people as people, nor expected to detest the physical world and the structures of society. We *are* to resist the attraction of a life lived in opposition to God's rule.[5] The world in this context signifies the reign of lust and pride, something John teaches is antithetical to God's purposes.[6]

In this connection, I believe the stress should be on attitudes, not things (possessions, gadgets and goods). If my friend pulls down a six-figure income and I scrape by on $20,000 a year, I may be jealous enough to be the more worldly of the two of us. If Christians I know make a judicious use of attractive homes, automobiles I can't afford and clothing that definitely didn't come "off the rack," I may be the worldly one in my bitter craving for what others enjoy. The stress must be on attitudes. The world is not far away, not miles away from where I struggle and sweat and labor. The temptation to be thoroughly worldly arises from within me as my response to the ways in which culture expresses pagan values.

If we evangelicals are happy to be free of nit-picking legalism, have we blundered into a thicket of attitudes that are by any consideration worldly? Fundamentalists are right about some things, aren't they? Jesus did counsel his disciples, "you do not belong to the world, but I have chosen you out of the world" (John 15:19). Here is surely a legitimate doctrine of separation. We have been chosen out of the world. Evanglicals who are seeking to put as much distance as possible between themselves and fundamentalist mores need to remember that God works among imperfect human beings in particular historical settings. Whatever their failures in developing a Christian lifestyle, fundamentalists made the effort (and paid the price) to be authentically Christian, as they understood Christianity. We may hope that future historians who critically assess our efforts at finding the balance between freedom and lawful behavior will be charitable when they uncover our gaffes and limitations.[7]

The Reasons

John's commands to abstain from loving the world is followed by two reasons for such a command (2:15b-16). First, we simply can't love God and the world. We are compelled to make a choice: one way or the other. The world is in revolt against God's authority; if we love what is worldly, we have aligned ourselves with God's enemies. This is the point James makes in his searing rebuke, "you adulterous people, don't you know that friendship with the world is hatred toward God? Anyone who chooses to be a friend of the world, becomes an enemy of God" (James 4:4).

The second reason provides a sharper focus on what John earlier called "anything in the world" (2:15b). A trio of vices exhibits the sort of attitudes that the writer insists do not come from God: "the cravings of sinful man, the lust of his eyes and the boasting of what he has and does" (2:16).

The first of these I understand to be *self-centeredness*. When John speaks of the flesh (*sarx*), he is not disparaging the human body as inferior or sinful. With his Hebrew background, John would view *sarx* as the whole person in all human weaknesses. He utilizes *sarx* in a more positive sense in writing, "the Word became flesh and lived for a while among us" (John 1:14); this is saying that the Word became human -- with the weaknesses, needs and limitations of humanity. While Paul seems to stress the ethical side of *sarx* (describing the lifestyle of nonbelievers), John views *sarx* as "all that satisfies the needs and wants of human beings."[8]

Those needs and wants are often legitimate, but if they rule us, we will behave like unconverted people. Persons who are mastered by their out-of-control desires become self-centered and sinfully independent. If they crave something, they intend to acquire it, no matter the consequences. Only Christ is to be master of the believer (I Cor. 6:12-13); to live otherwise is to be worldly. Perhaps I can heatedly defend every purchase I make, every activity I enjoy; still, if the basic orientation of my life is less what others need and Christ desires and is more a question of what I insist *I* must have, I am becoming worldly, whether or not I am willing to admit it.

The second vice to avoid I would call *greed* or *sensuality*: "the lust of the eyes." If what I see arouses uncontrollable cravings, I am (by John's definition) a worldly individual.[9] If I covet someone else's spouse, this is a worldly approach to life (Mt. 5:27-29). If I covet another person's goods, the external trappings of success or the means by which I can impress another, I am trapped in the snare of worldliness. Langdon Gilkey describes being imprisoned during the Second World War and surviving on a subsistence level diet. When he was repatriated after the war, he returned to America and was overwhelmed by the abundance we casually accept as normal. When he walked down the aisles of a supermarket, he was surrounded by cereals, breads, canned vegetables, fruit, meats; the food was stacked, piled, spilling over in crates and boxes. Gilkey felt engulfed, drowning in wealth, stuffed and bloated.[10] I fear that greed comes on us so quietly, gradually and unobtrusively, we consider it normal. Regardless of how it appears, craving all we see is still a perverse manifestation of worldliness.

A third dimension of the worldly approach is "the pride of life" (*he alazoneia tou biou*). In ancient times an *alazon* was a wandering braggart. The wandering sophist was also nicknamed *alazon*.[11] Paul uses *alazones* in II Tim. 3:2 in a list describing the vices of ungodly people in the last days and advises Timothy to "have nothing to do with" such people (II Tim. 3:5). James castigates merchants who make their clever plans for material gain without seeking God's approval and sovereign care: "As it is, you boast and brag (*kauxasthe en tais alazoneiais humon*)" (4:16). In the passage we are considering, *alazoneia* describes a pretentiousness that makes us greedy for advantage, status and materialistic gain.[12]

This empty pride is a complex hydra-headed monster affecting all of us. How easily we are caught up in vain boasting, showing off, pompous posturing. True, the desire for excellence is commendable. Students should do well in their studies, craftsmen should exhibit art and grace in their work, company managers should fine-tune their management skills, etc. Mediocrity, banality, shabbiness and all that is drab are far from Christian. Nevertheless, how frequently we seek to impress others or to look better than others without being able to conceive of ourselves as ostentatious. It was not without reason that a wise father, in counseling his son regarding seven things the Lord hates, placed at the top of the list "haughty eyes" (Prov. 6:16ff).

The Warning

On the heels of this list of vices, John gives a final warning: what we see is on the way out (2:17a). In some ways the world is like a corpse yet to be buried, already putrifying.[13] The world system is marked for destruction. Its end is tragic and certain. Does it make any sense to put so much stock in something so ephemeral?

By contrast, our search for permanence is assured, if we are committed to doing God's will (2:17b). Ultimately the followers of God will be separated from the citizens of the worldly kingdom. Wheat and chaff, sheep and goats are images used to convey fixed distinctions and destinies (Mt. 3:12; 25:31ff). The crucial time for decision-making is already here, and the consequences of our decisions are not far ahead. Judgment is not something other people face. Listen to Paul's warning to believers: "...we will all stand before God's judgment seat...each of us will give an account of himself to God" (Rom. 14:10,12).

Have we managed as evangelicals to steer clear of a worldly perspective? We not only must, we may. I know the tug and pull of anti-Christian values is nearly irresistible at times. Yet I remain convinced that legalistic lists and detailed codes of behavior will not forestall the encroachment of Satan's realm into our churches.

The alternative to worldliness is not legalism (as tempting as that might be). We must never trample Christian freedom underfoot in our frenzied haste to escape the seduction of the world. The biblical way is to arm ourselves with Scriptural principles -- principles flexible enough to work in a variety of situations. We have to put the question to ourselves: Does this attitude, this mindset, even this debatable activity constitute for me the lust of the flesh, the lust of the eyes or the pride of life?

Not many years ago, Dr. Kwame Nkrumah in a public inscription modified Jesus' classic words in Matthew 6:33 to read, "Seek ye first the political kingdom..."[14] My reaction to Dr. Nkruman's inscription was righteous indignation against his tampering with Scripture. But am I guilty of the same charge -- tampering with Scripture -- in my way of living? To what extent am I carrying out the intent of Jesus' teaching? What am I seeking first?

Certainly I don't have to follow the herd and be stampeded by popular consensus. I may influence, rather than always be influenced. I have the right to set the course, to say "no!", to go the way I must go. I have the right; the question is, do I have the nerve?

Notes

1. James Barr, in his forward to the American edition of *Fundamentalism* (Philadelphia: Westminster Press, 1977), points out that American Christianity is "creative" in finding ways to escape fundamentalism. He writes approvingly of the metamorphosis of evangelical thinking and urges evangelicals in this country to resist the notion that one is not truly evangelical unless one accepts the fundamentalist position (page v).

2. John Stott calls the less important (*not* unimportant!) concerns of legalism "micro-ethics," as opposed to "macro-ethics," the highly significant moral and social issues of the day (*Between Two Worlds* Grand Rapids: Wm. B. Eerdmans Publishing Co., p. 156). Neglecting the pressing problems of racism, militarism, "yuppie" covetousness, poverty, illiteracy and many other matters while focusing unduly on largely cultural concerns (how shall we dress? what music shall we listen to? shall we drink alcoholic beverages, etc?) is to be avoided!

3. By addressing "children," "fathers," and "young men," John seems to be employing a rhetorical device to instruct believers who are at various stages of spiritual growth.

4. I John 4:9-10.

5. I. Howard Marshall, *Epistles of John* (Grand Rapids: Wm. B. Eerdmans Publishing Co., 1978), p. 143. Sometimes we speak of "the world system," though that may imply more order than is apparent in human civilization. If human beings are often chaotic and capricious, at least Satan is at the helm of this unwieldly craft, guiding it with determined purpose.

6. Allen Verhey, *The Great Reversal: Ethics and the New Testament* (Grand Rapids: Wm. B. Eerdmans Publishing Co., 1984), p. 229.

7. cf. George Marsden, *Fundamentalism and American Culture* (New York: Oxford University Press, 1980), p. 230.

8. Raymond Brown, *The Epistles of John*, The Anchor Bible (New York: Doubleday & Co., 1982) p. 308.

9. cf. also Jesus' discussion of the eye as the "lamp" of the body in Mat. 6:22ff.

10. cited by David G. Myers, *The Inflated Self* (New York: Seabury Press, 1980), p. 10.

11. E. Guting and C. Brown, "Pride," in *The New International Dictionary of New Testament Theology*, ed. Colin Brown (Grand Rapids: Zondervan Publishing Co., 1975-1978), vol. III, p. 28.

12. F. F. Bruce, *The Epistles of John* (Grand Rapids: Wm. B. Eerdmans Publishing Co., 1970), pp. 61-62.

13. Glenn W. Barker, "1, 2, 3 John" in *The Expositor's Bible Commentary*, ed. Frank E. Gabelein, (Grand Rapids: Zondervan Publishing Co., 1978), vol. 12, p. 332.

14. cited by Bruce, *Epistles of John*, p. 64.

The Quiet Assassin: Godlessness, Christian Liberty and Values

Fran C. Sciacca

It wasn't an unusual day. Our pastor's friend left the John Wayne Airport in Orange County, California, on a short, routine hop to San Diego. His new plane performed superbly. It was a wise purchase. The Pacific Ocean gleamed its approval as he looked below. Then suddenly, his engine sputtered and quit. He had to make a split-second decision. The plane was designed to survive an aquatic crash, but it would sink. His life would be secure, but he would lose his new prize. In those few moments, he decided to attempt to glide back to shore. He radioed the airport and informed them of his decision. His plane approached a golf course, the wing snapped a large tree, and he crashed into a nearby home. Our pastor's friend died that day. His decision had been clouded by an over-attachment to his plane. His judgment became misjudgment. Sometimes a wrong perspective, a sincere misjudgment, is tragic.

I believe that a significant portion of the personal and corporate casualties visible in the evangelical community today -- the epidemic of divorce, the loss of personal integrity, and the disintegration of biblical values -- may be traced to a wrong perspective on Christian freedom. Just as the young pilot misjudged the seriousness of his choice because of his attachment to the plane, so too we may misunderstand the plan and will of God because of erroneous assumptions about the nature of salvation and the Christian experience.

We have unconsciously substituted a doctrine of autonomy for the doctrine of liberty in reference to our relationship with God. Autonomy has all the appearances of liberty because of its emphasis upon independence. And certainly the clear teaching of Scripture is that the Christian has been "set free" from a variety of bondages (cf. John 8:32-6; Rom. 6:18; Gal. 5:1; 1 Peter 2:16; 2 Cor. 3:17). Yet, it is a tragic error to equate being set free in Christ with independence. The truth is that our release from bondage was the necessary prerequisite for becoming God's servants. Consequently, a Christian is not an independent creature. In fact, just the opposite is true. It is the genuine believer who becomes increasingly aware of the disparity between one's own sinfulness and God's holiness. The proper response to this process is a growing indebtedness to God's grace. It is the genuine Christian who progressively becomes more attached to God and less attached to this world and its goods. The believer says with the Psalmist, "As the eyes of slaves look to the hand of their master, as the eyes of a maid look to the hand of her mistress, so our eyes look to the Lord our God, till he shows us his mercy" (Ps. 123:2). In short, we become more aware of our actual dependence as we realize the true nature of our relationship with God.

In contrast to this stands the autonomous Christian. Believing that being "set free" in Christ means being "let loose," such a person acts independently of God, but becomes more and more attached to this world system. Because we are *creatures* made in the image of a Creator, our proper place by design is in a subordinate role. When we attempt to shed this arrangement, we become like the Jews in Jeremiah's day: "My people have committed two sins: they have forsaken me, the spring of living water, and have dug their own cisterns, broken cisterns that cannot hold water" (Jeremiah 2:13). Seeking to be independent of God, they entered a more severe servitude, namely, bondage to the inadequacy of their supposed freedom. The Christian who seeks autonomy faces a similar dilemma. In the quest to be independent, one actually becomes dependent -- dependent on this world and its goods.

The issue of Christian liberty involves, then, two inseparable components, dependence and independence. How we assign these two to God and this world system will determine whether or not we are acting and living in true biblical freedom or autonomy. True biblical freedom results from dependence on God and independence from this world system. Autonomy, in contrast, is the product of independence from God and dependence on this world system.

My experience as an educator in a Christian school representing children from families of over 100 different churches has provided a unique window into the "heart" of the body of Christ. A sort of "suburban captivity" of the church has yielded a proliferation of Christian autonomy within the evangelical community. I have witnessed and experienced a mutation of Christianity, consisting of motion without meaning and, in the truest sense, form without freedom. This is a Christianity that sounds and "smells" genuine. But once "backstage" one discovers it is a religious perpetual motion machine -- impressive and active, yet ultimately unproductive. This Christianity is autonomy dressed in attractive evangelical garb, but autonomy nonetheless. It is not a malicious carnivore, rampaging Godzilla-like through the structures of God's kingdom. Rather, its effect is more like a chain letter, quietly recruiting, constantly spreading, offering goods it will never deliver.

God has addressed this spectre in his Word. He calls it "godlessness." Godlessness. The word conjures up stereotyped mental images of blatant sin, people devoid of moral sensibilities engaging in overt acts of unrighteousness. Yet, the individual God holds in his Word as an illustration of godlessness is Esau (Heb. 12:16). What was this man's heinous crime? He exchanged his birthright for a bowl of soup! For this he is called a "profane" (godless) man. Esau was "profane" in that he threw away the privilege of the firstborn, which in this case involved the promises of God through Abraham and Isaac for all humanity. A godless man or woman, then, is not one who deliberately disregards or defies God's law or God's person, as reprehensible as both of those are. A godless person is one who relegates the God of the universe to the status of everyday people. A godless individual simply lives as though God were unimportant.

Like Esau, we in the church may have become a "profane" people. We may be leading moral, upright lives that are actually autonomous existences under a mask of Christian freedom. We may, in the final analysis, be godless. I see godlessness manifested primarily in five ways in the Body of Christ.

Self-Worship, not True Worship

Godlessness substitutes self-worship for true worship. Genuine worship is captured for us in the confession of John the Baptist, "He must become greater; I must become less." (John 3:30). True worship is much like watching someone walk into a blazing sunrise. Soon that person is totally eclipsed by the growing brilliance. The more I approach true worship, the less others will notice me. Godlessness reverses this truth; I become the focal point in my relationship with God. Esau vividly illustrates this. It was his hunger, needs and circumstances that were crucial. The plan and promises of God were silent spectators during that dramatic moment.

Today a set of self-worship twins are often present -- self-abasement and self-absorption. Paul cautions Timothy about godless theology in the context of both of these forms of self-worship (cf. 1 Tim. 4 and 6).

I fear that some of the underlying attitudes of "simple-life theology" (i.e., sacrificing in the name of spirituality) may be a form of godlessness. An emphasis on what the individual is giving up or is doing without has an improper focus. I vividly recall a speaker at a Christian high school who, while attempting to plead the cause of the Third World, boasted about his $2.00 sportsjacket from the Salvation Army, after saddling 300 students with guilt for their jaded lifestyles. High schoolers have an uncanny ability to "see behind the curtain" and perceive the hypocrisy of contemporary Wizards of Oz. These students sensed the false pride of the speaker; he justly lost his audience. While it is true that many Christians are virtually permeated with materialism, unless our message turns the gaze of others toward the Lord, a sacrificial lifestyle is not true worship. It is godlessness.

Paul also warned Timothy about those who seek to become wealthy because of their faith. The current health and prosperity theology has resurrected this Ephesian heresy. An emphasis on what God wants to do for me, or has promised me, also has an improper focus. Although the supposed basis for this orientation is the goodness of God, the question remains, who is exalted, Jesus or I? Paul describes godless people in 2 Timothy 3 as self-lovers, money-lovers and pleasure-lovers. True worship always centers on Jesus Christ; it exalts and glorifies Him. A godliness that centers on self is godless; we might even call it a godless godliness, which is simply autonomy.

Bible Knowledge, not Spiritual Growth

Godlessness substitutes the accumulation of Bible knowledge for true spiritual growth. Some have estimated that over 1 million pages of information are generated daily. The world has scrambled to meet this challenge in a proliferation of journals, newsletters and seminars. The pressure to "know" has never been greater. The people of God have joined this endless marathon as well. At this writing I see eight seminar notebooks on my shelves, and five newsletters arrive regularly. Seminars and newsletters are wonderful vehicles for distributing predigested information and have a valid and necessary place in the life of the Christian. But we must be careful that we are not lulled into believing that mastering information is the equivalent of spiritual growth. This method of "vicarious learning," of assimilating somcone else's discoveries, has some unfortunate side effects in the life of a believer. One such effect is a reduced sense of accountability. When a truth is presented "second hand," there is an inherent tendency to disregard its applicability and impact on one's own life. We become "information junkies." Our main enjoyment comes from accumulating the truth, not obeying it. We demand to be "entertained" by those who teach the Scriptures; yet we walk away unchanged. We resemble those in Ezekiel's day:

> My people come to you, as they usually do, and sit before you to listen to your words, but they do not put them into practice. With their mouths they express devotion, but their hearts are greedy for unjust gain. Indeed, to them you are nothing more than one who sings love songs with a beautiful voice and plays an instrument well, for they hear your words, but they do not put them into practice (Ezekiel 33:31-32).

Oswald Chambers has appropriately said, "Teaching is meant to stir up thinking, not to store with goods from the outside."[1] The apostle Paul's stated desire for the spiritual growth of the Christians at Colossae included a deep, personal involvement with God himself, never simply with information:

> My purpose is that they may be encouraged in heart and united in love, so that they may have the full riches of complete understanding, in order that they may know the mystery of God, namely, Christ, in whom are hidden all the treasures of wisdom and knowledge (Col. 2:2-3).

If our primary source of biblical input is radio preaching, seminars and our pastor's weekly sermon, we are robbing ourselves of the joy of personal discovery and the opportunity for God to speak to us firsthand. My own exposure to Christian adults is extensive, and I am frightened at the growing chasm that is developing between them and the Bible. I am finding that more and more people know less and less of what God wants for them as individuals. As a Bible teacher I find myself continually facing this battle. It is tempting to assume, after spending hours preparing to teach God's Word that, having mastered the information, I have grown a commensurate amount.

If our perspective on true spirituality consists almost exclusively of information gathered vicariously, various illusions result. One is an illusion of true fellowship. There is a temptation to equate talk about similar content with genuine fellowship. Yet, genuine fellowship involves the mutual sharing of our inner selves, the secret joys and sorrows of walking with God. The current resurgence of interest in small groups has the potential of neutralizing this form of godlessness. But there must be a commitment to accountability and transparency, an openness to be exhorted and a willingness to be honest.

Another illusion relates to our growth. When we see our "data bank" of biblical knowledge enlarging, we may sense that we indeed are growing in our Christian experience. This is dangerous. Paul said that knowledge "puffs up" and "passes away" (1 Cor. 8:1; 13:8). Raw information, which cannot last, provides a false sense of spiritual maturity. I continually need to remind myself that the possession of a seminary degree does not mean I am a member of an elite spiritual group. This form of godlessness becomes preoccupied with facts independent of their relationship to personal life. Perhaps this is why we have brilliant, informed Christians who abandon their spouses, and believers who become more cynical and insensitive rather than broken and caring. We are speaking more factually about God in the twentieth century, but less affectionately.

This form of godlessness substitutes how much I know for how much I grow. But because the outcome of the process is not a deeper sense of my dependence upon the Lord, it is a counterfeit type of growth, masking my actual autonomy.

Common Sense, not God's Will

Godlessness substitutes sanctified common sense for seeking the will of God. We live in the era of the "planners" -- family planning, financial planning, church planning, ministry strategies, marketing schemes, ad infinitum. Isn't it biblical to plan? Yes. Doesn't God consider it a matter of proper stewardship to plan? Of course. But the issue must not simply be what appears "best," rather, what is "right." King David in 2 Samuel 7 is a prime example. He was living in a palatial mansion, whereas the God of all creation dwelt in a tent. Struck by the absurdity of this situation, David decided to build for God a permanent home better than his own. He sent for Nathan, seeking divine approval on his plan. Nathan assured him the plan was right and told him to proceed. But later that evening, when Nathan returned home, he discovered that he was wrong. The Lord told Nathan that although David's intentions were noble, his logic sound, and his plans proper, he was wrong. David had assessed the situation and made his decision on what he could see. The problem was, what he could see did not encompass the specific will of God.

Lot provides us with another vivid illustration of this fallacy. When he and Abram were dividing up the land, he based his choice on what he could see: "Lot looked up and saw that the whole plain of the Jordan was well-watered, like the garden of the Lord..." (Gen. 13:10). "What a lovely place to build a house and raise a family!" he probably thought to himself. Yet nestled in that lush green plain were two cities where sin ruled, Sodom and Gomorrah. Little did he suspect that a consequence of this choice would be the loss of his wife and his land in God's swift judgment upon these cities. Paul's statement, "we live by faith, not by sight" (2 Cor. 5:7), is especially crucial in this area.

Decision-making that is based simply on weighing the evidence is a far cry from genuine faith. "Sanctified" common sense is not a synonym for God's will. How many children should one have? How far apart should they be spaced? Do we adhere to the advice of the leading psychologists of the day and determine our family's destiny based on their discoveries? Should we wait to have children until we are "financially secure"?

We had three unplanned pregnancies, one of which was a biological enigma. The comments made to us by well-meaning Christians frequently were condolences rather than blessings, especially when the last pregnancy resulted in twins! The message communicated to us was that God could make something good out of this tragedy, rather than the fact that God was the Sovereign Lord of our lives and that this was part of his will for us. Since this experience, we have become sensitive to the actual contents of comments made by Christian couples regarding children. The alarming reality is that very few of them include any type of acknowledgment that they are servants of the Most High, whose will is their highest priority.

Often our first answers to questions such as these come from Christian authorities, specialists in a particular field or our "feelings" of what we think we can handle. Rarely are they the product of secluded moments before God in prayer, fasting and Scripture reading.

Probably the easiest way to distinguish if our plans are made on the basis of sanctified common sense or the Spirit's leading is to monitor our response when our plans change or when we are faced with insurmountable difficulties. Godlessness frets and pushes because it cannot see beyond the plans themselves. The dependent Christian bends and adapts while at the same time seeking the face of God.

Obviously God wants us to plan and to seek wise counsel from his people. But at the same time we must cultivate an attitude of dependence, trust God, and act in obedience to him. Circumstances will often come in which we, like the One whose likeness we are to assume, will need to concede, "Not my will, but thine be done." Autonomy overemphasizes the fact that God gave us minds to think, conveniently neglecting the fact that he also gave us wills to obey.

Morality, not Biblical Values

Godlessness substitutes moral conduct for true biblical values. I believe this form of godlessness could very well be the single greatest threat that the church will face in the remainder of this decade. As an educator in a Christian matrix, I frequently hear "secular humanism" attacked with the vigor and valor of the Inquisition. Some declare that it is the most virile enemy of the people of God. But I fear that we, like the passengers of the Titanic, may be moments away from disaster, while resting comfortably on our convictions. The erosion of genuine biblical values while maintaining moral conduct is a frightening threat to the health of the church today.

For the most part, we are a people of appearance, attentive to how we look and behave. We maintain that Christians ought to behave in certain ways, or perhaps more specifically, ought not to behave in certain ways. There is a biblical basis for this mentality, to be sure. Jesus is our model, and he certainly engaged in specific activities and abstained from others. I suspect, however, that in reality a larger number of Christians do all the right things for the wrong reasons. I see this increasingly prevalent in the lives of Christian young people, especially those whose parents are in the professional ministry. We need to face the fact that God is not merely interested in moral and appropriate behavior. He longs to transform the part of us that controls our values, our thoughts, our decisions, and our feelings. The clear message of the Bible is that a changed heart produces a changed life.

I am not interested in raising children who are simply "nice youngsters" and who will eventually become merely "responsible adults." I want my children to grow up valuing the very things that God values. Out of their values will emerge conduct that is genuinely moral. And what does God value above all else? God values people. Paul praised Timothy as one who valued the same things as the Lord -- people (Phil. 2:19-21). Paul himself said that the Thessalonians would be his "joy" and "crown" at the return of Jesus Christ (1 Thess. 2:19). He could make such a sweeping exclamation, because he knew he would see the Thessalonians again. In fact, he knew they would spend eternity together.

People last forever, "things" don't. This world and all its goods will eventually be destroyed by fire (2 Pet. 3:10). Yet people, who are in the image of God, will live forever, either in his presence or in utter torment. This truth shouldn't illicit guilt feelings, but awaken us to what really counts to God and therefore ought to count to us as well.

A seven year old child in a Christian family faced a dilemma. He had been invited to a birthday party at one of those establishments that condense the noise and excitement of a Ringling Brothers Circus into a 45-minute experience! But the party was the same time as an evangelistic puppet show at church. He had been praying for the salvation of a neighbor friend for many months. After outlining the choices, the boy's father told him he would honor and support the child's decision, whatever it would be, but the child must choose. The child considered the options for five minutes, before announcing, "Dad, I've decided to take Michael to the puppet show." When his father asked why he made that choice, the boy responded, "Parties are only for a day, but Christians are forever."

It is possible for us to say all the proper things, even jump through all the right hoops, but yet have the same values as the unbelieving world -- status, finances and physical beauty. To cultivate Christian behavior without instilling biblical values is ultimately to nurture an entire generation which will eventually shed this carefully cultivated "good" behavior, like Esau did his birthright, when it infringes on their underlying worldly value system.

Escape, not Endurance

Godlessness substitutes escape for endurance in trials. Woody Allen once said, "It's not that I'm afraid of death, I just don't want to be there when it happens."[2] No one enjoys suffering. But I believe we may have lost sight of the place suffering has in the plan of God. We are immersed in a cultural obsession that is almost monolithic: "I am entitled to a full, happy, healthy life." The effect of this message is a human race trapped on a treadmill, increasing its pace with no possible destination.

Happiness, the state of being fulfilled and satisfied, is unattainable if sought. Jesus said, true happiness (blessedness) is a byproduct of hungering and thirsting for righteousness (Matt. 5:6). Those whose goal is to become increasingly conformed to the likeness of Jesus Christ will discover genuine happiness. However, the uncomfortable corollary of this axiom is that Christlikeness is most often produced in the crucible of suffering. Paul commanded rejoicing in the midst of sufferings because of their positive effect (Rom. 5:3-5). He even went so far as to assert that the circumstances of life which threaten to cripple and crush are the very things God uses to renew us spiritually and allow the life of Jesus to be manifested in us (2 Cor. 4:7-12, 16-18). To offer God's elect deliverance from suffering as a benefit of being "set free" in Christ is to rob them of the very vehicles necessary for the completion of the work of God in their lives. And to separate ourselves from his plan and purpose is to be independent of him. That is godlessness.

These are five manifestations of counterfeit freedom. Doubtless there are others, but I believe these five need to be exposed and addressed because they are dangerous. They provide a faulty barometer of our spiritual health. We slowly drift into the Laodecian delusion that we are healthy and well, while we are spiritually sick and needy (Rev. 3:14-18). Godlessness is preoccupied with externals, the outward appearance, the "form." But because we thereby become autonomous from the plan and purposes of God, our lives slowly degenerate to a "form of godliness" separated from the power of God (cf. 2 Tim. 3). It is indeed dangerous to assume good health, if one is in actuality sick.

This counterfeit freedom is also dangerous because it is an integral part in Satan's scheme to attack the child of God. C.S. Lewis captured this truth in the *Screwtape Letters*:

> My dear Wormwood,
>
> Obviously you are making excellent progress. My only fear is lest in attempting to hurry the patient you awaken him to a sense of his real position. For you and I, who see that position as it really is, must never forget how different it ought to appear to him. We know that we have introduced a change of direction in his course which is already carrying him out of his orbit around the Enemy; but he must be made to imagine that all the choices which have effected this change of course are trivial and revocable...You will say that these are very small sins; and doubtless, like all young tempters, you are anxious to be able to

> report spectacular wickedness. But do remember, *the only thing that matters is the extent to which you separate the man from the enemy*. It does not matter how small the sins are, provided that their cumulative effect is to edge the man away from the Light and out into the Nothing...Indeed the safest road to Hell is the gradual one--the gentle slope, soft underfoot, without sudden turnings, without milestones, without signposts (emphasis mine).[3]

Godlessness is indeed a powerful weapon in Satan's arsenal. If he can effectively separate us from the power and person of God under the guise of being "free" in Christ, he has greater liberty to vandalize the work of God in our lives. Being misled about our true spiritual condition and giving Satan freer access to our lives are serious consequences of this godless autonomy. But by far the most serious is that godlessness is totally contrary to the specific will of God.

In Scripture there are only two categories of people who live as though God were not God, the fool and the wicked (Ps. 14:1; 10:4). Neither of these terms is an appropriate ascription for members of God's family. God's will for every Christian is to become more like his Son (Rom. 8:29). And the sobering truth is that in his incarnation, Jesus was dependent on, never independent of, the Father. He spoke only what the Father instructed (Jn. 12:49), and did only what the Father commanded (Jn. 6:38). He is held before us as the one whose obedience to the will of God entailed the role of a servant, a dependent. For a Christian to flaunt freedom as a mask for autonomy is a mockery of the very life of Christ.

An Evangelical Response

As serious a malady as godlessness is, however, it need not be terminal. It is significant, I believe, that of the seven occurrences of the word "godlessness" in the New Testament, four are in the context of pastoral responsibilities. Paul spoke of godlessness to Timothy in both of his letters to the young pastor. He warned Timothy of people who as a consequence of godlessness were "wandering from the truth" or "wandering from the faith."

Wandering is a process. It appears innocuous because its movements are slow and nondramatic. The tragedy lies in the final outcome -- being helplessly and perhaps irretrievably lost.

The nature and scope of godlessness must become a priority for evangelical pulpits and a focal point in Christian classrooms. We need to see ourselves once again in reference to the character and overall plan of God. Our leadership must call us back to our primary responsibility and our first love -- conformity to the likeness of Jesus Christ. The initial responsibility, then, for turning back this tide lies squarely with the leadership of the evangelical community: seminaries, colleges and universities, parachurch organizations, and the local church.

There needs to be a renaissance of personal piety: not an irrelevant asceticism, but rather the cultivation of what used to be the touchstone of genuine Christianity -- a deep personal relationship with the God of all creation. God's people need to be taught *how* to have a relationship with God, one that will cultivate dependence rather than propagate autonomy. It was a *pastor* that Paul instructed about godlessness and admonished concerning the importance of combatting it. This is significant. It means that Christian leaders have the responsibility to preach, to teach, and most importantly, to model lives that are antithetical to Christian autonomy.

There is, however, another institution to which God has given an even higher charge: the home. The home is the primary medium for instilling values, a consequence that occurs regardless of the parents' orientation. The goal of the Christian home must be to cultivate biblical values that are congruous with the Christian education the home provides. The lifestyle of the parents is the "informal curriculum." It is from this curriculum that the children assemble their value system. The actual words or instruction the parents give is the "formal curriculum" from which the child derives a doctrinal system. When the two are incongruous, the product is a child with a secular value system and a sacred vocabulary.

A daughter that is told the imperative of respecting authority should not be exposed to a continual verbal assault on the pastor, the boss or the law. The father who regularly speeds is teaching disrespect for authority, regardless how vocal he is about respect. On the other hand, the man who praises his wife within earshot of the children communicates a definite positive message about the dignity of marriage. How parents respond to suffering has a permanent effect on the view their children develop concerning God's sovereignty and love. Each ought to ask, "Do I fear and dread God's dealings with me, squirming always to escape, or do I submit, trusting that my heavenly Father cares and knows what is best?" We need to talk to our children about what God is doing in our lives. They need to see and hear that our relationship with God is not simply a matter of behavior, it is our very life. The influence on the child exercised by the life of the parent can never be underestimated.

I believe Jesus himself knew that the "informal curriculum" would always win out over the "formal curriculum," if the two are incongruous. He instructed the people to do what the Pharisees taught because the Pharisees spoke the words of Moses, but not to do what they did (Matt. 23:1-3). He knew that followers imitate leaders' lives more than their words. As parents we must realize that the greatest inheritance we can leave to our children is a biblical value system, the product of a vibrant faith and a dependent life.

In our personal lives the single most effective curative and preventative for godlessness is regular, personal Bible study on one hand, and a constant vigilance over our sensory input on the other. David said it so simply: "How can a young man keep his way pure? By living according to your word...I have hidden your word in my heart that I might not sin against you" (Ps. 119:9,11). Firsthand daily exposure to the Scriptures with an eye toward internalizing and applying the truth is the best remedy for godlessness. Reading, meditating, and memorizing for the sake of becoming more like Jesus Christ instead of enlarging one's biblical "data base" is the best curative.

Paul warned the Corinthians that they might be led astray from their pure and simple devotion to Christ. He highlighted their minds as the vehicle Satan would use. What we allow into our minds becomes a part of us. Petra, a contemporary Christian music group spotlights this truth in their song, "Computerbrains:"

> Everything that you do and see,
> One more event in your memory.
> Every bit takes another bite,
> Without control over wrong or right.
> You must screen every entry made,
> The consequences must be weighed.
> The only way to security,
> Is every thought in captivity.[4]

Jesus adds further insight when he asserts that we speak out of the "overflow" of our hearts (Matt. 12:34). What we put into our minds has an effect on what comes out of our mouths. Paul instructed Timothy, "Avoid godless chatter, because those who indulge in it will become more and more ungodly" (2 Tim. 2:16). Godless input leads to godless output, and godless output leads to ungodly conduct, sin. We rarely "fall" into sin. Usually we walk in, arms outstretched and eyes wide open. Affairs don't simply "happen;" marriages don't simply "die;" children don't simply "run away." Often, visible sin is only the flower of a well-established root of godlessness. One of the ways, then, that we can battle our tendency toward godlessness is to strive to eliminate godless input in our lives wherever possible.

The literature we read, the TV we watch, the music we listen to, the places we frequent, the conversations we have, and the people we associate with all prompt feelings and thoughts of autonomy or dependence. We must choose to "screen every entry made" in regard to what we allow access to our minds. To believe that such input has no ultimate effect on our values and conduct is naive and dangerous. We will always need to lean in the direction of dependence on the Lord to remain truly free in Christ.

Godlessness is an assassin. It robs us of our birthright as children of the Most High, it kills the next generation and destroys the purposes of God. But its success is totally dependent on its anonymity. If the leadership of evangelicalism will expose this villain and provide adequate instruction, challenge and modeling, I believe that godlessness will be nothing more than a temptation that blossoms for a season but then withers on the vine, fruitless and futile in the enemy's strategy against the children of God.

Notes

1. Warren Wiersbe, "The Apostle of the Haphazard," in *Victorious Christians You Should Know* (Grand Rapids: Baker Book House, 1984), p. 57.
2. Colin Chapman, *The Case for Christianity* (Grand Rapids: Wm. B. Eerdmans Publishing Co., 1981), p. 29.
3. C. S. Lewis, *The Screwtape Letters* (New York: MacMillan Publishing Co., Inc., 1961), pp. 53 and 56.
4. Petra, "Computerbrains," from the album, *Beat the System*, Star Song Records, 1984.

The Ethics of Political Decision-Making

Richard Cizik

Does a Christian public policy exist? Does our faith dictate a common response to political issues? Although 16 centuries have passed since Augustine wrestled with these questions in *De Civitati Dei*, the issues he raised about Christian responsibility in the public arena remain fundamental. Every generation must answer them anew. The difference is that today our moral choices are made more difficult by a complex and rapidly changing world. So it is that many believers in the twentieth century, as in the fifth, do not find fulfilling their civic duty an easy task. John Courtney Murray, the Jesuit analyst of church and state, recognized the complexity of making ethical judgments, but counseled against handwringing:

> It is as if a surgeon in the midst of a gastroenterostomy were to say that the highly complex situation in front of him is so full of paradox ("The patient is at once receiving blood and losing it"), and irony ("Half a stomach will be better than a whole one") and dilemmas ("Not too much, nor too little, anesthesia") that all surgical solutions are necessarily ambiguous.[1]

The remedy to this kind of paralysis, Murray believed, was to face our problems frankly and then to get on with the task: "Complicated situations, surgical or moral, are merely complicated. It is for the statesman, as for the surgeon, to master the complications and minister as best he can to the health of the body, politic or physical."[2]

Christians should be similarly motivated to master the complications. We must live out our confession of faith in every area of life; to do otherwise violates conscience and betrays our Lord. The task of addressing "complicated situations" is formidable. Secularists denounce the application of biblical values to politics as a violation of their rights. Religious partisans often tell believers what to think; they discourage individual thought and responsibility by insisting, "This is the only answer." Those without firm convictions can find themselves tossed to and fro with uncertainty.

Nonetheless, it is possible for responsible Christians to minister to the body politic. By following three guidelines -- moral absolutes, social principles and prudent judgments -- we can offer answers to a society struggling in its search for enduring values.

The Guideline of Moral Absolutes

The historic confession, "Jesus is Lord," is the church's primary message. To proclaim it is a profoundly political act. When the message was first spoken, an emperor was considered the supreme civil and divine authority. Imagine, then, the impact of Jesus' claim. Pilate asked the mute Jesus, "Do you refuse to speak to me? Don't you realize I have power either to free you or to crucify you?" Jesus' reply was radical: "You would have no power over me if it were not given to you from above" (John 19:10-11). The "above" here refers to God, not Caesar.

Political authority, according to the Christian faith, is not derived from the people, as taught by contemporary thought. All nations and governments are subject to a higher law. For emphasis the apostle Paul wrote three times that the state's "authority" is God's authority (Romans 13:1, 4a, b, 6). This does not mean that God has endowed the state with divine infallibility or that he appoints individuals to political office. Rather, it means that the state is accountable to God, the ultimate source of law and morality.

As the ultimate source of truth, God has laid down objective, eternal standards of what is good and evil. He will hold rulers and citizens accountable to these standards. Many people scoff at such an idea, of course; the Enlightenment has convinced them that all human beliefs about good and evil are culturally and historically relative. "You have your values, and I have mine" is a commonly heard statement. Humankind is said to have suffered enough from religion and doctrines, whose adherents on all sides were convinced that they were the carriers of absolute truth.

Secular skepticism, with its revolt against any external standard of values, laid a foundation for a pluralist and tolerant society. It has led, however, to an inability to distinguish between good and evil, or at least to an unwillingness to do so, which for all practical purposes amounts to the same thing. It is much easier to say in the abstract that absolutes are naive and obsolete than clearly to admit that slavery is as good as freedom, granted that there are no moral absolutes. This mindset produces what has been described as a "naked public square" -- a society in which there is no absolute, transcendent prohibition against evil.[3]

In contention is the "first question" of government, namely "How should we live?" According to Aristotle, "politics" is humanity responding to the question of how society ought to be ordered. This is essentially a moral question, for at stake are the moral judgments and standards we will use to decide what is fair and just and what constitutes the common good. In this debate moral absolutists appeal to some external standard, such as the Bible, to advance their views in the political arena; moral relativists appeal to every society's right to define good and evil. For example, witness this exchange on the U.S. Senate floor: In heated debate about abortion Senator Jesse Helms asserted that "there was a little set of instructions, ten of them, that came down from Mount Sinai" and still have relevance for contemporary lawmaking. Senator Lowell Weicker derisively replied, "We are not running this country by divine commandment or instructions from [Mount]

Sinai."[4] The colloquy raises an important question: what are sufficient standards for legislative action in a pluralistic society?

Appeals to tradition, majority rule or natural law all fall short of providing an unambiguous standard for the ordering of society. Tradition is invoked on both sides of many issues, as was the case during the debate over race discrimination. The will of the majority is not self-justifying; it can even be wrong. Natural law, a universal and eternal law discernible by reason, is helpful, but too ambiguous to settle specific questions of public policy.

It is the Word of God that ultimately provides the only sure standard for law and morality. The precepts and prohibitions needed for guiding the moral order are supplied with propositional clarity. Secularists and others reject revelational authority but enjoy no immunity from its moral claims. All persons are subject to God's moral laws through divinely given reason and conscience. Unfortunately, many efforts to communicate these truths in the public arena ignore this fact. Appeals to moral absolutes from Scripture are often made at face value without any further exegetical ado and in the search for solutions reason is afforded little place of importance. The result is all but certain: grounding political values solely in religious sources will make inevitable the religiously sterilized public life that we so ardently protest. Since there are many people who are not moved by arguments from biblical orthodoxy, the retention of absolute values in society requires an approach that nonetheless convinces such people of the merits of these values.

An ethical apologetic appropriate for this task will defend the relationship between religion and morality in public affairs. Those who try to break this connection by insisting that it is a violation of the separation of church and state are surely wrong. On the other hand, effective moral reasoning calls for more than simply repeating injunctions of the Decalogue or the Sermon on the Mount, particularly in the complex field of public affairs. Certain beliefs, even considered noble for moral reasons, can be disastrous when translated into political acts, let alone into rules of politics. Moreover, without good moral arguments, bad moral argument will have the field to itself.

The assertion of absolutes is thus utterly necessary, but qualified. It is necessary, for as T. S. Eliot expressed, "If you will not have God, who is a jealous God, you should pay your respects to Hitler or Stalin."[5] What qualifies the task in the political arena are the "rules of the game" we have agreed to play through our acceptance of our citizenship. The role of government is not to stipulate absolutes, but to define what is unlawful in order to preserve justice in society. While moral wrongs are sin, not all should be unlawful. In order to make a case for legislating against immoral acts we must show that they present a danger to society. If evangelicals want to outlaw pornography, abortion or homosexual practices, we must convince society in terms that society understands; that is, at this time, under these circumstances, such practices are a threat to society in some demonstrable sense.

In order to persuade the non-Christian citizen our justifications for legal or political action must be based on civil, rather than theological grounds. We use such reasoning -- even though our own positions are informed by, and impelled by our devotion to Jesus Christ and Christian truth. It is possible, for example, to argue for the "right to life" on scientific, social and ethical grounds, recognizing that those arguments derive from biblical roots. In this way, even if unbelievers are unpersuaded, they can at least see that believers are making their case on grounds that are legitimate in a pluralistic society.

This kind of ethical apologetic is not universally accepted. It requires cultivating a divided consciousness, to recognize the differences between the "two cities," as Augustine called them. The terms of discourse in each (the city of God and the human city) are not always interchangeable. Some believers unjustifiably regard using extra-biblical arguments as succumbing to a humanistic ethic. Even so, most Christians are initially exposed to an ethical problem, such as world hunger, from secular sources and only then take up the issue in a biblical context. As long as the primacy of biblical authority is adhered to on matters about which Scripture is clear, the use of non-biblical information sources should be accepted. It should not surprise us that it is possible to establish common ground with non-Christians on many issues of public importance. God has written his law not only on stone tablets but also on the human heart. While the law "written on their hearts" (Rom. 2:15) is often suppressed it is not alien to humanity. By effective moral reasoning it is possible to convince society that moral absolutes serve the public good. This is the art of government -- so to order life that self interest prompts what justice demands.

The Guideline of Social Principles

The church has been more successful in limiting the state's claim than in guiding its policies. A misunderstanding of the role of biblical witness in the social order is partly to blame. For some, a belief that "there is no Christian view" on issues makes any attempt to influence government pointless. Just as unfortunate is the converse -- viewing the Bible as a slot-machine (put your money in, out comes an answer) that mandates explicit answers for ordering government. In either case, as John Stott has said, "To assert that there are no solutions or to offer slick solutions are both dishonoring to God."[6]

The Bible is not a manual for government or a blueprint for the ideal political or economic system. The Old Testament was given to people living in a theocracy, and the New Testament was given to those living under the yoke of Rome. In spite of the fact that it was directed to cultures and eras different from our own, the Bible offers principles that serve to guide us in our 20th century political decision-making. God has revealed his will, but not in a simple set of rules. Instead, the principles of Scripture must be worked for, much as an understanding of Christian ethics has to be diligently sought after. The process is highly individual. Just as believers interact with culture in different ways they also read the Bible with diverse approaches. Philosopher Richard Mouw has pointed out that American Protestants tend to read Scripture in one of, or in a combination of, four ways: doctrinally, morally, devotionally or culturally. Over the centuries believers have seldom consciously read the Bible for cultural insight. Yet, this method, looking for guidelines to structure institutions in society, is precisely what is necessary to see the first principles of social ethics.

Scripture affirms that government should pursue fundamental objectives of order (protection against violence to life and property), justice (what each man is due), and freedom (the condition for all other action). A number of social principles help clarify these priorities, including religious liberty as a divinely given right, sacredness of human life, justice for the impoverished and oppressed, dedication to peace and opposition to war, stewardship over the environment, and the inviolability of three ordained institutions -- family, church and state.

An overarching community philosophy, what Peter Berger called a "sacred canopy," requires basic orientations, touchstones of normative principle, to edify and guide the body politic. A society held together by these social principles can balance individual rights (freedom) against social authority (order) by rooting both in transcendent purpose (justice). While these value sources pull against each other, they also reinforce one another. Compare the effectiveness of these principles to the proposals of philosophers, religionists and political ideologies. Jean Jacques Rousseau's "civil religion", the theistic version of the "social contract" within liberal Christianity and the God-less social order of Marxist-Leninism are but a few examples. None of these is capable of balancing freedom, order and justice in a unified value system.

For Christian principles to guide our society successfully requires attention again to methodology. The church must address certain political issues, yet avoid captivity to any single political ideology. It needs to articulate clearly social principles without appearing to be an interest group, opposition party or government in exile. To avoid the pitfalls of social activism, the church must deal with matters of principle only where the principle is very clear. In *Politics and Protestant Theology*, Rene de Visme Williamson suggests, "Few Christians, if any, would find fault with the Declaration of Barmen in which the German Confessing Church condemned nazism. Again, few Christians, if any would deny that church pronouncement condemning compulsory racial segregation in the United States was right."[7] In our day the moral implications of the destruction of prenatal life, the repression of religious freedom internationally, and the nuclear arms race clearly mandate a church response. These are a few issues, by no means complete, in which the principle at stake is unmistakable and the need for guidance is obvious.

No less an obligation exists for the church to translate its social principles into laws and programs. History demonstrates that Christian beliefs can powerfully influence the political order. The common law (rooted, as Justice Joseph Story pointed out, in Christian moral assumptions) is one conspicuous example of how eternal values have shaped temporal ones. In the political process, people equally committed to biblical principles will often disagree on which policies best implement any particular social principle (e.g., the pursuit of peace). The role of the church at this point must necessarily be one of restraint. It should clearly articulate the principles that legislators and citizens should consider in lawmaking, but leave it to them to decide what policy prescriptions best accomplish that goal.

This distinction can be summed up as follows: the church is responsible for communicating biblical principles, the Christian citizen for applying them to society, and the machinery of the state for legislating them. In this framework of role division the church does not itself engage in direct political action by advocating specific programs or policies. That is left to individual believers active in the political and public-policy process. Confusing these roles casts doubt upon the witness of the church in the political arena. A public witness, for example, in behalf of peace points a direction for political leaders, even though it may never be fulfilled in this world. But to jump from principle -- the call to be peacemakers -- to specific policy recommendations, such as support or opposition to the MX missile, jeopardizes the church's integrity (the church lacks expertise, though its members may have it), wisdom (it may be wrong) and fairness (since believers hold differing opinions, it ought not side with a majority against an equally loyal minority).

The lack of a clear moral imperative from Scripture on a host of issues as diverse as nuclear power and genetic engineering mandates individual freedom and liberty of conscience for believers. On issues like these, where "facts and motives are mixed and consequences contradict the principles involved," Williamson declares, "the church should remain silent, letting individual Christians and Christian groups decide themselves what Christian witness means."[8]

Freedom to decide is not license, however. Even on these issues the Bible should play a role in decision making, providing a moral framework or boundaries that suggest and limit possibilities for action. This means that we cannot simply convert our sociological or political preferences into moral absolutes. Inconsistencies in our decision-making often occur for this very reason: we profess some issues as simply matters of personal opinion and reserve our moral absolutes for other issues. Thus we can be relativists about the nuclear arms race, but moralists about abortion, or vice versa. This is the idolatry of politics, the creating of gods for an ad hoc use in political debates. It is as dangerous to the gospel as the converse -- a world-denying spirituality that views religion and politics as separate from, and irrelevant to one another.

The Christian must resist using the gospel for political purposes or making it hostage to any political person or cause. Some sixty times in the New Testament the death and resurrection of Christ are described as liberating and the Christian life as one of freedom. The Apostle Paul declared, "It is for freedom that Christ has set us free. Stand firm, then, and do not let yourselves be burdened again by a yoke of slavery" (Galatians 5:1). A burden of political conformity is a form of legalism that must not characterize the body of Christ; neither should any judgmental or unloving attitudes over differences of opinion be present. Disagreements, moreover, should be regarded not as "off limits," but as legitimate and even healthy. They offer the opportunity to discuss regularly conflicting ideas with a spirit of prayer, openness to the Holy Spirit and unconditional submission to God's Word. In this way the church is a community that transcends, while never denying, its internal differences. Here is victory over the last great temptation (as the Book of

Revelation intimates), that of making politics more than itself -- to make it everything.

The Guideline of Prudent Judgments

The enemy of prudent judgments is the outlook that anyone can run the state. "Politics," jested Robert Louis Stevenson, "is perhaps the only profession for which no preparation is thought necessary." Many of our fellow citizens concur, at least until confronted with making actual choices themselves. Then they discover what political philosophers have told us: politics is more difficult than one thinks.

The pursuit of values -- personal, social and transcendent -- is what both religion and politics have in common. Yet modern humanity seems bent on prying the two apart. Legislators are told not to let their "private" religious views influence their political tasks. The perceived danger is that religion and politics do not mix well, although both make claims on our loyalties. That is why Jesus described our twin obligations, "Give to Caesar what is Caesar's, and to God what is God's" (Matthew 22:21). Jesus implied that Caesar has a role that religion must respect; conversely, politics ought not to pretend that religion does not exist. Determining what is Caesar's due and what is God's has always been difficult, and the children of God have often been wrong.

One critic sarcastically observed that "Hard-boiled politicians know, as did Boss Tweed, that 'this God-business' may have little to do with politics." Both motives and methods are suspect. He adds that the Judeo-Christian tradition, when carried to its logical conclusion in politics, suffers from excessive moralism: "Religious men and women can be excessively moralistic in defending the righteousness of their cause but singularly ineffective in reaching positions of consensus in a sinful world."[9] The church's history abounds with instances of believers taking portions of Scripture out of context, endowing them with absolute moral authority, and then acting in error. Perhaps this is why writer Harold Nicolson described religious people as "the worst diplomats."[10]

A widespread appreciation of politics would significantly alter this reputation. Called the "art of the possible," politics is impossible without compromise. Compromising is seemingly impossible, though, for those who think they have a monopoly on truth. For them compromise is just that, compromising. The word "compromise," however, is derived from *compromittere*, which means to promise mutually to abide by an arbiter's decision. Compromising, then, is not a defeat or striking a deal so much as it is an act of trust, offering up a conflict to the Arbiter Absolute.[11] After all, that is what being a nation "under God" means. Understood in this sense, compromise is not the abandonment of morality, but a moral act itself. It is a willing and unselfish choice to settle for less than is personally desired in order to resolve conflict. Professor Lon Fuller's distinction between the "morality of aspiration" and the "morality of duty" is helpful:

> As we consider the whole range of moral issues...there is an invisible pointer that marks the dividing line between where the pressure of duty leaves off and the challenge of excellence begins. The whole field of moral argument is dominated by a great undeclared war over the location of this point.[12]

In short, legislating values has an optimum point, beyond which it is not possible to move. Most political arguments, in fact, are usually about degree. Prudence is knowing how far to go in pursuit of a good that may, at some point, conflict with other goods.

Decision-making even then can be an arduous task. Politics does not easily allow allegiance to any single moral principle. American jurist Learned Hand once said, "There is no democracy among human values, however each may cry out for an equal vote."[13] Most political decisions pose a conflict of values, that is, the situation in which one moral principle pulls one way and another pulls the other way. The divergencies among Christians on political ethics often reflect their differing emphases on the objectives of order, freedom and justice. To balance or choose among these objectives does not necessarily signal a retreat from principle; choice means that perfect solutions to political problems are few.

Many politicians liken the dilemma of King Darius (Daniel 6) to their own. A coup d'etat attempt by his chief ministers, with Daniel as the victim, places the king in an unenviable position. He signs a decree prohibiting prayers to anyone but himself. To revoke his decree, even for a friend, is to relinquish the crown. His moral choices are clear: yield the kingdom to evil men and save Daniel or sacrifice Daniel and save the kingdom. Save the man or the empire? Neither is entirely satisfactory, although King Darius must make a decision. Edward John Carnell labeled a dilemma like this a "tragic moral choice."

The issues confronting legislators today are no less morally ambiguous than those King Darius faced. Welfare programs designed to sustain life create dependency; defensive weapons made to deter aggressive powers are used to make war; trade policies designed to protect some workers hurt others; technology created to protect the environment is used to destroy it; and on and on. They must choose among less than perfect options knowing that every piece of legislation has countless effects, some adverse and some beneficial.

Given these limitations, what are legislators and citizens to do? One thing is certain. Even though our political choices fall short of the norms of Christian ethics, we are still obligated to make proximate or less than ideal, ethical judgments. When basic claims conflict, we ought not resort to a merely utilitarian ethic ("the greatest good for the greatest number"), because what brings about the most good is but one factor to consider. All principles do not make equal claims on us; a stronger claim should not automatically be surrendered for a weaker one. This means, for example, that the central political value, justice, ought never be surrendered. But justice is only possible when other political values -- such as freedom and order -- are in balance and not pursued beyond their appropriate limits.

To give specific answers to all the conflicts that occur among values is impossible. But at least the following can be said: The prospects for prudent decision-making are open to us when we acknowledge an obligation to a Higher Law and its directives. In light of this truth, we need to develop both the character traits and political reasoning to choose wisely between conflicting principles. As Justice Oliver Wendell Holmes, with his eye on politics, explained, "Some people admire the man of principle. I admire the man who can find his way through a maze of conflicting principles."[14]

Several leaders have admirably demonstrated this ability. During the Civil War, Abraham Lincoln was visited by a group of Presbyterian ministers who brought a petition calling for the emancipation of all slaves. To clarify his thoughts he wrote on a slip of paper: "The will of God prevails. In great contests each party claims to act in accordance with the will of God. Both may be, and one must be, wrong. God cannot be for and against the same thing at the same time."[15] Lincoln went on to ask why, if God had revealed his will to others, he would not have similarly revealed it to him. Lincoln said he was most anxious to know the will of God and to follow it, but he did not expect any miracles. In politics he had chosen to study the plain facts, ascertain what is possible and do what is wise and just. No less is required of our leaders or ourselves, although all too often we are content to settle for less.

Politics, for all its ambiguity, is not a subjective art. To make political judgments we must try to understand their empirical complexity. This requires a full and fair hearing for both sides of an issue and a calm, reasoned and objective judgment of all the facts, interests and arguments involved. We are not entitled, however intense our concern, to substitute sincerity of intention for accuracy of knowledge. To avoid the temptations of the terrible simplifiers we should bear in mind Aristotle's great maxim: "Look for precision in each class of things just so far as the nature of the subject admits."[16]

To assist in unravelling complex issues certain standard tests for ideas and decisions are helpful: (1) Does our opinion conform to the rules of logical consistency? We should not hold contradictory ideas. (2) Does our opinion adhere to all the established, relevant facts? Factual accuracy means that no evidence is suppressed or denied. (3) Does our opinion relate to reality? Our opinions must have the function of bringing us into relationship with reality. A true idea or opinion helps to draw everything together into a comprehensive whole. These tests suggest some approaches for making decisions and evaluating ideas. They will never guarantee that our political judgments are right, only that we are prudent in the decision-making process.

Conclusion

As argued here, Christians can effectively address the ambiguities of decision-making in the public sector. The assertion of moral absolutes is altogether necessary but dependent on an apologetic befitting a pluralistic society. Even then our legislative enactments need grounding in a social framework. Such a framework, a vision of the polity, is supplied by biblical principles. Not least of all, prudential judgments make the art of politics a more manageable and noble task.

In the end, though, ministering to the body politic will not usher in true justice. This should neither surprise nor discourage us. Like Augustine, we know that it is achieved only in the city of God and not in any earthly city. Nevertheless, as citizens and ambassadors of that city, we are called to witness to it in an alien world. May we be faithful to that duty.

Notes

1. John Courtney Murray, *We Hold These Truths: Catholic Reflections on the American Proposition*, cf. "The Margin Makes the Difference: John Courtney Murray on Morality & Foreign Policy," George Weigel, *Catholicism in Crisis*, December, 1985.
2. Ibid., p. 8.

3. Richard John Neuhaus, *The Naked Public Square* (Grand Rapids: Wm. B. Eerdmans Publishing Co., 1984), p. 188.

4. *Congressional Record*, May 21, 1981, S 5469-71.

5. T. S. Eliot, *The Idea of a Christian Society* (New York: Harcourt Brace, 1940), p. 63.

6. John Stott, *Issues Facing Christians Today* (London: Marshall Morgan & Scott, 1984), p. 31.

7. Rene de Visme Williamson, *Politics and Protestant Theology* (Baton Rouge: Louisiana State University Press, 1976), pp. 176-77.

8. Rene de Visme Williamson, pp. 176-77.

9. Kenneth W. Thompson, "Religion and Politics in America: An Overview," *The Annals of the American Academy*, January, 1986, p. 16.

10. Harold Nicolson, *Diplomacy* (London: Oxford University Press, 1955), p. 50, cf. Kenneth Thompson, "Religion and Politics: An Overview," *The Annals of the American Academy*, January, 1986, p. 16.

11. Richard John Neuhaus, *The Naked Public Square* (Grand Rapids: Wm. B. Eerdmans Publishing Co., 1984), p. 124.

12. Lon Fuller, *The Morality of Law* (New Haven: Yale University Press, 1964), cf. George Will, *Statecraft As Soulcraft* (New York: Simon & Schuster, 1983), p. 79.

13. Leonard Hand, *The Spirit of Liberty*, Irving Dilliard, ed. (New York: Alfred A. Knopf, 1952), cf. George Will, *Statecraft As Soulcraft* (New York: Simon & Schuster, 1983), p. 92.

14. Oliver Wendell Holmes, *The Common Law*, ed. Mark De Wolffe Howe (Cambridge: Harvard University Press, 1963), cf. Kenneth W. Thompson, "Religion and Politics: An Overview," *The Annals of the American Academy*, January, 1986, p. 15.

15. Abraham Lincoln, *Second Inaugural Address*, March 4, 1865.

16. Whittle Johnston, "Ethics, Power and U.S. Foreign Policy," *Christianity and Politics* (Washington: Ethics & Public Policy Center, 1981), p. 90.

Christian Freedom and Third World Realities

Roger E. Hedlund

Spiritual freedom, said Jacques Ellul, is a neglected theme. It has "vanished from the Christian horizon."[1] The advent of liberation theology may be viewed as a partial corrective to this situation, one which, however, is not without its own limitations. Perhaps it is more correct to view Christian freedom as a largely Western issue arising from the religious, social and political struggles of Europe and North America. Thus, for example, a book about the makers of religious freedom merely traces the struggles for religious liberty of the Puritans in seventeenth century England.[2] But the contemporary Third World focuses on somewhat different problems. Massive social, economic and political problems confront many of the developing countries. Western democracy is not for everyone. "Of the 161 nations in the world today, only fifty-one enjoy complete freedom."[3] Some of these nations restrict religious liberty, others restrict political freedom. Economic insufficiency is a major factor in much of the world today. Another reality is a resurgence of Hinduism, Buddhism and Islam in a number of countries. Small wonder, then, that themes other than "spiritual liberation in Christ" are at the forefront of the church's agenda in much of Asia, Africa and Latin America.

A pertinent question, therefore, concerns the relevance of themes of Christian freedom in light of the realities of Third World poverty, injustice and exploitation and the challenge of the world's non-Christian religions and ideologies.

Before offering a brief discussion of some of these issues, this article will center on definitions of certain key concepts.

What is Freedom?

Christian freedom, according to Helmut Thielicke, "arises as a result of my being empowered to be a responsible child of God and to learn to will what God wills. Freedom here becomes the unimpeded spontaneity of love."[4] Christian freedom is not antinomian. Freedom from enslavement is not without constraints. Unrestricted freedom would disguise a worse form of tyranny: "freedom can be realized only within the confines of certain limitations."[5] The human person is a victim of one's own incapability, hence the Reformation doctrine of justification by *grace* alone. Liberation to be what I should be comes from outside myself: "I have received my self from the hands of God...therefore I must give myself back to Him."[6] But the human problem is that persons are not capable of doing this, for they are bound. Liberation must come from God; it is the freedom of grace. As Thielicke said, "In the state of free, mature worship to God, into which we have been called...we enter into the bondage that makes us free of all the bondages and false empowerments we meet in the created world."[7] The parable of the prodigal son teaches that lack of restraint leads not to freedom but to bondage. We must choose, states Thielicke, "between bondage to the Father, which makes us free, and bondage to the powers of the world, which enslaves us."[8] Christian freedom is characterised by a response of love. The love ethic teaches the Christian how to live with the gift of forgiveness: "It shows us how the prodigal lives after he has forsaken the servitude of the far country and after he has outgrown the virtuous legalism of the brother who remained at home."[9]

As delineated by Thielicke, Christian freedom is spiritual, having its origins and base in God. This starting point contrasts with liberation theology's excessive preoccupation with human and social dimensions of liberation. Thus, for Metropolitan Bishop Geervarghese Mar Osthathios of Orthodox Syrian Church, freedom means the creation of a classless society.[10] According to John Desrochers, freedom entails a radical transformation of social structures.[11] The social manifestation of freedom is predominant in these writers. Gutierrez distinguishes three approaches or interdependent levels in the process of liberation: first, the aspirations of oppressed peoples; second, an understanding of history; and third, the biblical understanding of Christ as the Saviour who liberates from sin. He writes, "Christ makes man truly free, that is to say, he enables man to live in communion with him; and this is the basis for all human brotherhood."[12] Gutierrez rightly relates the issue of freedom to Jesus Christ. Many liberation theologians, however, tend to emphasize the human aspects of liberation. T. Paul Verghese, for example, argues that human growth is a process involving both authority and freedom which requires structures in which love can develop.[13]

By way of contrast Ellul understands human freedom as a gift of God, as does Thielicke. Moreover, this is related to Christian hope:

> God is the liberator and on this ground man is authorized to have and to live out hope. Because he has experienced the act of liberation this man knows that hope is not vain. Only the free man can hope.[14]

Freedom, then, is a spiritual relationship in which we are placed in fellowship with Christ. Hope finds expression in freedom, that is to say, spiritual freedom is lived out here and now. The Christian, who has been freed from bondage of the Powers, has freedom to live out the Christian virtues.[15] Freedom in Christ must be lived out visibly.[16]

Christian freedom, then, means a Christian *presence* in the world, including the world of politics. Political involvement is a complex issue. As a citizen of two kingdoms the Christian should give careful consideration to one's Christian obligations as a citizen of the state. The Christian must be discerning, adopting "the relativity of politics."[17] One dare not identify any political party as

"Christian," for the believer should always remain a creative critic of all systems. One should be particularly apprehensive toward any totalitarian or oppressive regime, since "means which negate freedom can never lead to freedom."[18] This is a sensitive point in much of today's world. There are no simple solutions to global injustices and brutal demonstrations of human inhumanity toward others.

Jurgen Moltmann asked the question, "How can an inhuman brute be transformed into a true human?"[19] The usual answer is the law. Yet the effort to practice the law produces a new legalism. "So he becomes the slave of a law which holds up to him a humanity it refuses to grant and demands of him freedom without setting him free."[20] Moltmann raises the problem, but the gospel provides the remedy. The best and only solution seems to lie in the evangelical doctrine of *grace* ("faith", in Luther's understanding). The gospel sets one free for joyful, obedient service. This has important ramifications in the world of revolutions and of benevolent, but regimented and manipulative systems.

Religious Liberty

Closely related to the issue of freedom in Christ is the Baptist principle of liberty. One aspect of this emphasis is the doctrine of "soul competency." To be responsible, each individual must be politically, intellectually, and spiritually free. As one author noted, persons "must be free to decide their attitude to God for themselves, and they must not be victimized for their opinions."[21] The gospel is never forced on the individual will; it must be accepted as a free act without compulsion. Liberty means not only the ability to choose, "but the use of that power of choice to enter through Christ into the life of the Spirit."[22] The human person is morally free. Therefore, Baptists insist on the necessity of religious liberty. Religious freedom on its positive side, states E.Y. Mullins,

> is God appealing to the soul through truth and calling forth the soul's intelligent and obedient response. It is the soul's approach to God through faith and prayer and fellowship and obtaining grace to help in time of need.[23]

A corollary emphasis is the Baptist axiom of a free church in a free state, which stems from the Baptist understanding of the church as a company of believers who have entered into personal relationship with Christ through voluntary covenant:

> The Church, in fact, is a society of a special kind. It exists within the State, and its members are generally citizens of the State. But their membership in the Church is not created by their citizenship in the State.[24]

This characteristic Baptist stance cost a number of early Baptist leaders their freedom and their lives in a struggle against the European state-church system. Even today Baptists in some countries are in prison for their faith. The Baptist witness to freedom is relevant in the present world context in which religious and other personal freedoms are openly denied in many societies and violated in others.

Third World Realities

From the evangelical viewpoint, says Domingo Diel of the Philippines, Asia's rapid population growth means that more and more people in Asia die without Christ and without hope. Therefore, the church must use all means possible to carry out the missionary commission. Mission in Asia must also take seriously the traditional religions of Asia. A *dialogical* understanding of the task is valid in the face of Asian religions which question the authority of the Bible and the absolute claims of Christ. A third reality is the context of poverty and social injustice. Christians must be responsive to the struggles of the poor for liberation.[25]

Dehumanization, prevalent in many Third World countries, is offensive to concepts of Christian freedom and dignity. India, for example, is a democracy with a population of 750 million of which more than 50 percent live below the poverty line,[26] and some 200 million may be considered socially and economically oppressed. The latter consist of the outcastes ("untouchables") who live "far below the subsistence level, virtually living on a single, inadequate meal a day...with no work opportunities."[27] Questions about social, religious and political freedom hardly seem a priority for people whose economic freedom is denied.

Nevertheless, as Indian theologian Sebastian Kappen asserts, Jesus is a source of light and inspiration to the oppressed millions of India.[28] Jesus is the Prophet of the New Age (which presupposes the initiative of God) which he preached. Jesus' response to cosmic bondage was a "no" which took the form of miracles. Jesus "went around doing good and healing all who were under the power of the devil" (Acts 10:38). This fact has been well summarized: "God's reign as mediated by Jesus makes humans free *from* all alien forces and free *for* wholeness, personal as well as social.[29] What Jesus began is germinal and anticipatory and will come to consummation in the New Heaven and the New Earth. Meanwhile, we must work to remove the evils of unhealthy conditions, hunger, disease, and death among all, including the underprivileged in India. We do so guided by the Spirit of God, for "liberation from cosmic evils...is a task that mankind has to accomplish in dialogue with the Lord of history."[30]

Both Hinduism and Marxism have failed to lead the Indian people out of bondage, says Kappen. Jesus' call is to all to become His disciples irrespective of caste, creed, community, race, region or culture. "What distinguishes the Jesus' community is its belief in the New Humanity which does not admit any distinctions."[31] Jesus' teaching is remarkable in that "He views divine forgiveness as something that man can mediate to his fellowmen."[32]

But has the church not also failed? "A true Christian will share everything to create an egalitarian, brotherly and sisterly world of freedom and peace with justice," declares Geervarghese Mar Osthathios.[33] In India, however, charges the Rev. M. Azariah of the Church of South India, Christians of Scheduled Caste (i.e. outcaste) background are discriminated against in the church and oppressed by fellow Christians.[34]

A church which would proclaim liberty should itself manifest Christian freedom. Unfortunately, it is often true that the church displays problems similar to those in society. Hierarchial leadership, which needs to motivate groups and facilitate "grass roots" participation, becomes oppressive and self-seeking. Competitive power struggles and internal politics discourage local initiative and stifle emerging leadership. Concerns of the gospel which need to be voiced at the local level are overlooked because centralist tendencies in the church neglect the "little" people who are the real leaders in the congregations. Village pastors, for example, should be encouraged to minister Christ among the people. This spiritual dimension should be a first priority. Yet it is largely overlooked in the competition for positions of power which control and give access to sources of funds poured into Third World churches from the West. Power structures do not bring freedom; they may in fact enslave. Frequently they divert from the priority task of proclaiming freedom in Christ.

The problem is compounded by the presence of insensitive international Christian organizations which pre-empt local initiative, siphon off choice leadership, and create an inflated parachurch economy. The foreign mission agencies of the past apparently were more sensitive to local conditions and personnel needs than are a number of their bureaucratic successors. Many churches in the Third World have been diverted from their mission. Rather than being liberating forces in the Name of Christ, they have become captive to the very principalities and powers they were called to rebuke and disarm. No longer are such churches outposts of the Kingdom of God; they have become the private domain of ambitious persons. It is not only the ecumenical church that has been subverted: (so-called) evangelicals have their own empire-builders, self-seekers, embezzlers, and petty crooks who attend world conferences and serve on international committees.[35] The spiritual renewal of a degenerate church is essential if the people of God are truly to fulfill their destiny as mediators of the freedom of Christ in the world.

Christians too are in need of conversion. As Kappen declares, "The roots of man can be healed only if he is open to the forgiving love of God."[36] Mother Theresa is loved and respected in India because she models the compassion of Jesus for every human being. Her exemplary sacrificial service respects the dignity and personhood of the poorest of the poor. Despite the failures of the church, the world is attracted to Jesus, whose call is to both rich and poor. Both groups must meet his conditions; they must put his kingdom first.[37]

Evangelization is an affirmation of personhood and freedom. Pope John Paul II, addressing the bishops of the Roman Catholic Church in India, reiterated the classical mission of the church in bearing witness to and proclaiming salvation, mercy, and compassion to all, but especially to the poor. The pope also asserted that evangelization cannot be separated from issues of development and liberation, peace and justice, dialogue and inculturation.[38]

Evangelization in Asia takes place in an arena of human suffering. The Suffering Messiah of Isaiah and of the gospels is poignantly attractive in the Asian scene of suffering, violence, and dehumanization. As Diel declares, he "must be genuinely incarnated again in the context of the suffering in Asia, so that such suffering with all its consequences can be taken up again unto himself, as in the cross".[39] Moltmann also emphasizes the crucial importance of the cross. The liberated are healed not by Jesus' happy life but by his wounds.[40] A theology of suffering seems particularly relevant to issues of faith and freedom in light of the sorrow and suffering in the two-thirds world. In conducting its mission of evangelization the church of Jesus Christ cannot be aloof to human need. Since the poor are near to God,[41] humanization must always be a concern of mission.[42] Evangelization respects the dignity of persons and the values of culture, while opening the way to true freedom in Jesus Christ.

World Religions

Jesus came, he said, to set people free (John 8:32,36). What, then, of the religions of the world: are they to be viewed as vehicles of salvation or as instruments of bondage? Both possibilities have been attempted by various theologians. By defining religion vaguely as "a way of liberation or of salvation," R. Panikkar seems to endorse any religion as a possible means of "salvation," which in turn is defined as the fullness of humanity in any sense.[43] Panikker's reconstruction includes revolution, which he says aims at a particular kind of liberation.

The Hindu approach is different. According to Vivekananda, "religion is the manifestation of the Divinity already in man."[44] Religion functions to bring out this internal divinity and entails self-control and self-denial: "Freedom *from* the senses is true freedom."[45] In the Hindu view, freedom is a denial which is said to lead to fulfillment and self-affirmation. "Religion does not mean indifference to the things of the world. It means non-attachment."[46] But is this freedom?

Consider the following "Poornakumbha" advertisement which appeared in *The Hindu* (March 13, 1986):

> After twelve long years comes the opportunity to purify your soul -- "Poornakumbha"...It is believed that anyone who takes a dip in the sacred Brahmakund on this particular day gets complete absolution for all worldly deeds.
>
> This year, people belonging to all walks of life, from all over the country, will throng to Hardwar on 13th. April, the day of Poornakumbha.
>
> Make your plans well in advance and join them to take the holy dip that provides salvation.

Is this freedom or bondage? St. Paul warned the Colossian converts, "do not let anyone judge you by what you eat or drink, or with regard to a religious festival, a New Moon celebration or a Sabbath day" (Col. 2;16). To the Galatians he wrote,

> Formerly, when you did not know God, you were slaves to those who by nature are not gods. But now that you know God -- or rather are known by God -- how is it that you are turning back to those weak and miserable principles? Do you wish to be enslaved by them all over again? You are observing special days and months and seasons and years! I fear for you...(Gal. 4:8-11).

Though the religions of the world may contain manifestations of light, the highest expression of the human quest for God, they also display aspects of human depravity. In the words of the Dutch missionary theologian, Kraemer, "The world fails to know God even in its highest wisdom, although it strives to do so. Man seeks God and at the same time flees from Him in his seeking."[47] In Kraemer's judgment, "the universal religious consciousness of man has everywhere produced also the most abhorrent and degrading filth that perverted human imagination and lust can beget."[48]

The contemporary, controversial Roman Catholic theologian, Hans Kung, takes a more tolerant attitude toward the world religions, which he views as possible ways of salvation for non-Christian humanity: "A man is to be saved within the religion that is made available to him in his historical situation"; hence, one should seek God "within that religion in which the hidden God has already found him."[49] In this way Kung can deduce that salvation is available to all humanity. Nevertheless Kung also finds that the religions contain error as well as truth: "Though they are far from God, God is not far from them."[50] God, Kung declares, can be known in these religions. Idol worship may be the "concealed" worship of God. Conversion does not require renunciation of the true and pure (Phil. 4:8) in the world religions:

> Since God seriously and effectively wills the universal salvation history of the whole of mankind, although he does not, indeed, legitimize every element (some being erroneous and depraved)...yet he does sanction the *religions as such* -- as social structures."[51]

Ultimately, however, Kung is forced to concede that the world's religions need demythologizing and that the preaching of Christ is necessary to dissipate darkness and to bring light and freedom.[52] Elsewhere Kung calls for an authentic local (Indian, Chinese, Japanese, Indonesian, Arabic, African) Christianity, the unique, distinguishing figure of which is the historic Christ.[53]

According to the New Testament, Jesus Christ has brought freedom. "It is for freedom that Christ has set us free"(Gal. 5:1). "Because through Christ Jesus the law of the Spirit of life set me free from the law of sin and death" (Rom. 8:2). "You, my brothers, were called to be free" (Gal. 5:13). If this be so (and according to the inspired Scriptures, Christians must so believe), the followers of Christ are responsible to proclaim this unique message.

In today's world, however, this prerogative is disputed. It is questioned first of all by other religions, which also claim to offer spiritual and social freedom. The search for liberation is found in all schools of Hinduism and in Buddhism.[54] Secondly, there is the secular materialistic challenge: "Is not religion itself, even when it speaks of liberation, still a prison? The movement toward a non-religious secular humanism presents itself as the final exodus to human freedom."[55] What shall we say, then, to the challenge of a modern pluralistic world? Is there hope? Can modern humanity become truly free? Or are we bound by the inexorable laws of a mechanistic universe? Are we captive to the demands of fear or the fatalism of kismet and karma? Are we hopeless victims of universal injustice and suffering?

Even Paul cried in spiritual anguish, "What a wretched man I am! Who will rescue me from this body of death?" (Rom. 7:24). But the Apostle also grasped the answer to the dilemma in Christ: "Thanks be to God -- through Jesus Christ our Lord!"(Rom. 7:25)

Toward a Solution

The ultimate question concerns the relevance of the gospel. The world asks, "Does Jesus Christ bring freedom?" An entire conference of the World Council of Churches (Nairobi 1975) was devoted to the theme, "Jesus Christ frees and unites." But its conclusions were only tentative.[56] Yet convinced Christians, along with Paul, believe that the quest for liberation is fulfilled in Jesus Christ. How, then, are they to mediate Christian freedom in a questioning world?

The place to begin, says Fr. Josef Neuner, is for Christians to acknowledge the common aspirations of all ages to find freedom.[57] Triumphalistic attitudes will not do in today's world. The Eastern religions have come to the West where they challenge the inadequacies of Western culture. In a decadent and crumbling society, Eastern ideologies offer an attractive spirituality: "Most significant for our time is the shifting of freedom into man's interiority."[58] The West is following this characteristic of the Eastern religions. The result is a tendency to retreat from the world. But for Neuner the crucial Christian critique arises out of the declaration that "Christian freedom is liberation of the whole man,"[59] and not a flight from the world. Therefore, "Freedom and responsibility must remain together."[60]

The standard of measurement is Christ. As Neuner rightly suggests, "God has shown once and for all in Jesus Christ what man is and what human freedom means. In Him the true meaning of freedom is shown for all men."[61] Christ is the norm for all that is human. Jesus Christ is not isolated from the world. Ultimately there are no "rival" messages of freedom, says Neuner, so the Christian should not be astonished at the message of freedom anywhere God is at work in the world. Yet believers need discernment to distinguish the genuine from the false. The Christian "is able to judge these ideas of freedom through the Word of God and the inner testimony of the Spirit that makes him experience the freedom which is in Christ Jesus."[62] In the world, the church of Christ is to champion freedom for all. The church itself must manifest freedom in Christ, and Christians are called to involvement for the cause of the oppressed and to proclaim liberty in Christ.

Christians are to announce the Kingdom of God and call people to hope and freedom in Christ. Mortimer Arias believes that kingdom evangelization is relevant and essential: "To evangelize is to announce the coming kingdom" which gives meaning to the present as well as hope for the future.[63] Kingdom evangelism centers on the proclamation of Christ. "The Kingdom of God has come!...It has a face and a name: Jesus Christ."[64] Arias believes in conversion. He recites his own conversion experience at age 18 and then observes, "Conversion to Christ means conversion to the neighbor."[65] Proclamation of the Kingdom is to be taken seriously by Christians themselves. "There is no genuine evangelization...without kingdom discipleship. It is not only a matter of *credibility* but of *authenticity* and *faithfulness* to the Gospel."[66]

Samuel Rayan holds that Christian developmental, liberation, and humanizing activities are an evangelizing witness to Christ in India: "To evangelize is to help transform heart, life, person, group, world and the entire network of human relationships according to God's own best wishes on our behalf. It is more than a matter of words, rites and registration in a church."[67] Rayan cites the Jesuit experience at Ranchi, North India to substantiate this viewpoint. Rayan's argument implies that social ministries *are* evangelization. Without denying the evangelistic impact of any activity carried out in the name of Christ, it may be questioned whether deeds alone are an adequate announcement of the gospel. Some restatements of the Christian mission negate the distinctiveness of the Christian message. Exclusive emphasis on humanization loses the full sweep of the gospel. The evangelical must opt for a full-orbed proclamation -- in word as well as in deed -- of the person of Jesus Christ who has come into the world and who sets his people free (John 8:32,36).

Notes

1. Ellul, Jacques, *The Ethics of Freedom*, translated and edited by Geoffrey W. Bromiley, (Grand Rapids: Wiiliam B. Eerdmans Pub. Co., 1976), p. 105.
2. Loane, Marcus L., *Makers of Religious Freedom in the Seventeenth Century*, (Grand Rapids: Wm. B. Eerdmans, 1961).
3. *U. S. News and World Report*, 4 Feb., 1980, cited by Kane, 181:127.
4. Thielicke, Helmut, *The Freedom of the Christian Man* , translated by John W. Doherstein, (New York and Evanston: Harper and Row, 1963), p. 15.
5. Ibid., p. 14.
6. Ibid., p. 21.
7. Ibid., p. 27.
8. Ibid., p. 28.
9. Ibid., p. 157.
10. Ibid., p. 37.
11. Desrochers, John, *Christ the Liberator*, (Bangalore: Centre for Social Action, 1977), p. 52.
12. Gutierrez, Gustavo, *A Theology of Liberation*, (Maryknoll: Orbis, 1973), p. 37.
13. Verghese, T. Paul, *The Freedom of Man*, (Philadelphia: Westminster Press, 1972).
14. Ellul, Jacques, *The Ethics of Freedom*, p. 13.
15. Ibid., p. 144.
16. Ibid., p. 222.
17. Ibid., p. 382.
18. Ibid., p. 405.
19. Moltmann, Jurgen, *Theology and Joy*, (London: SCM Press, 1973), p. 65.
20. Ibid., p. 65.
21. Cook, Henry, *What Baptists Stand For*, (London: Carey Kingsgate Press, 1961), p. 164.
22. Ibid., p. 172.

23. Mullins, E. Y. and Tribble, H. W., *The Baptist Faith*, (Nashville: Convention Press, 1962), p. 73.

24. Cook, Henry, *What Baptists Stand For*. p. 201.

25. Diel, Domingo Jr., "An Asian Theology of Mission and Evangelism," *Review and Expositor*, 82/2 (Spring 1985), pp. 217-224.

26. Rajshekar, V. T., "Hinduism vs Movement of Untouchables in India." (Bangalore: Dalit Sahitya Akademy, 1983), p. 11.

27. Azariah, M. "The Un-Christian Side of the Indian Church: The Plight of the Untouchable Converts," (Bangalore: Dalit Sahitya Akademy, 1985), p. 17.

28. Kappen, Sebastian, *Jesus and Freedom*, (Maryknoll: Orbis Books, 1977), p. 143.

29. Ibid., p. 74.

30. Ibid., p. 79.

31. Ibid., p. 151.

32. Ibid., p. 143.

33. Geervarghese Mar Osthathios, *The Sin of Being Rich in a Poor World*, (Madras: Christian Literature Society, 1983), p. 4.

34. Azariah, M. "The Un-Christian Side of the Indian Church," p. 10.

35. This harsh-sounding judgment is based on twelve years of observation and experience, as well as candid evaluation by responsible Christian leaders in India. There is little tangible difference between the "evangelicals" and the supposedly "non-evangelical" ecumenicals.

36. Kappen, Sebastian, *Jesus and Freedom*, p. 180.

37. Ibid., p. 92.

38. John Paul II, "You are Called to Bear Witness to the Gospel," *Proclaim* (Bulletin of the Pontifical Mission Organizations, Bangalore) 7/3 (March, 1986), p. 5-7.

39. Diel, Domingo Jr., "An Asian Theology of Mission and Evangelism," p. 224.

40. Moltmann, Jurgen, *Theology and Joy*, p. 50.

41. Jeremias, Joachim, *New Testament Theology*, (New York: Charles Schribner's Sons, 1971), p. 222.

42. DuBose, Francis M., *God Who Sends*, (Nashville: Broadman Press, 1983), p. 155.

43. Panikker, R., "Philosophy and Revolution: the Text, the Context, and the Texture." *Philosophy East and West*, 23/3 (July, 1973), p. 215.

44. Vijnananda, Swami, "What is Religion?" *Prabuddha Bharata*, 77/7 (July, 1972), p. 299.

45. Ibid., p. 301.

46. Ibid., p. 305.

47. Kraemer, Hendrik, *The Christian Message in a Non-Christian World*, (Grand Rapids: Kregel, 1961), p. 126.

48. Ibid., p. 113.

49. Kung, Hans, *Freedom Today*, (New York: Sheed and Ward, 1966), p. 140.

50. Ibid., p. 139.

51. Ibid., p. 140.

52. Ibid., p. 144.

53. Kung, Hans, *On Being a Christian*, (New York: Doubleday and Co., 1976), pp. 114, 174.

54. Neuner, Joseph, "No Monopoly in Promoting Freedom" in Schillebeeckz, Edward, and van Iersel, Bas (eds.), *Jesus Christ and Human Freedom*, volume 3 of *Concilium -- Religion in the Seventies*, New Series, (New York: Herder and Herder, 1974), p. 33.

55. Ibid., p. 34.

56. Paton, David M. (ed.), *Breaking Barriers, Nairobi 1975*, (Geneva: World Council of Churches, 1976), pp. 35-37.

57. Neuner, Joseph, "No Monopoly in Promoting Freedom," p. 36.

58. Ibid., p. 37.

59. Ibid., p. 38.

60. Ibid., p. 39.

61. Ibid., p. 40.

62. Ibid., p. 41.

63. Arias, Mortimer, *Announcing the Reign of God*, (Philadelphia: Fortress Press, 1984), p. 89.

64. Ibid., p. 69.

65. Ibid., p. 112.

66. Ibid., p. 119.

67. Rayan, Samuel, "Evangelization and Development," in Anderson, Gerald H., and Stransky, Thomas (eds.), *Mission Trends No.2: Evangelization* (New York: Paulist

Press and Grand Rapids: Wm. B. Eerdmans Publ. Co., 1975), p. 104.

Ministering to Women in Mid-Life Transition: A Challenge to Evangelicals

Jim Conway

Today's mid-life woman is healthy, ambitious, educated, and has a new sense of who she is as a woman. She may have 20 to 30 very productive years ahead of her. She is not ready to rock herself through these next years pretending to be contented with her former roles.

Her great-grandmother had a life expectancy of 48 years. Today's mid-life woman will probably live into her eighties. The mid-life woman of today is radically different from her great-grandmother. We must understand this drastically changed woman and help her to realize the full utilization of her gifts that God intended.

In this article we will look at various aspects of a woman's development and at the attitudes of Christ and others toward women. This article is an appeal for recognition and freedom for the mid-life woman, an appeal for Bible-believing people to allow the mid-life woman a fuller role in the planning, ministry and outreach of the local church.

The Development of Adults

The study of adult development is a rather new phenomenon. Before the late 1920s, it was generally assumed that adults could not learn or change after their early twenties. In 1928 Thorndike[1] shocked the educational world with his studies of adults in their thirties. He discovered that they were capable of learning.

Charlotte Buhler[2] was one of the early researchers looking at the process of adult development (1939). Erikson (1950),[3] Havighurst (1953),[4] Neugarten (1964),[5] and a host of others in the late 60s through the mid- 80s have expanded the research and study of adult development and learning from both an educational and psychological point of view.

Research has resulted in the adult era being divided into many sub-periods. The adult era, which had been previously considered very stable, has important times of change. These times of change help to identify the different adult periods. A large group of researchers and writers, such as Knox,[6] Levinson,[7] Gould,[8] Lowenthal,[9] and many others, have helped more precisely to delineate these adult stages.

It is now commonly accepted that there is a young adult era, a mid-life era, and an aging era; but each of these broad stages has also been more finely divided. For example, in the young adult era of 18-34, there are major differences between the early 20s, the late 20s, and the early 30s.

Mid-life, roughly age 35-55, also has several sub-stages. The mid-30s male, who quite often is an aggressive, single-focused individual trying to make his mark in the world, is very different from the early 40s male who is now wondering what life is all about and which values and lifestyles he should change. The 50s man is different from both groups. He more classically fits Erikson's classification of "generative." He is more mellow, more willing to invest himself in the lives of younger people.

The mid-life woman also has distinctly different stages during her middle years, and these distinct periods do not necessarily coincide with what is happening in men during their middle years. The church, as well as educational and psychological groups, has tended to define women's stages as being the same as men's stages.

We have assumed that women think and respond to life in the same way and at the same time as do men. Perhaps we erroneously believe that women are the same as men, because until recent years much of the research in theological and educational circles has been done by men. It is difficult, perhaps even impossible, for a man to think as a woman.

A mid-life woman in her mid-30s and early 40s is experiencing the beginning of the empty nest, the absentee husband consumed by his career goals, and her own sense of cultural displacement as society begins to classify her as no longer "young and beautiful." The sense of loss that she is experiencing in many areas of her life causes her to reassess her life values. The Christian woman may ask, "What do the church, the Scriptures, and God have to say to me in this new era of my life?"

The evangelical or fundamentalist church is often not making a positive statement about the worth, value, and contribution of women to society or to the body of Christ. Women are relegated to being mothers, homemakers, bakers-of-cookies for church parties, and communion-glass-washers. Women's input into ministry direction and emphasis is often ignored.

The Biblical Basis of Relationships

In order to understand the mid-life woman of today we need to look at Creation and see God's perspective on women. One of the results of the Fall was the sharp distinction that rapidly developed between men and women. The Bible says before the Fall:

> So God created man in his own image, in the image of God he created him; male and female he created them. God blessed them and said to them, "Be fruitful and increase in number; fill the earth and subdue it. Rule over the fish of the sea and the birds of the air and over every living creature that moves on the ground."[10]

In Genesis 1 there is no distinction between men and women for authority or responsibility. God created both in his image. In fact, God's image in humankind was not complete until he had made both male and female. In the centuries following the Fall the outworking of the fallen condition of men and women is evident. It is expressed in damaged interpersonal relationships, which have become exploitive rather than mutually nourishing as God had intended.[11]

Genesis 2:18 says, "The Lord God said, 'It is not good for the man to be alone. I will make a helper suitable for him.'" The words "suitable for him" are probably better translated "corresponding to him." The woman is not a cute little geisha girl who waits on Adam hand and foot and provides the opportunity for his ego needs to be met through male dominance. Rather, she is an equal, a companion, a person who is different, yet not his inferior.

"Helper" in our Western culture usually denotes a person of lesser power, influence, or capability. We seldom think of the term as referring to someone who is equal or superior. "Helper" in our twentieth century context is the waterboy on the baseball team, the plumber's trainee, Mommy's little helper. A helper is an inferior person, who must be supervised because he/she does not have the experience or the authority to be self-directed.

The word "helper" is used 21 times in the Old Testament. Sixteen times it refers to one who is greater than the person being helped. Frequently, God himself is the helper, as in Psalm 54:4, "Surely, God is my help; . . ." There is no instance in the Old Testament where "helper" refers to a person who is inferior to the person being helped. Unfortunately, we load up this word "helper" in Genesis 2:18 with our authoritarian Western concepts. We impute to all women the qualities of inferiority, incompetence, inequality, and we generally assume that women must be led by the superior being, the male.

In Genesis 2:18, God for the first time says of his creation that something is *not* good, "It is not good for the man to be alone. . ." Adam was created with the need for relationships. Without another human with whom to communicate, Adam was incomplete, and it was on this basis that God said the situation was *not* good. People are created with relational needs. No person is complete alone.

An unconscious conviction of many men is that they are complete within themselves. They do not need anyone else, least of all the insights and perspectives of a woman. This male arrogance is a direct violation of God's creation. God did not create another man to be in relationship with Adam; he created a woman. She was not merely created for reproduction and the continuation of the race, but to meet the aloneness need of Adam and to give a perspective on life that was female.

Genesis 3 relates the sad account of the Fall. In the first glimpses of the male-female conflict, Adam blames Eve for his violation of God's will. God then outlines what the results of the Fall will mean for their experience in the world and with each other. It is interesting to notice that God predicts the domination of men over women when he says, "And he will rule over you."[12] This is a predictive statement and not a command; God is not the author of the evil of male dominance.

Husbands and wives were intended by God to be companions, to meet the aloneness need of each other; but, instead, they have become competitors, often driving each other into a deeper sense of aloneness. The message of the New Testament is a message of equality in Jesus Christ and of restored relationships. Redemption through Christ means that relationships between God and believers, men and women, husbands and wives, parents and children, can be relationships of companionship similar to that which was experienced by Adam and Eve and God before the Fall.

The History of the Treatment of Women

Women have not fared well in most religious systems and cultures around the world. Sayings about women attributed to Buddha include: "Women are evil, jealous and stupid;" "Avoid the sight of them;" "Do not speak to them."[13]

Women were treated no better under Hinduism. A woman was thought to have no soul. It was a sin for a woman to read the Vedas, the holy scriptures. If a Brahman is reading the Vedas and a woman walks by, he must stop reading them. "In Hinduism, to be born a woman was regarded as evidence of some failure in the previous life."[14]

Women did not fare much better under the Muslim religious system. A sign commonly posted outside a mosque was "Women, dogs, and other impure animals not permitted."[15]

The Talmud, the Jewish law book, said, "Blessed be God who has not made me to be a heathen, a slave, a woman." The Apocrypha said, "A man's wickedness is better than a beneficent woman."[16]

The Greek and Roman world was not much better. It was common in those cultures for the wife to be the servant. She certainly never ate with her husband when there were guests in the home.

The Greek poet, Hipponax, is supposed to have said, "It's hard to get a wife who will bring a good dowry and then do all the work" and "Only two days that your wife gives you pleasure, the day you marry her and the day you bury her."[17]

Jesus' intrusion into the world was a radical departure from the cultures of his day. He treated women with respect, gave them responsibilities, and included them in his entourage.

The dramatically different status of women promoted by Christ and in the New Testament was, however, only shortly lived. Within a few years, even in the Christian communities, much of the liberty granted to women in the New Testament was eroded away as men dominated the church and wrote the rules. For example, the teaching about marriage has largely been passed down by a celibate priesthood who essentially believed that sex was evil and that women were inferior.

Thomas Aquinas, the father of medieval theology, said, "As regards the individual nature, woman is defective and misbegotten, for the active force in the male seed tends to the production of a perfect likeness in the masculine sex; while the production of women comes from a defect in the active force or from some material indisposition . . ."[18] Aquinas is also attributed to have said, "Nothing so casts down the manly mind from its height as the fondling of a woman."[19]

In the mid-1980s we think our world is rather enlightened, but Wolfgang Mider's *New Encyclopedia of World Proverbs* published in 1986 with 18,000 human proverbs from around the world shows that women are still viewed negatively. Some of these proverbs are: "To educate a woman is like placing a knife in the hands of a monkey;" "he who listens to the words of a woman will be accounted worthless;" and "a woman has long hair but short brains."

Two thousand years have passed since the liberating words of Christ and we have not seen much impact in bringing about a respect for women. They are often viewed as necessary evils, things to be tolerated, not as persons who make a positive contribution in society, to the lives of men, or to the church.

The Current Evangelical View of Women

There are a number of statements, inferences, or common assumptions that are widely held as truisms among evangelical or fundamentalist groups. They are repeated or inferred so frequently that, tragically, people begin to believe them.

1. *All women are to be submissive to all men.* This false concept is often built by inference from the husband and wife relationship outlined in Ephesians 5. Because the wife is directed to be submissive to her husband, it is inferred that *all* women are to be submissive to *all* men, which is not true. The submission spoken of in the Scripture is directed to a *married* woman who is to be submissive *only* to her *own* husband. It is not directed to *all* women, instructing them to be submissive to *all* men.

2. *Wives are to be submissive to their husbands, but husbands are not to be submissive to their wives.* This false idea is based on Ephesians 5:22 and is usually discussed while totally ignoring the truth of equal submission taught in verse 21.

A basic principle of scriptural interpretation is that verses are not to be lifted out of context. Verse 21 -- "Submit to one another" -- is the basic teaching; the verses that follow are merely elaborations concerning how that teaching is to be carried out. Nowhere in Ephesians 5 is the husband absolved from submitting to his wife. Nor does Ephesians 5 give the husband the position of "boss."

3. *Women are to exercise their spiritual gifts (especially those which include staying barefoot, pregnant, and in the kitchen).* Ephesians 4:7 and I Corinthians 12:7 tell us that God gives gifts to every person in the body of Christ, and God expects these gifts to be used. We must realize that women are not given merely inferior or non-leadership gifts. Leadership is not reserved only for men. Remember, it is men who have translated and interpreted the Scriptures to us. They see the words of the Scripture through the screens of their male eyes.

4. *Women are not to exercise the gift of teaching or exhorting men.* This false "truism" is taught by massive numbers of evangelical and fundamentalist leaders. Women are not allowed to teach classes where there are men. They are also excluded from teaching in the pulpit, serving on major leadership boards and committees in the church, and holding positions such as elder, deacon, or pastor.

Is it strange that the same church that will not allow a woman to teach men will allow women to teach boys. When does a boy become a man? Can a woman still teach him if he is 17 or 18?

Even more difficult to understand is the church which restricts a woman from full service in her local church but supports a woman missionary overseas. Her job may be to reduce the language to written form, translate the Scripture, start Bible study groups with men and women, and lead men, women, and children to Jesus Christ. She then disciples these new believers into the total Christian life. In short, she is involved in the full role of pastor and discipler. Yet, when the woman missionary comes home, she is not allowed to speak from the pulpit because she would now be "teaching men."

5. *God's order for the church, the family, and society is the chain of command.* This doctrine erroneously holds that women are to be unquestionably subservient to their husbands and that children until death are to obey absolutely their parents. The chain of command philosophy has

resulted in women being put under the thumb of their "boss" husband and ignores the clear teaching of mutual submission found in Ephesians 5:21.

Jesus' Radical View of Women

The general method of Jesus' teaching included the use of parables. These illustrations do not exclude women. They were equally applicable to males and females. Jesus gave as many parables using women as examples as he did using men.

It is not recorded that on any occasion in his public ministry he taught that women were second class nor did he state that the woman's place was only in the home. Jesus never told Mary and Martha they needed to be married nor did he rebuke mothers who were present at the feeding of the thousands.

Matthew 12:46-50 and Mark 3:31-35 are records of people telling Jesus that his family was outside asking for him. He responded by asking, in essence, who is my family? They are the ones who do my Father's will. "For whoever does the will of my Father in heaven is my brother, and sister and mother." He did not merely use the word "brother" as a generic term meaning people, but he specifically used additional words to show the inclusion of "sister" and "mother" on an equal basis.

Mary, the mother of Jesus, is an example of God's trust of women. Comparing the Matthew and Luke accounts of the angel speaking to Joseph and Mary, we see that the angel spoke to Mary first. She was the first person to know that God was at this time going to introduce his Son into the world.[20] The angel came to Joseph after "she was found to be with child through the Holy Spirit."[21] Mary was not an uninformed, ignorant woman. She was aware of what God was going to do in her life.

When Mary entered the home of Elizabeth, the baby in Elizabeth's womb, John the Baptist, leaped when he heard Mary's voice. Then Elizabeth was filled with the Holy Spirit and made a profound prophetic statement. God trusted these women.[22] God's attitude toward us is, "There is neither

Jew nor Greek, slave nor free, male nor female, for you are all one in Christ Jesus."[23]

Christ's contacts with Mary and Martha exemplify Jesus' attitude toward women. Mary was allowed to sit at his feet and to receive his teaching just the same as all the other disciples.

Martha creates a problem for pastors who hold a low view of women. She is criticized by pastors for not spending time at the feet of Jesus as Mary did, and yet she was busy doing the "homemaking things" encouraged by many evangelical leaders. Sometimes pastors forget that Mary was being discipled on an equal basis with men who were present.

Martha, on the other hand, is frequently overlooked in the account of the raising of Lazarus. Jesus spoke directly to her, giving her one of the fullest statements to date of himself: "I am the resurrection and the life. He who believes in me will live."[24] She responded by saying, "Yes, Lord,...I believe that you are the Christ, the Son of God."[25]

The Easter morning revelations were given to both men and women, but the revelation came first to the women. The point is not that women are superior; the point is that Jesus did not exclude women. In fact, it was so common for women to be included in the ministry of Christ that when the 120 were praying and waiting for the coming of the Holy Spirit, Scripture records, "They all joined together constantly in prayer, along with the women and Mary the mother of Jesus, and his brothers."[26] Acts 2 continues, "When the day of Pentecost came, they were all together in one place."[27] . . "All of them were filled with the Holy Spirit and began to speak in other tongues."[28]

A revolution had taken place on behalf of women with the coming of Christ into the world. Women who were previously treated as possessions, servants, things, were now elevated to equals with men. They were equals in standing before God in ministry, equals who could be trusted with revelation, and equals who could prophesy. The New Testament church did not seem to blink an eye. They continued the radical new direction for women.

Comparing the rapid, radical social change that took place on behalf of women with the coming of Christ, we see that

Jesus and the church were light years ahead of their culture. The church today in its attitude toward women is, in fact, behind the New Testament. We are less open than the radical teachings of Jesus.

Research on the Church's Effectiveness in Ministering to Mid-Life Women

For more than ten years my wife and I have carried out several research studies on men and women at mid- life. Our research has yielded certain significant findings concerning women.

In one of our national studies of 373 evangelical mid-life women, 41.4% said they were experiencing a moderate to severe mid-life reassessment time called a mid-life crisis.[29] The age identified for mid-life crisis was the late 30s and early 40s, approximately ten years earlier than the stresses associated with menopause.

These mid-life evangelical women identified twelve causes for mid-life crisis and were then asked to identify resources that had been helpful in the reduction of their stress during mid-life. Sixteen different resources were pinpointed as important in helping women work through mid-life stress.

Across the top of Tables 1a and 1b are listed twelve of the contributing causes to mid-life crisis. These include low satisfaction with work, fear of growing older, problems with raising children, problems in marriage, low self-esteem, financial pressure, feeling unattractive, husband's affair, menopausal stress, divorce, general restlessness and confusion, and problems with aging parents.

The items listed at the left-hand side of the tables are the helpful resources women identified. These include talking with close friends, discussion with relatives, being alone and thinking, attending a seminar, professional counseling, personal prayer, small group support, listening to a sermon, reading the Bible, taking a class at a local high school, taking a class at a college or university, attending a retreat, attending a church service, listening to a radio or TV program, reading a book or magazine, and attending church school.

The items listed in **bold type** in the left-hand column of the tables are resources commonly supplied or encouraged by the local church: prayer, Bible reading, seminars, small groups, retreats, church services, church school and sermons.

The data in the tables are correlations between problems causing mid-life crisis which are listed across the top of the tables and helpful resources listed along the left-hand side. It is especially important to notice the numbers in **bold** type. These indicate either a strong positive or negative relationship between items on the table. For example, sermons are correlated negatively with low satisfaction at work, which means that sermons tend to have a negative relationship to a woman who is struggling with low satisfaction in her work or career. On the other hand, sermons have a positive correlation for women who are struggling with menopausal problems, and a very positive relationship for women who have been divorced or are working through restlessness.

The tables can be used in another direction. For any problem listed across the top, look down the column to see which items have been identified by the women as important resources for helping them during this stressful mid-life era.

If a woman is struggling with her husband's affair, feeling unattractive, or having financial problems, the church is essentially unhelpful. If a woman is struggling with low self-esteem, the church is counterproductive. The same is true of the woman who is struggling with a sense of low satisfaction at work. She actually feels worse because of church ministries.

The tables can help people who minister to mid- life women to use frequently the resources that have been identified by women as helpful, as well as to identify the areas where the church appears to be counterproductive. Other statistics (multiple regression) generated by this study identified professional counseling and secular education outside of the church as more positively correlated to the stresses of women during the middle years than the ministries of the church.

Suggestions for a More Effective Ministry to Mid-Life Women

Perhaps the question we need to ask is, "How must the church change in order to minister more effectively to mid-life women?" Some of the following considerations may help.

1. *Eliminate male bias.* The programs and ministries of the church are basically male-dominated. As a result, the male approach to life, interpretation of Scripture, and thought patterns control what will be done for people and how it will be done.

An example of this bias is Romans 16:1-2, "I commend to you our sister Phoebe, a servant of the church in Cenchrea; . . ." The word translated by many translations is the same word used by Paul 22 times in the New Testament. Eighteen times it is translated "minister," three times it is translated "deacon," but only here is it translated "servant." The other passages all refer to men but this passage refers to a woman. Did God intend some kind of stepped-down interpretation?

It is important to point out that the word can legitimately be translated as "servant." But the question is, why was it translated servant only when referring to a woman? The same word was used for Epaphras, Timothy, Apollos, and Paul himself.

Another example of the male bias is seen in verse 2, "I ask you to receive her in the Lord in a way worthy of the saints and to give her any help she may need from you, for she has been a great help to many people, including me." This verse also speaks of Phoebe who was called a "servant" in verse 1 instead of "minister" or "deacon." Now she is referred to as a "great help." The word here clearly means "one who presides."

Unfortunately, "great help" is ascribed to Phoebe, but the same word is used in Romans 12:8, I Timothy 5:12, I Timothy 3:4 to refer to a leadership position of ruling. Why would this reduction of title and authority be put in the translation? Part of the answer seems to lie in male bias, either unconscious or overt.

The problem becomes even greater when we realize that the last part of verse 2 also says that Phoebe had been a "great help to" Paul himself. Is there a suggestion here that Paul had allowed himself to be under her authority at some time in his ministry? Or is that thought unthinkable?

Is it really unthinkable? Jesus taught mutual submission and accountability. Each person was to serve the other.

Many males tend to view themselves as the norm, the center of the universe, and women as abnormal. God designed women to make a unique contribution to men. He created men and women incomplete. They both need the unique contribution of the other. Men say, "If women would just straighten up and be more male-like, things would be OK." If men are going to minister more effectively to women, they must begin to listen to women and begin to think as women think. They must incorporate her approach to life, to the Scriptures and to people as an equal and significant part of church ministry.

2. *Specifically study women's concerns.* The church is still assuming that mid-life women are basically mothers. But by mid-life, women have completed the mothering job. They need a new challenge in life. They are looking to the church, but the church is saying, "Stay home and be a good wife and mother." This is an inappropriate challenge for mid-life evangelical women. Studies repeatedly show that the women with the highest degree of depression are the women who are following a mother-only role. The women with the least amount of depression are those who have combined marriage, parenting, and career.[30] The mid-life woman has 20 to 30 productive years ahead. She is more self-assured and assertive. She does not want to be patronized. She wants a significant challenge and opportunity to serve.

The mid-life woman is extremely perceptive. She knows when she is being talked down to. She understands when her pastor says, "Yes, God has gifted everyone in the body of Christ, but women's gifts tend to fall more in line with homemaking responsibilities, like Martha." Women have been so convinced by the church that it is God's plan for them to be second-class citizens that most of the time they never resist.

Women must be valued on an equal basis with men. Their contributions are important. Women need to be encouraged to share their perceptions and understanding of the Scriptures. Women think differently from men. Important nuances and shades of meaning will come to life as we allow the other half of the body of Christ to contribute their insights from the Holy Spirit filtered through their female approach to life. It is not enough for a pastor to say, "I want to understand you." He must go further to say, "I want to understand you because if I don't understand you, then I have less of God's truth."

The woman's contribution is not an optional accessory like a compact disc player for a car. She is a crucial and integral part, such as the frame is to the car. Without those parts, there is no car, and without women fully contributing in the body of Christ, the church is distorted and we labor with a less than complete interpretation of the Scriptures, of God and of methods of ministry.

Some men fear that granting women full status in the body of Christ might threaten their position. Some feel they have too much at stake. I have been a pastor for almost thirty years and a seminary professor for five more years. As I have understood women and allowed them to contribute fully, I have not found them exploiting me. Rather, I have discovered the opposite. They encourage and build me up. The more I have recognized women, the more they have been able to exercise freely their gifts without hostility and suspicion, and the greater their respect has been for me. Men have nothing to fear, only enrichment to enjoy.

3. *Become more relational.* Men like ideas; women like relationships. If we are truly seeking to minister to women, our ministries must be slanted toward relationships and less toward cognitive thinking. Men feel they have resolved the problem if they have shared an idea with someone. It is true that the idea is important, but for an idea to have an effective impact in the life of a woman, it frequently needs to be couched in a relationship.

It is not enough for a woman to know that statistics show she is going to survive the emptying of her nest. It is not even enough to know that God cares for her in all the experiences of life. She also needs skin wrapped around those promises and ideas. She needs people who will pray with her, who will let her express loneliness, who are not embarrassed to hug her, and who can lift her spirits by expressing their love for her.

Our model is not our culture nor the male perception of life. Our model is Jesus himself. Jesus did not simply move from event to event or place to place through his ministry -- he moved from person to person. The gospels are an account of Jesus' interaction with people.

It is difficult to change our minds. A male with a vested interest in his position and pride may find change even more difficult. I urge such men to interact with their wives or with a group of women in the church concerning this article. Encourage them to identify the important issues that men and women in the body of Christ need to confront together, so that women today can become full partners in the church and in the world.

Table 1a. **Relationships Between Contributing Factors of Mid-Life Crisis with Learning Resources for Women Between Age 34-45**

	Work	Aging	Child	Marriage	Esteem	Financial
Friend	-.08	.12	.23+	-.06	-.03	.18
Relative	.21+	.09	.08	-.08	.07	.29*
Thinking	-.02	-.20	-.00	.04	-.11	-.14
Seminar	-.08	-.14	.15	-.13	.08	-.09
Counsel	-.18	-.27*	-.08	.37***	.19	-.10
Prayer	**-.26***	**-.26***	.07	-.16	**-.27***	.11
Sm Group	.03	.01	**.24+**	**-.23+**	.01	-.06
Sermons	**-.31***	-.17	.21	.03	.12	-.04
Bible	**-.22+**	-.19	-.10	-.05	-.08	.05
HS Class	-.06	-.09	.07	.26+	-.04	-.32*
College	.10	.26+	-.06	.05	.14	-.04
Retreat	-.10	.13	**.31***	-.21	.08	.14
Ch Serv	-.24+	-.15	.16	**-.23+**	.01	.20
Radio/TV	.05	.21	.01	.05	.29*	.36***
Book/Mag	-.16	-.07	-.10	.14	.27*	-.05
Ch School	-.04	-.03	.24	**-.23+**	-.03	.15

Table 1b. **Relationships Between Contributing Factors of Mid-Life Crisis with Learning Resources for Women Between Age 34-45**

	Unattrac-tive	H Affr	Meno	Divorce	Restless	Parents
Friend	.10	-.28*	.16	-.11	.11	.18
Relatives	.11	.13	-.16	.15	.22+	.01
Thinking	-.03	.08	-.08	-.05	.08	-.16
Seminar	-.16	-.19	.14	-.00	.11	.09
Counsel	-.05	.24+	-.09	.19	.10	-.15
Prayer	-.13	.11	.07	.19	-.10	.02
Sm Group	.08	-.04	.14	-.05	.13	.13
Sermons	.09	.15	**.27***	**.35*****	**.24+**	.12
Bible	-.02	.14	.20	.11	-.10	.09
HS Class	-.13	.24+	.06	.55***	.00	-.17
College	.09	.04	.11	.26+	.42***	.07
Retreat	.07	-.19	**.25+**	-.15	.09	**.48*****
Ch Serv	.07	.07	**.35****	**.31***	.11	**.22+**
Radio/TV	.17	-.07	.19	.02	.19	.19
Book/Mag	.27*	.23+	.07	-.14	.07	-.18
Ch School	.14	.10	**.23+**	**.24+**	.01	.02

+ $P < .10$
* $P < .05$
** $P < .01$
*** $P < .005$

Notes

1. Edward Thorndike, *Adult Learning* (New York: Macmillan Company, 1928).
2. Charlotte B. Buhler (Malchowski), Edeltrud Baar, Lotte Danzinger-Schenk, Gertrud Falk, and others, *The Child and His Family*, (New York: Harper, 1939).
3. Erik Erikson, *Childhood and Society* (New York: W. W. Norton and Company, Inc., 1950).

4. Robert Havighurst and Ruth Albrecht, *Older People* (New York: David McKay Company, 1953).
5. Bernice Neugarten, ed., *Personality in Middle and Late Life* (New York: Atherton Press, 1964).
6. Alan B. Knox, *Adult Development and Learning* (San Francisco: Jossey-Bass Inc., Pub., 1977).
7. Daniel J. Levinson, *Seasons of a Man's Life* (New York: Alfred A. Knopf, Inc.,1978).
8. Roger Gould, *Transformations* (New York: Simon and Schuster, Inc., 1978).
9. Marjorie Lowenthal, Majda Thurner, and David Chiriboga, *Four Stages of Life* (San Franscisco: Jossey-Bass Inc., Pub., 1975), pp. 49-50.
10. Genesis 1:27-28.
11. Genesis 2:18-25.
12. Genesis 3:16.
13. Dorothy R. Pape, *In Search of God's Ideal Woman*, (Downers Grove, IL: InterVarsity Press, 1976), p. 24.
14. Ibid, p. 24-25.
15. Kathleen Storrie, "Women, Dogs, and Other Impure Animals," *HIS* 38:8 (May 1978):17-20.
16. Russell C. Prohl, *Woman in the Church* (Grand Rapids, MI: William B. Eerdmans Publishing Company, 1957).
17. Ibid.
18. Susan G. Bell, *Women from the Greeks to the French Revolution* (Belmont, CA: Wadsworth Publishing Company, Inc., 1973), p. 122.
19. Vern L. Bullough and Bonnie Bullough, *The Subordinate Sex* (New York: Penguin Books, Inc., 1974), p. 174.
20. Luke 1:35.
21. Matthew 1:18.
22. Luke 1:42, 43, 45.
23. Galatians 3:28.
24. John 11:25-26.
25. John 11:27.
26. Acts 1:14.
27. Acts 2:1.
28. Acts 2:4.

29. Jim Conway, "Early Mid-Life Women: A Study of Self-Reported Mid-Life Crisis Among Religious Women Age 34-45 and Their Likelihood to Participate in Learning Experiences," Doctoral dissertation, University of Illinois, 1986.

30. Judith Abelew Birnbaum, "Life Patterns and Self-Esteem in Gifted Family-Oriented and Career-Committed Women," in *Women and Achievement* by Martha Tamara Shuch Mednick, Sandra Schwartz Tangri, and Lois Wladis Hoffman, eds. (New York: John Wiley and Sons, Inc., 1975), p. 418, and Pauline B. Bart, "Depression in Middle-Aged Women," in *Women in Sexist Society*, Vivian Gornick and Barbara Moran, eds. (New York: Basic Books, Inc., 1971), p. 110.

When It's Time to Confront

Marshall Shelley

The intertestamental book, Bel and the Dragon, describes a confrontation between Daniel and a great living dragon the Babylonians revered. When Daniel was pressured to bow before the monster, he said to the king, "If you will give me permission, I will slay the dragon without sword or club." The king agreed.

As verse 27 relates, "Then Daniel took pitch, fat, and hair, and boiled them together and made cakes, which he fed to the dragon. The dragon ate them, and burst open."

That's one kind of effective confrontation. Unfortunately, it's an approach that probably should not be used with dragons in the church. Unlike Daniel or Saint George, the goal of a pastor is not to slay but to tame the beast, to prevent further destruction on either side.

Such work is rarely easy, never fun, but it is possible. Before looking at the important elements of effective confrontation, we must clarify what dragon taming is *not*.

It is not suppressing differences of opinion. These are inevitable and even desirable -- one person's insights balance another's quirks. The church is stronger when its unity comes out of diversity, when the body of Christ is more than birds of a feather flocking together. Unless the differing opinions are outright heresy or vitriol, they need not be feared.

Controlled friction produces energy, and energy is essential for creativity and effectiveness in church life. Different ideas should be allowed to coexist and God allowed to take the lead, thereby raising one opinion to prominence. A person is not a dragon because of different ideas, but because of destructive actions.

Neither is confrontation the silencing of all complainers. Chronic complainers need to be deflected, not destroyed. Most gripers are low-octane hostiles who merely like to share their misery. Generally they're not destructive, unless they're given the spotlight or made into martyrs. While their complaints aren't pleasant to hear, remember that complainers are rarely leaders themselves; their gripes are usually a symptom of their sense of powerlessness.

How do you handle complainers? Not by arguing -- they're rarely willing to be convinced -- but by letting them know there are other ways of looking at the situation. "You think Fred's solo was rotten? That's interesting, I enjoy that kind of medley now and then."

On the other hand, taming dragons is not giving in, becoming a doormat, appeasing them so they won't spew their wrath throughout the church. Simply because leaders are servants doesn't mean they must passively accept injustice or ignore threats to the body. Just a few sentences after writing those lofty verses on imitating Christ's humility and servanthood in Philippians 2, Paul warns, "Watch out for those dogs, those men who do evil, those mutilators of the flesh" (3:2). Hardly kind words, but the words of a servant dedicated to protecting his Father's house.

What then is dragon taming? What is the point of any confrontation? Not stifling people's ideas but protecting the church from those *acting* in destructive ways. In that effort, the right attitude, atmosphere, and approach are essential.

The Attitude in Confronting

Often the greatest damage is not done by the dragons themselves but by the overreactions they provoke in others. When attacked by dragons, our normal response is to become upset or defensive, and when we feel threatened, we usually wind up dousing the fire with gasoline.

In most disputes neither side is entirely innocent. And even if our cause is completely right, we lose if we respond wrongly. The situation only gets worse.

The confrontation of dragons has to be carried out in love -- smart love. "Always view the other person as a child of

God like yourself," said one Arizona pastor. That is, of course, easier said than done.

The trick is to accept dragons as persons of worth while not approving of their controlling tactics. It means trying to maintain an open relationship and keeping it current. Knowing what's going on in the lives of difficult members often proves helpful. Smart love also means trying to see the church and its perceived problems from their viewpoint.

One pastor resisted his impulse to ignore a young man who openly criticized him for moving too slowly to establish a small-group ministry. Instead, he spent time with the young man and discovered his doctors had recently found malignant cells in his blood. Suddenly he understood the young man's impatience and desire for community.

Pastors have discovered several helpful keys in establishing the right kind of attitude for dragon confrontation. First, as early in the conflict as possible, someone must verbalize what Norm Shawchuck, in *How to Manage Conflict in the Church*, has called the three P's of conflict management:

Permission: Everyone involved must be told that disagreements are OK. No one should feel guilty about offering a dissenting view.

Potency: Each person must be allowed to state one's position with strength and clarity. There's nothing unhealthy about airing feelings as long as we respect one another.

Protection: No one will be intentionally hurt, nor will anyone be allowed to inflict needless hurt.

Unless these ground rules are openly stated, conflicts will often be prolonged as people avoid the real issues, until they feel secure enough to speak up without risking irreparable damage to the church or themselves.

Second, if possible, *reframe the dragons*. The natural response when under attack is to put up defenses, if not visibly, at least emotionally. We're hurt, and like any injury, our hurt makes us more sensitive to the slightest pressure. Things that before wouldn't have bothered us now make us recoil. Reframing how we see the dragons can help keep us from overreacting.

One Sunday when Howard Warren stepped into the pulpit, his glance fell upon the Millers in the fifth row, Mike on one end, Erika on the other, and four kids in between. Suddenly Howard found his mouth dry, he couldn't seem to breathe, and he couldn't remember what he'd intended to say.

The Millers were irregular attenders, but they had started a Bible study in their home and were teaching some things in direct conflict with the church's statement of faith. Howard had had some bad experiences with outside groups preying on church people in the past, and he feared the Millers would make their way through the congregation spreading unrest if not outright heresy.

Something had to be done. He didn't know what he was going to say, but he had made an appointment to visit the Miller home Tuesday evening. He wasn't looking forward to the encounter.

He managed to get through his sermon, but his delivery was rough, disjointed. He doubted if many people sensed his discomfort, but he knew he wasn't getting through.

Afterward Jeff Duncan, the youth pastor, came into the office and asked, "Was something bothering you today?"

"I was hoping it didn't show," Howard said. He told Jeff about his dread of confronting the Millers. "I looked at them in the pew, and all I saw was two lions on either side of the path. I felt like they were going to devour me, and if not me, then everything else in the church."

"Don't look at them as lions," Jeff said. "Look at them as wounded sheep."

The simple difference worked. In a moment, Howard's fear was gone. "I've never taken them out of that frame," he says now, three years later. "Jeff's observation was true, not that the Millers' lives were in disarray, but they had come through some difficult times and needed to be encouraged. I assumed they were wounded sheep, I loved them, and when we talked about the Bible study, they happily agreed not to teach those doctrines."

The Millers have joined the church, and Howard Warren enjoys a growing relationship with them. Reframing doesn't change the dragons, but it can change the way we treat them. And sometimes that's enough.

Third, *pray not only about, but for the dragons*. It's easier to publicize foibles and faults than to pray for them. But when you genuinely pray *for* the person hurting you, a whole new dimension enters.

Samuel offers a marvelous model. He had been the God-appointed judge and unquestioned leader of Israel, but when he was old, the people turned against him demanding a king instead. Samuel tried to dissuade them. But when they insisted, he didn't resign or shake his fist or whine over his blemished career. Instead he said, "For the sake of his great name, the Lord will not reject his people, because the Lord was pleased to make you his own. As for me, far be it from me that I should sin against the Lord by failing to pray for you. And I will teach you the way that is good and right" (1 Sam. 12:22-23).

Even after his defeat in the "business meeting," Samuel recognized that God's people deserve prayer, simply because they are God's. How difficult it must have been to continue to pray and teach. But if he could do it for a nationful of obstinate dragons, might it be possible on behalf of a churchful?

Finally, *be gentle but firm* . If you're a church leader, the authority is on your side and people expect you to take the initiative.

This is particularly necessary with people who want to be the convicting voice of the Holy Spirit for other people's lives. One pastor was taken aside by a young man and told, "You're working in the wrong area. Your spiritual gift is evangelism, not church planting or nurture. You should be on the road as an evangelist."

After two or three of these jabs, the pastor was torn. Was he right? *Am I really doing what God wants me to do*? Because the young man was a sincere and committed worker, the pastor's emotional upheaval was even greater. After two months of self-doubt, the pastor finally said, "I've listened to your advice, and I appreciate your input, but I cannot accept it. It has caused confusion in my life that didn't exist before you spoke, and I don't think God wants us to continue in confusion. If God wanted me to change ministries, he'd probably tell me, wouldn't you think? Especially after you sensitized me to the issue."

The young man accepted the pastor's judgment. He apologized for being so forward and putting the pastor through two months of turmoil. This rather harmless dragon was tamed largely because of the respectful but firm way he was approached by the pastor.

A tougher situation is when certain church members are devoted to a national religious figure who has different views from the pastor. They want the church's teaching, vocabulary, and style to parallel that of the prominent personality. How can a pastor who speaks to hundreds dare disagree with someone who speaks to hundreds of thousands?

What is the best way to respond? "Attacking the views of the personality does *not* work," says a Nebraska pastor. "The moment you do that, you become the bad guy. You don't have the credibility to attack a 'hero of the faith.' Besides, I appreciate 95 percent of what the celebrity says; it's just the 5 percent and the way people want to apply it in our church that becomes divisive."

Again, a gentle but firm attitude is the best response. The direction and style of ministry are the responsibility of the pastor and board. In this situation, the battle to be fought is not over the particulars but over the authority and decision-making process in the church.

"The only thing that's worked for us is pointing out that as pastor, I, along with our board, have been given the responsibility for this congregation," says the Nebraska pastor. "When we hear them out but gently explain that we have to make hard decisions about what *our* church can do in *our* situation, they accept that more readily."

The spirit needed for confronting dragons is not one of fear and withdrawal nor of arrogant power. It is gentleness and firmness -- an attitude of smart love.

The Atmosphere for Confronting

The climate of any encounter with dragons can be an important factor in improving or damaging the relationship. A setting where no one is likely to lose face -- a private, unhurried conversation -- is most effective in restoring relationships. Two important aspects of creating the right atmosphere are timing and location.

The *timing* must be planned with an eye on the emotional barometer. Confrontations are usually precipitated by a particular experience that cannot be ignored, something that makes us say, "Now he's gone too far."

If we respond too quickly, while the emotional barometer still reads too high, both we and the dragon risk not being able to see all sides of the issue. The prophet Nathan waited a year after David's sin with Bathsheba before confronting the king. While it probably wasn't a case of Nathan needing to calm down, perhaps it took that long for David to be open to receive Nathan's accusation. On the other hand, if we wait too long, the unresolved situation can raise the frustration level until we lose emotional control.

"Before I confront anyone, I call a fellow pastor and talk through the situation," says an experienced minister. "That calms me down, helps me clarify the approach to take, and helps me get my motives straightened out."

The *location* of a meeting can also help or hinder the cause. Holding a meeting in the pastor's office gives a definite advantage, if we want to exert our authority, negotiate from strength, or exercise discipline. It is *our* turf -- our desk, our chair, our pictures, our calendar. We can control the seating, and unless there's a separate seating area, we'll probably be in the ultimate power position -- behind a desk. Most people who enter will feel they have entered our realm and grant us the right to set the agenda and take the initiative.

It's a good situation for a showdown, but probably not the place to build or restore a relationship. It makes many people feel defensive, insecure, unable to open up fully. A Lutheran pastor admitted the breakdown in a relationship with one man in the congregation was partially caused by an office conversation. The man had been overstating his position in church business meetings, and the pastor thought a gentle word about diplomacy would help. But the man misinterpreted the gesture and told his friends the pastor had "tried to silence me."

"I found out later this man had often been called in and reprimanded by his boss at work," says the pastor. "That's how he interpreted my action. Another setting would have helped."

A second option is neutral turf -- a restaurant, for instance. While not offering the home field advantage, it proves a better setting for building relationships or negotiating as equals. "I use several coffee shops that have a back table or quiet room where we can have a private conversation," says a Covenant Church pastor. "I always tell them I'm picking up the tab, and we make small talk until we place our orders. Then I bring up the issue we need to discuss. The neutral turf has almost always proven beneficial in working through differences."

A third option is meeting on the other person's home turf. Some pastors report this works best for first getting acquainted with newcomers or, in the case of dragons, when coming to them on their terms. This can be effective when we sense something is wrong and want to take the first step toward reconciliation, or when we need to apologize. In their own house or apartment, people are more likely to feel free to talk, to air their strong emotions. They feel more in control.

Many meetings, of course, are also held at the church -- in conference rooms around a table or in the sanctuary pews. These are usually attended by more than two or three people. Each location establishes its own atmosphere.

One principle, however, does seem to hold true whatever the room arrangement: If you anticipate problems from someone at the meeting, sit right next to that person, rather than across. It is very difficult to argue with someone when you're not in the traditional positions of confrontation. Breaking down the physical distance seems to chip away at the emotional distance. If you want a direct confrontation, however, sitting directly across from the person is the most effective arrangement.

These are all generalizations, of course, but when dealing with dragons, the nonverbal communication is important.

The Approach to Confronting

The procedure offered by Jesus in Matthew 18 for dealing with "your brother (who) sins against you" -- talking privately, meeting with witnesses, and finally telling it to the church -- is also a good order to follow with dragons. But between the private conversation and church action, there are several other intermediate steps that can be taken.

Private conversation. Initially, this is not a confrontation, but an attempt to understand the other person and see that one as Christ does. The goal is to emphasize the many ways you are alike, to see some glory in one another's life. More people are changed by attention and understanding than correction and coercion.

The book *The One-Minute Manager* makes the point well: If you're going to correct someone effectively, every criticism has to be accompanied by a compliment -- in the same context and with virtually the same breath. People are more willing to change when they know they're appreciated, understood, and valued.

Then represent your view clearly and concisely. Try to remember your larger mission -- to build the whole church body, including this person -- and explain the spiritual issues involved.

If the areas of disagreement are significant, a *willingness to bend* is the next step. Some members of a Southern Baptist church in Louisiana were angry with the pastor because the church didn't have a Women's Missionary Union. His past experiences with them had been negative, and he didn't want to drain the energy from the outreach to the unchurched he was emphasizing. When he met with the malcontents, he went willing to bend, willing to adjust to any needs he hadn't seen before. He asked why they felt a WMU was important. "We need Bible study and fellowship for women" was the reply.

"Fine," he said. "Why don't we start a morning Bible study for women, with baby sitting provided by the church? It will give women a chance to invite their neighbors to take a break from the kids. It will offer fellowship, Bible study, *and* evangelism opportunities."

Everyone was happy with the solution.

The most common mistake in dealing with dragons is approaching them judgmentally, assuming theirs is a sin problem. "I used to say, 'If you don't quit what you're doing, we're going to have to take action against you,'" says an Oregon pastor. "But our first approach should be one of compassion, because nine out of ten sinners in the church are hurting more than we imagine. Now I'll put my arm around a man and say in private, 'Jim, I've heard some things, like... Is there any truth to this?' Often he'll break down and acknowledge it. But my key question is 'How can I help you?' It usually takes them by surprise."

If understanding, willingness to bend, and compassion don't work, try at least to *agree on how you'll disagree.*

One outspoken matron, a charter member of an independent congregation in Wisconsin, habitually and openly criticized the pastor's sermons, board decisions, and anything else she didn't care for. She was an accomplished parliamentarian and often used the church constitution to frustrate the desires of the majority.

One day the pastor told her, "Marion, let's agree on one point anyway: When you have a complaint, come to me first. Do not talk to anyone else. Maybe we'll be able to solve the problem without getting the whole church upset." She made the promise.

But within a month, as the pastor suspected she would, she was carping after church about the way the new lines were painted on the parking lot. The pastor invited her into the office. "We've had disagreements in the past, Marion. But one thing I've never accused you of is lying."

"What to you mean?" she asked.

"You promised me you'd see me first with your complaints, and yet you were telling Mildred Hansen your objections to the work in the parking lot."

Marion, an honest person, admitted she broke her promise. Being caught in the act surprised her. She stopped complaining, and within months she was one of the pastor's strongest backers, occasionally to his embarrassment, when she continued to use technical parliamentary procedure for his benefit.

Witnesses. Sometimes private conversations, even with all the peacemaking techniques we can muster, are not enough. At that point, witnesses are necessary. Especially if the conflict involves us personally, other people can be used to resolve the problem. Those in the church who are respected by the dissidents and yet willing to defend another position can be effective in confrontations with rampaging dragons.

Pastor Roger Smalley had a policy that he would not perform the wedding ceremony of a Christian marrying a non-Christian. When Roger explained the policy to Ed Hogan's daughter, who wanted to marry a man who had not accepted Christ, Ed was irate. In the adult Sunday school class, he stood up and asked how the pastor could get away with not doing his job and refusing to perform a wedding for a member of the church.

Roger, who wasn't in the class at the time, felt that since he was the object of Ed's wrath, perhaps the Anders, long-time members of the church and friends of the Hogans, could be more effective peacemakers. Roger explained the reasons behind his policy to the Anders and asked them to visit Ed.

They did, explaining the biblical instructions against being "unequally yoked" and pointing out that the pastor had counseled many people coming from this kind of spiritual mismatch whose marriages later fell apart. They said the pastor was convinced it was a mistake even from a practical point of view. The Anders succeeded in getting Ed to concede the pastor did have a point. In time, Ed and the pastor were able to repair their relationship.

At the point private conversations do not resolve the situation and witnesses become involved, two other cautions should probably be taken: *begin taking notes* and *inform the board.*

Note taking is a defensive move. Often dragons are in the business of collecting injustices, real and perceived. They may charge us with breaking promises, or perhaps they'll later misrepresent conversations.

After the relationship has broken down, pastors should have a witness present in any subsequent extended conversation. But in addition, it is wise to keep a written record of the content of the conversation and any conclusions reached. The lightest ink is better than the longest memory. Not only does it help both sides keep the facts straight, but it also saves lost sleep trying to recall the order of events, if things heat up later on.

As soon as a dispute doesn't respond to personal persuasion, and definitely if any specific action is going to be attempted, it's time to inform the board. Without the support of the board, firm action is impotent if not impossible.

In one Texas church, an elder was very nonchalant about his duties. He stopped attending worship services, and even his attendance at board meetings was sporadic. The rest of the board recognized the problem, but no one was willing to risk losing the man's friendship by confronting him.

The pastor saw no choice but to take action himself. He visited the man and suggested he needed to become more active or else resign his board position, or take another position in the church that didn't require so much time. The encounter seemed to go smoothly, with the elder agreeing to "think it over."

The following day, however, the pastor received several phone calls from church members wanting to know "why you asked Brother Rod to leave the church." The elder and his family left the church "because of the preacher." The next month was spent trying to correct the false rumors.

"My mistake was acting alone," says the pastor. "The situation could have been avoided if I'd insisted that at least one other elder accompany me. If no one was willing, I should have waited until someone was. The leadership as a whole must be willing to administer discipline for it to be effective."

Tell it to the church. What do you tell? You do *not* treat the situation as a trial with the congregation as jury. "Our elders made a mistake by, in essence, *trying* a woman before the congregation," says one Church of Christ minister. "They told specific times, dates, places -- and seemed to be building a case, trying to convince the congregation this woman needed discipline. That's the wrong spirit."

What should they have done?

"Explain simply that reconciliation and restoration were needed and efforts up to this point had not been successful."

Telling the church is not punishment; it is enlisting the help of the whole body in reconciliation. According to the Church of Christ minister, "The spirit needs to be, 'We have dealt personally with this matter and have failed to reconcile.

We have gone with two or three others, and that has failed. Now we're taking the next step and asking you, the congregation, to work with us toward restoration. Perhaps you can succeed where we have failed.'"

Treat him as you would a pagan or tax collector. If the entire church cannot bring reconciliation, the final step, according to Matthew 18, is recognizing that the person is no longer part of the body. Almost always this is merely an acknowledgement of what has, in fact, already taken place.

"In sixteen years of practicing church discipline," says one West Coast pastor, "we have never reached this step without the person leaving the church on his own, but we still recognize publicly what has happened -- that this person is no longer part of us. Not to do so would be tacit acceptance of that person's behavior, and that's hypocrisy -- teaching one thing, accepting another."

Treating a person as a publican or pagan, however, is not shaming or despising that individual. Jesus was known for loving publicans and sinners. But neither did he pretend they were soul mates. This is the delicate balance the church must walk with unrepentant dragons -- to love them as outsiders to be won over.

In dealing with dragons, public action is a last recourse, obviously. "Never get in a spittin' match with a skunk," says the folk wisdom. "Even if you win, you come out smelling bad." Dragon/pastor conflicts can normally be settled behind the scenes. Even most dragon/church conflicts can be settled without a public show of force.

The only time public action is ever appropriate is for continuing, confirmed, and unconfessed sin. Even then, however, the leadership of the church must support the move. Bringing things into the open too quickly is more dangerous than waiting too long. Rather than forcing the issue publicly, often more is gained by learning to minister in an unresolved situation.
